the series

Patricia A. Wasley
Coalition of
Essential Schools

Ann Lieberman
NCREST

SERIES EDITORS

Joseph P. McDonald
Annenberg Institute
for School Reform

Surviving School Reform:
A Year in the Life of One School
LARAINE K. HONG

Eyes on the Child:
Three Portfolio Stories
KATHE JERVIS

Revisiting "The Culture of the School
and the Problem of Change"
SEYMOUR B. SARASON

Teacher Learning:
New Policies, New Practices
MILBREY W. McLAUGHLIN and
IDA OBERMAN, Editors

What's Happening in Math Class?:
Envisioning New Practices Through
Teacher Narratives (Volume 1)
DEBORAH SCHIFTER, Editor

What's Happening in Math Class?:
Reconstructing Professional Identities
(Volume 2)
DEBORAH SCHIFTER, Editor

Reaching for a Better Standard:
English School Inspection and
the Dilemma of Accountability
for American Public Schools
THOMAS A. WILSON

Restructuring Urban Schools:
A Chicago Perspective
G. ALFRED HESS, JR.

The Subjects in Question:
Departmental Organization
and the High School
LESLIE SANTEE SISKIN and
JUDITH WARREN LITTLE

Authentic Assessment in Action:
Studies of Schools and Students
at Work
LINDA DARLING-HAMMOND, Editor

School Work: Gender and the
Cultural Construction of Teaching
SARI KNOPP BIKLEN

School Change: The Personal
Development of a Point of View
SEYMOUR B. SARASON

The Work of Restructuring Schools:
Building from the Ground Up
ANN LIEBERMAN, Editor

Stirring the Chalkdust:
Tales of Teachers
Changing Classroom Practice
PATRICIA A. WASLEY

This series also incorporates earlier titles in the
Professional Development and Practice Series

Surviving School Reform

A YEAR IN THE LIFE OF ONE SCHOOL

Laraine K. Hong

FOREWORD BY PATRICIA A. WALSEY
AFTERWORD BY DEBORAH MEIER

Teachers College, Columbia University
New York and London

Published by Teachers College Press, 1234 Amsterdam Avenue, New York, NY 10027

Copyright © 1996 by Teachers College, Columbia University

All rights reserved. No part of this publication may be reproduced or transmitted in any form or by any means, electronic or mechanical, including photocopy, or any information storage and retrieval system, without permission from the publisher.

Library of Congress Cataloging-in-Publication Data

Hong, Laraine K.
   Surviving school reform : a year in the life of one school /
Laraine K. Hong ; foreword by Patricia A. Walsey ; afterword by
Deborah Meier.
      p.   cm. — (Series on school reform)
   Includes bibliographical references and index.
   ISBN 0-8077-3521-3 (alk. paper). — ISBN 0-8077-3520-5 (pbk. : alk. paper)
   1. Hong, Laraine K. 2. Elementary school teachers—Washington (State)—Biography. 3. Educational change—Washington (State).
I. Title. II. Series.
LA2317.H67A3 1996
372.11′0092—dc20
[B]   96-3791

ISBN 0-8077-3520-5 (paper)
ISBN 0-8077-3521-3 (cloth)

Printed on acid-free paper
Manufactured in the United States of America

03 02 01 00 99 98 97 96   8 7 6 5 4 3 2 1

For my grandparents—
Han Sik and Hyei Cha Hong
Hyung Koon and Nancy Saba Chun
In loving memory of their journeys

Writing a story . . . is one way of discovering *sequence* in experience, of stumbling upon cause and effect in the happenings of a writer's own life. This has been the case for me. Connections slowly emerge. Like distant landmarks you are approaching, cause and effect begin to align themselves, draw closer together. Experiences too indefinite of outline in themselves to be recognized for themselves connect and are identified as a larger shape. And suddenly a light is thrown back, as when your train makes a curve, showing that there has been a mountain of meaning rising behind you on the way you've come, is rising there still, proven now through retrospect.
—Eudora Welty, *One Writer's Beginnings*

Contents

Foreword by Patricia A. Wasley	xi
Acknowledgments	xiii
Introduction	xv

1 A School and a Program   1

    An Unremarkable School   3
    New Arrival   5
    A "School for the Twenty-First Century"   7
    Not Alone   10
    Gathering Together—August 1990   16

2 1990–1991, The First Half   23

    The School Council Meets (and Meets, and Meets . . .)   26
    But *Why* Do You Want to Move?   30
    Teachers—Teams and Individuals   33
    Learning and Changing   37
    Mentorship and New Teachers   40
    Meanwhile, Back at the School Council . . .   42
    Consensus?   44
    The School Council: Informed and Informing   46
    Breaching the Process   48
    Deciding to Press On   52
    "Making Progress . . . Needs Improvement"   56
    Life Goes On . . .   58
    Settling Emerson   60
    Time Out   64

3 1990–1991, The Second Half   67

    And Word from the Governor?   69
    Staying Calm   70
    Decision Making Continues   71

	The Question of "Good Teaching"	74
	A Teacher Struggles	77
	Maintaining Perspective	79
	Hearts, Flowers, and Brickbats	85
	One Teacher's Estrangement	87
	If It's Conferences, It Must Be Spring	94
	Early Warnings	98
	Heading for the State Capitol	99
	Stay Close. . . . "Who Has the Picket Signs?"	102
	The Classroom—Age Group or Family?	107
	As We Were Saying . . .	111
	Again, the Matter of "Good Teaching"	112
	A Principal	114
	Struggling Toward Consensus	119
	We're Still Teaching	122
	Continuing the Process	123
	The Will of the Few	131
	Involved Parents	132
	Whose Class?	136
	Visit from the Intervention Team	138
	Checking the System	139
	Our Turn	141
	Last Phase	143
	Final Business	144
4	**Distillation**	**148**
	Defining Ourselves	149
	Changing Roles, Shifting Power	152
	Maintaining Order	168
	Staying Centered	176
	Continuing On	178
5	**An Activist School**	**179**
	Individual Schools, Practical Solutions	180
	Flourishing	184
Afterword		187
References		191
Index		193
About the Author		196

Foreword

One of the most frustrating dimensions of learning about school reform is that all too often the literature produced to guide us is all too distant. Readers cannot smell the chalkdust, see the insides of desks stuffed with last month's orange peels. Nor can they sink down onto the sagging couch in the faculty room that supports the brief moments of respite between changing one's practices, teaching one's classes, and meeting with parents. Because teachers are busy teaching, it is difficult to get firsthand accounts of the cataclysmic changes whole language instruction can wreak on one's 20-year repertoire, or a realistic sense of what it is like to deal with anywhere from 25 kids for the whole day or 25 kids each of six hours of the day. As Seymour Sarason reminds us repeatedly, we find ourselves trying to learn about complicated things—such as changing schools—from oversimplified description and too readily offered prescription. While I am one of the outsiders who write about schools, I am among the first to find a quiet corner to relish the opportunity to read an insider's firsthand account.

It was with just those sentiments that I commandeered the couch for a quiet Sunday read and, in a day, spent the year inside a resilient and courageous school plagued with all of the turmoil and trauma of those who dare to build a school where everyone learns. And as I moved back and forth between Hong's explanation of what they were trying to do, who the people were and what they were like, how decisions were made, descriptions of daily faculty life, and the reactions of parents, school board members, and district administrators, I was keenly aware that to attempt change is a gargantuan task. This is, unfortunately, far less clear in research reports that synthesize their findings for busy policymakers into a series of lists and maxims.

While *Surviving School Reform* is surely about larger issues of school reform, it is most importantly an autobiography. It is a participant's account of an important time in her own life. She does not pretend that it is anything else. Nor does she suggest that she is offering anyone's perspective other than her own. While she hints that many faculty shared her perceptions, she also lets us know quite clearly that she cannot represent the perspective of some—Fran, a teacher who wants to maintain a more traditional approach, or _____, a parent who does not agree that the school needs to move ahead. She lets you know whom she likes, whom she thinks less of and why. She tells the story to get it down, to make sense of it for herself, to capture an important time, to gain from it what she can.

On closing the book, I found myself asking two questions. First, why is this perspective so important? For decades, school reform has been mandated by those who work outside of schools—university professors, state legislators, school board members, among others. Over time, unfortunately, well-intentioned policies and practices put in place by distant friends of education have borne sparse fruit. Classrooms across the country look much as they did when we were children, despite huge and costly effort. Dr. Hong's account reminds us that if we really want change, we must bridge the gap between those who think they know what should be done and those who are doing it. What better way to build stronger mutual understanding and more realistic plans than to invite those who work outside in—to share what it feels like, what appears to be going on from a participant's vantage point.

And second, what role can such a personal account play in fostering school reform? Besides illuminating the complexity for all involved, Hong's story demonstrates a kind of willingness to relive in public what happened so that others can examine it—to learn from her mistakes and those of her colleagues, to draw conclusions of their own. It is this kind of honesty about one's self and one's work that we so badly need in the midst of efforts to change. While most of us excel in planning new things and in defending them once they've been put in place, we lack the kind of critical facility required to reflect on what happened or to determine what might be gained from it.

My hope is that many will read this book, and use it as a stimulus to think about their own personal narratives, to better understand multiple perspectives, and to learn to analyze the workplace dramas that affect us all. I am appreciative that an insider has so honestly allowed us to come in. And I am hopeful that this excellent writer will invite us in again.

—Patricia A. Walsey

Acknowledgments

Jefferson Elementary is a pseudonym for a very real school, no less complex than any other school. Each individual in this story contributes something singular. Together they constitute a community of enormous talent, energy, generosity, and life-saving humor. I have changed all of their names and a few personal details in order to protect their privacy, but I hope that if and when they read this story, they will recognize that it is indeed "theirs." For "Anne," my fellow teachers, staff, parents, and the children, I offer this story as acknowledgment of their great daring, for change in these times requires daring as much as wisdom.

In my ongoing but sporadic efforts to pull this book together over the past few years, I have been supported and encouraged by several patient and thoughtful individuals. There probably would be no book without Pat Wasley, whom I appreciate as both friend and colleague and someone who never underestimates the role of the classroom teacher in making a difference for schools. With his own special understanding of school change, Robert Hampel contributed invaluable comments and suggestions, as well as much-needed levity along the way. And providing that final push to finish, Maurice Holt offered lovely enthusiasm, generous mentoring, and a reminder that the world turns on the efforts of those who can act as well as of those who generate ideas.

I also wish to acknowledge my parents for their never-failing support and faith. I suspect that it is because of their own strength and philosophical acceptance in confronting difficult change over the years, that I have learned to accept change as both necessary and replete with the promise of something better.

Introduction

This book tells the story of one year in the life of Jefferson Elementary School, one of many schools across the country struggling to alter some age-old rituals in public education. This is a school that was once indistinguishable from thousands of other elementary schools; but instead of holding to predictable paths, we decided in 1988 to turn some corners. We knew there were better ways of teaching than cradling a teacher's manual in one arm. As a result, we probably experienced more frustration, doubt, and daily stress over the ensuing years than any of us could have imagined. Yet, I think most of Jefferson's staff would say it was a fair enough exchange for what we now share—the sense that we can determine the course of our own professional lives, a feeling of abiding mutual support, and the belief that we have come closer to helping every child realize the best within him- or herself.

Library shelves overflow with books on school reform. Why one more? My presumption is that even at their most insightful, most discussions fail to convey the sweat and tears of school reform, and fail to convey how bold change can affect a specific school and community in the deepest, most personal ways. There is a huge emotional gap between an academic exposition on the difficulties of school reform and a tension-charged meeting of parents and teachers to discuss a proposal for multiage grouping. A polite seminar discussion does not begin to touch the bewildering pain a teacher may feel when confronted with instructional changes that upend 20 years of practice.

The first three chapters of this book strive mainly to tell the story of the 1990–91 school year at Jefferson Elementary. I did not want formal analysis and interpretation to intrude upon the description of events and their effects on those involved. Stories are most affecting when they can be told and heard of a piece, whole, without stops along the way. And this particular year for Jefferson held its own particular momentum and intertwining of events. For each significant change that we tried to initiate we faced a ripple of repercussions, sometimes slight and manageable, but other times marked by anger and resentment. It was a constant struggle explaining to parents, reassuring each other and ourselves that what we were doing was ultimately the best for our students. And, whether by dint of stubbornness, good fortune, or design, for the most part we were able to work through each issue as it arose—cooperative learning, mainstreaming, whole language, hands-on math, technology, multiage grouping.

The third year of our revised program proved to be an unexpected crucible. The confluence of events simply may have been too much for one school community to absorb. In a span of 9 months, from September 1990 to June 1991, not only did we have to grapple with a proposal to move our school to another building and with the issue of extending multiage grouping, but there was also the Gulf War, a blizzard that closed the schools for three days, a statewide teachers' strike, the threat of a lawsuit from one of the new teachers, and a small cadre of parents seeking the principal's removal.

Each year we had sailed out farther and farther, testing the waters, clear about our direction if not always certain we would be able to keep our craft intact and afloat. If we were ever going to find ourselves splintered among the rocks, 1990–91 should have been the year. Instead, at the end of those 9 months the ship appeared not only intact but even more seaworthy than before. Much had happened, but we knew that much also had been learned. There was some regret that no one had been recording events as they had occurred, because this is a story that we would want to tell and retell, listen to again and again to remind ourselves of what we had experienced and how much work still remained.

As with any account of individual school change, this one has many pieces underlying and overlaying external events. Capturing such a complex context is usually best achieved through formal on-site study, with systematic ongoing observations, field notes, and interviews. This story of Jefferson, however, relies entirely on a reconstruction of events from personal memory, my conversations with participants at the close of the school year, and reference to certain artifacts such as minutes and newsletters. Although I tried to give as fair an account of events as I could, my role as both participant and observer during the year meant that it was difficult for me to be totally objective in my recollections. By actually holding onto my own perceptions and feelings through this writing, I hope to have conveyed a sense of the personal stress and tension that are inevitable companions to school change.

I regret that the student's voice is conspicuously missing from this story. As much as I wanted to add this narrative layer, I found it impossible to construct purely from memory and a few notes. Children's daily lives are like a grand symphony of rhythms, tensions, dissonances, and harmonics. Accurately capturing any piece of it requires capturing the actual moments of experience, the immediate gestures and expressions, the words said, the feelings conveyed, the giggles shared. While I have vivid, affectionate, and often specific recollections, they would make a paltry, inadequate telling.

Still, the events that I do tell about are unique events, but unique only in the context of often mundane daily doings and the larger purposes of our professional lives together. While high drama may have been occurring on one level, life in the classroom maintained its own familiar pace. When together, children and teachers tenaciously held to the vital, often exuberant business of learning. I wish there were some way I could have captured here the small daily triumphs, those moments that push us to want to know more, do better each day that we walk into the classroom. For despite all of the seemingly overwhelming events of the year, the real story still lies within the walls of the classroom, within each teacher and each student struggling with and reveling in the pursuit of knowing.

My hope is that this book will have something to say to those individuals who are immersed each day in the odd juxtaposition of drudgery and exhilaration that comes with school change. Jefferson's story may provide insights and raise new questions about reform and what schools, staffs, and communities should be aware of as they make pivotal decisions and take their own tentative steps toward change. And it may give teachers, parents, and administrators some basis for extending their already ongoing conversations. Perhaps they will take heart in seeing that conflict need not be fatal to change but that, given sufficient time and candor, those involved may actually find themselves closer than when they began.

Chapter 4 in *Surviving School Reform* is called "Distillation." It was intended to be just that, a distillation of the most salient elements shaping and supporting Jefferson's year. What actually underlay the events as they occurred? What affected the course and outcomes of these events? And what meaning could be derived from the often emotional jumble of events? If there is anything remarkable in this chapter it is probably how unremarkable are the factors identified as making a difference for our school. By now so much has been learned about school change that the only real surprise is that major school reform still remains so elusive. As I described our own experience, however, with areas such as leadership, process, and time, I developed a fuller appreciation for how everything fit together like a kind of intricate puzzle construction.

Why did change have to be so comprehensive and simultaneous? Why not one piece at a time? Schools are too complicated to be transformed by timid tinkering. They are also exceptionally practical places, where hundreds of decisions are made every minute throughout a building. In the final chapter of this book, I tried to provide an explicit statement about how school reform, manifested in day-to-day issues, is essentially a practical challenge. Participants may be struggling to reconcile differences in beliefs, values, and attitudes, but to move forward at all requires agreement on initial actions, small steps on which to build a foundation for change and a basis for common understandings. Serious efforts to change the institution of the school have to lead to ongoing decisions that engender tangible action while also demonstrating a clear moral responsibility to the larger school community. None of this can occur without embracing the whole culture of the school, without accepting the school as its own special, often wondrous, entity.

The manuscript for this book has lived through countless drafts. It has been carried across town, across an ocean, and across the continent. In all this time, school reform appears no less easy than when Jefferson Elementary began its first tentative steps toward significant change. The hope, however, lies in the fact that Jefferson continues to flourish. If this can happen to one school, surely it can happen to thousands.

1

A School and a Program

Seven A.M. Although a few teachers often arrive before George, the day does not truly begin at Jefferson Elementary School until his lime-green, vintage VW van pulls into the parking lot. Robust, brown-skinned, George is a custodian of great habit. With an obvious air of proprietorship, he unlocks the outside doors to the main building, methodically switches on lights in the hallways, library, offices, and staffroom. Once the coffeepot is plugged in, George heads out to unlock classroom doors in the separate wings, turn on the heat, make sure all is in place, and that the night custodian has done his job.

By 7:30, the office manager is at her desk in the front office. Jeanne begins to answer the phones. They have been ringing intermittently for the past 20 minutes.

"Please tell Mrs. Vance that Carol will be late. She has a dentist appointment."

"Would you ask Mrs. Marshall to call me? I have a question about the field trip."

"We lost our school menu. What's the hot lunch today?"

"Can Tim bring his water pistol to school?"

Voices start to collect in the staff workroom as teachers dribble in to check their boxes, run off copies, gather up butcher paper, check materials out of the supply closets. Bodies flow in and out of the staffroom, filling coffee mugs, glancing at the lunch tables for a stray doughnut or piece of candy. Greetings are brief but friendly; some staff members take a moment longer to coordinate schedules, exchange an idea, ask about a student, share a funny story. Someone may grumble; others will sympathize, but they move on. Too much to do.

At about 9:15 A.M. the yellow buses pull up to the front of the main building to unload their jumble of passengers. The school day officially begins at 9:30. In each of 18 elementary (K–5) classrooms you can be assured that the lunch count is being taken, absences noted, announcements made, and the Pledge recited (usually). Work begins. Silent reading, astronomy, U.S. geography, place value, pattern blocks, stories, and more stories. Children work by themselves, in pairs, in groups of three or four, always shifting. Teachers listen, ask questions, and try not to talk too much.

Mr. Lee's fourth and fifth graders are grouped at different spots around the room for their daily "Decimal Jump." They take turns jumping, then measuring their distances.

"Do you measure up to the toe or the heel, Mr. Lee?" Alice asks.

"What do you think is more fair?"

"I guess the heel," she responds.

He nods. Converting the meters and centimeters to decimals, the students record their jumps on individual graphs. Later they will combine their data to produce the class average for the day, adding it to a class graph.

In a multiage third/fourth-grade classroom, students are pulling out their writing folders. Some immediately pick up where they left off the previous day. They know what comes next; it's just a matter of getting it down on paper. Others head for the computers to finish typing drafts or final copies.

"Miss Hill, there's no more computers!" moans Jason.

"Well, find out who's going to be finished soon. Can you work on your poem for a while?"

Still other children are scattered around the room, some in pairs to proofread a story, a few in groups just for the sake of company, and a couple of loners leaning back in their chairs, biting at their pencils, gazing at the ceiling, patiently waiting for inspiration to strike. Dave has already finished his personal story about a burglary at his father's camera shop, so he's engrossed in designing the cover and title page. It will take him all period to finish, but it will be colorful and imaginative. Something he'll want to share with the class later in the week.

No noise emanates from Ms. Dillard's room. It is silent reading time. Third graders are scattered around the clusters of tables, some reading picture books, others with "chapter books." Two girls sit hip-to-hip next to each other on the floor. Sometimes reading is most fun when you're scrunched up next to someone. Ms. Dillard is in her rocking chair, reading her own book. Once in a while an eye lifts off the page to take a quick glance around the room.

So it goes. Later there is morning recess. Mrs. Gaines's kindergartners are having their snacks, but before they start eating, they each have their morning crackers piled into different-sized stacks on their desks. Mrs. Gaines is at the chalkboard.

"Sarah, describe your stacks."

"Two crackers and three crackers," she answers, after carefully counting each stack.

Mrs. Gaines writes: 2 + 3 =
"What answer should I write?"
"Five!" the class answers together.
"Super. Now who has different stacks?"

Lunch doesn't come soon enough. The aides spend the year searching for ways to keep the noise level in the lunchroom down to something tolerable. Lunch recess is a half-hour, a good length of time for children to exercise limbs and vocal cords. The teachers grab their own lunches; some plop down in the staffroom ready to exchange stories about their morning. Others hurry back to their rooms, needing time to get those beans and cups set up for the afternoon, wanting to clean up paints and brushes, or simply looking for some precious quiet time. Recess ends. Where were we?

"Mrs. Brink, Tommy's not helping!"
"Do I have to use cursive?"
"I'm finished! Is this good?"
"Can I use my calculator?"
"How come plants have flowers?"
"So, are there Siamese triplets too?"

At 3:30 the bell rings. The walkways instantly flood with some 500 children, backpacks bouncing up and down, bodies leaning forward, their legs trying to keep up. The "walkers" head out through the neighborhood, while the luckier ones spot their parents' waiting cars. The rest pile back onto the buses, a little noisier and considerably less tidy than when they arrived 6 hours earlier.

Back in the classrooms teachers gather up papers, return materials to shelves and drawers, check their planbooks for the next day. Some take a few minutes to visit with others, find out how the day went, ask for advice, share a snack, simply express frustration or relate a success. They leave at different times. Some go home; others have meetings or workshops. At least half of the staff are still in their rooms at 5:00; and you can usually count on someone lingering until 6:00 or even later. The night custodian arrives, trundling his trash can through the school. The carpets will be vacuumed, the lights in the office turned off, all the doors locked. One day less of the 180 required by the state legislature.

AN UNREMARKABLE SCHOOL

Jefferson Elementary is part of a cherished but beleaguered national institution—the American public school system—that stands to measure our success as a society. Can it respect tradition and accept change, comprehend the past and embrace the future? Will it be able to reconcile diversity with a sense of community and common purpose? Will it be able to transform the relentless and complex demands of daily life into experiences and learning that will make a difference in the lives of children, while they are still children and as they become adults needy of delight, purpose, and some part of the human spirit? Jefferson is just one school among thousands trying to answer these questions. Each school shapes its answers differently, but the struggles and uncertainty are shared. Thus, a story of one school but perhaps encouragement for all.

In outward appearance, Jefferson Elementary School is unremarkable. It is nested within a quiet, residential community of middle-class and working-class families, primarily white but with a steadily increasing minority population. (Nonwhite enrollment at Jefferson increased to about 17% in 1989–90 from about 3% in 1985.) Many of the almost 500 children come from traditional nuclear families of mom at home, dad, and one or two siblings; but, following national trends, there are more and more students from single-parent homes, students with both parents working, students with stepparents and stepsiblings, immigrant families, families in precipitous economic situations. To better meet the needs of a more diverse student body, Jefferson acquired a full-time (versus itinerant) school counselor/psychologist and a part-time ESL (English as a Second Language) aide. Yet, as almost any school in this country will claim, such supplemental services are agonizingly inadequate. Too many children from all strata of society are still floundering, trying to survive each day with their anger and despair in check. These are the ones who steal your sleep, shatter your complacency, test the limits of your patience and the strength of your commitment.

When I first arrived at Jefferson in the fall of 1985, no one yet had realized how drastically our student population was changing or appreciated the elevated level of skill and education that society would demand from its future workers and the implications this held for our program. Nor did we have any accurate sense of the scope and depth of the changes that were emerging out of national initiatives on school and curriculum reform. A brief two years later, however, and we were miles out in the wilderness, trying to see what reform would look like in our own building.

While some of the staff and probably most of our community believed "nothin' was broke," and continued to trust in the familiar world of basals, ability groups, worksheets, memorization, and rote learning, others were less sanguine. Not only did our student population look different, but students insisted on behaving differently. A morning of circling answers and filling in the blanks on six worksheets was not keeping members of the Nintendo generation fixed to their seats and embued with the love of learning. Moreover, our instruction was not focused on helping students to think creatively and flexibly, to make decisions, or to work with each other and take pride in a sense of community. Instead of addicted readers, excited and competent writers, and math problem solvers, we were seeing, at best, indifference to learning and, at worst, overt antagonism. We were a school of dusty habits and traditions; and, as comforting as these may be for some constituents, it promised only frustration and detachment for our students, not to mention professional stagnation for ourselves. Granted, not everyone on the staff or in the parent community felt this way, but there were enough to form a beginning, and we were blessed with certain opportunities that year.

NEW ARRIVAL

Most schools in 1985 were conducting business not much differently than they had in 1955. Jefferson Elementary's own saga of change is the result of a confluence of events, fortuitous timing, and a core of people willing to look beyond tomorrow and risk their comfortable niches in order to see if there might be a better way to do what we were doing.

At the end of the 1985–86 school year, Jefferson's principal of many years retired. Arnold was a wonderful soul, a kind of favorite uncle to everyone, both children and adults. With his amiable, twinkle-in-the-eye manner, Arnold could always make you feel better with a handshake, hug, or hearty "How ya doin'?" I think in many ways Jefferson functioned as smoothly as it did because of Arnold's ability to make everything seem fine, to feel that instruction was fine, learning was fine, the children were fine, teachers were fine.

When Anne M. assumed Jefferson's principalship in September 1986, we knew immediately that things were going to be different. The changes began with staff meetings. No more time spent fussing about behavior on the walkways or where to store the construction paper. Staff meetings were to be used for inservice, classroom-related topics. It quickly became clear that Anne's first interest was instruction. She began to show up in our classrooms unannounced. Visits were brief but frequent. The likelihood of turning back to the class after writing on the chalkboard and suddenly seeing Anne at the doorway does a great deal to keep you on your toes. In the office, too, Anne was setting some new expectations. Not one for small talk, she made it clear that while she was going to be congenial, she would not have much time for casual chats and impromptu drop-ins. Some parents were miffed; they were used to the free and ready access that Arnold had invited. This seems an unimportant difference, but an accumulation of these small differences eventually sets the tone for the rest of the school.

Anne's first year at Jefferson was, in effect, a wakeup call to the staff, and perhaps a few alert parents. She was not moving fast, but she was moving deliberately, and her eye was on instruction. With a background in environmental education, many years of teaching, a doctorate in curriculum and instruction, and a previous principalship at an alternative middle school, Anne thrives on change. Her belief that change leads to growth and learning applies to individuals as well as to organizations. During her first year at Jefferson she was already suggesting that perhaps there were alternatives to basals and textbooks, that perhaps we could think about ways to overlap some of our curriculum. Did we really need a detention room? Were there alternatives? Had we heard about positive discipline and cooperative learning?

By the end of the 1986-87 school year staff conversations had begun to shift from idle staffroom chatter to more thoughtful exchanges about teaching and what was going on in the school. So much was going on: We were reassessing our approach to discipline (punitive or preventive?) and figuring out how to revitalize instruction; we were learning how to assume responsibility (each teacher had his or her own budget for the year); and, especially critical to future events, we were learning, sometimes painfully, how to make decisions as a group. In other words, we were beginning to take the first steps toward many of the significant changes that would eventually occur in our instruction, curriculum, decision-making process, and individual roles.

There was an extra factor in this process, however, which both accelerated and supported our efforts at school change. Typical of Anne, she would use a small, spontaneous moment as an opportunity to lead us into something larger than we could ever imagine. Perhaps this is a general characteristic of effective leaders, always being ready to take advantage of small windows into change and knowing, too, how to avoid setting themselves as sole instigators.

Betty and Mary, two of Jefferson's veteran teachers, longtime and faithful users of a basal approach to teaching, had been feeling restless and dissatisfied with the way they were teaching, even before Anne's arrival at Jefferson. They tried one published program, which was a few steps away from basals but still not different enough for the two teachers. By Anne's second year in the building, Betty and Mary had begun trying out some whole language approaches.

"We were moving," says Betty, "but there wasn't enough time for us to really plan together."

One afternoon some of the teachers were in the staffroom, agonizing about the lack of time. Anne happened to be sitting with them, and she told them about a proposal she had recently received from the state. She explained that they would have to apply, but there was the chance of receiving substantial funding and some extra planning days for the staff to work together. "We told her to go for it," Betty says. Anne probably received encouragement from other sources, but this incident illustrates her ability to take advantage of the opportune moment.

A "SCHOOL FOR THE TWENTY-FIRST CENTURY"

In the fall of 1987, the governor proposed a specially funded program to encourage innovative, perhaps radically innovative, approaches to schooling in the state. When the program, entitled "Schools for the Twenty-First Century," was announced and requested applications, we were ready. Along with the changes Anne had been initiating, we had already spent more than two years, in accordance with state department mandates, evaluating our existing curriculum, and with district inservice support we had begun applying new approaches using cooperative learning, manipulative problem-solving math, and technology.

Developing and writing the Twenty-First Century proposal consumed most of the 1987–88 school year and required the combined efforts of a group of 11 staff members (certificated and classified) and six parents. Through the winter of 1987 and into the early spring of 1988, we met in a drafty, cramped portable (a modular outbuilding) just outside the gym. We began with butcher paper and markers, brainstorming ideas, concepts, and goals. What we were really doing was piecing together a vision for our school—what kind of learning did we want for our students and how would we get there? There was endless discussion, balanced by both parent and teacher perspectives. We didn't limit ourselves to our own pool of knowledge; different individuals volunteered to read and share the available research on multiage grouping, mainstreaming, technology, and even the ideas of futurists.

Over the several months that we worked on the proposal, we periodically took drafts back to the full staff for reactions and input. The monthly school newsletter informed parents that copies of the draft were available in the office for them to read and respond to. While I don't recall any outspoken criticism of our work or even requests for major revisions in any of the drafts, I think it would be a mistake to interpret this as amiable agreement. I believe that if we tried today to initiate a new program with even just half the scope of the Twenty-First Century proposal, we would confront something considerably more than polite disagreement. In those first years of school change, neither staff nor parents were accustomed to active participation in decision making. Most of those not on the proposal committee seemed content to let us carry on, as long as nothing directly impinged upon their daily lives. In other words, the reality and implications of the proposal seemed too far removed to be considered seriously at that point. I imagine that many believed this was just another short-lived effort to "improve" education, and that it would eventually take its final resting place alongside all of the earlier fads and fizzled reform movements.

There were, indeed, staff members who would not be able to live with the program as presented in the proposal, and they would eventually transfer or retire. For the most part, these were teachers who had been with the district for many years. They preferred hanging on mightily to the status quo, but they did not openly express opposition to what was brewing out in the portable. I don't think it was an issue of intimidation but of custom and lack of practice. After too many years of professional docility, of keeping to their classrooms and quietly following the rules, they were not prepared to assert strong disagreement. Imagined or real, the perceived risk was too great, and they settled either for silence or for complaining among themselves. I believe, however, that if anyone had openly raised an objection in a staff meeting or gone directly to Anne, they would have been heard and their feelings respected; we would at least have engaged in more extended discussion and evaluation of the direction we were taking with this proposal. Absent such dissent, the sheets of butcher paper emerged as a 75-page proposal, printed, indexed, and personally delivered by Anne to the state department of education. So, it seems that as we began our march toward the twenty-first century, we did so to a great extent because those who could have set up significant obstacles chose instead to hold to the refuge of their classrooms and keep their own counsel. (Out of a teaching staff of 20 in 1990, four had transferred and eight had retired by the start of the 1992–93 school year. No one ever said restructuring would be easy.)

The proposal we finally submitted to the state was our blueprint for a "Developmental Community School." By "developmental" we meant that every individual, child and adult, would have a chance to learn at an appropriate pace and be provided with the environment, materials, and activities most compatible with his or her own style, needs, and abilities. Key elements in reaching this goal would include

- Whole language
- Cooperative learning
- Multicultural education
- An integrated curriculum
- Multiage grouping
- Technology
- Mainstreaming of special needs children

"Community" embodied the straightforward belief that closer cooperation and communication could be nurtured both within the school and between the school and its constituents. The term *community* has become particularly prevalent today in both education and other social/political contexts. Our adoption of the concept of community as part of the framework for our program was, however, something fully spontaneous and unique to the moment. I suspect that for the group cloistered in the portable for all those weeks, "community" simply became an inherent element of how we were working and what we hoped would eventually be deeply ingrained within the life of our school.

In the spring of 1988, with funding for the program approved by the state legislature, Jefferson was one of the initial group of schools selected as a "School for the Twenty-First Century." Each selected school would receive $50,000 a year, for six years, to implement its own particular plans for innovative education. To further support these plans, waivers of state regulations were available. Interestingly enough, few schools applied for such waivers; Jefferson required none. This suggests that significant change may be less problematic to initiate than is often perceived or assumed.

Since 1988 we have worked to develop not just an educational program, but an entire school ethos of decency and caring, where "every adult is responsible for every child," and where the simply stated but enduring guidelines for everyone are: "Be safe; be kind; be responsible; be respectful." We constantly struggle to take every student as far as possible in skills and knowledge, but we believe that academic goals will be reached only when children feel secure, and happy with themselves, when they care for one another and think that learning and their school are absolutely terrific.

NOT ALONE

School reform tends to be a lonely pursuit. It may be the hot topic of discussion and study for academics and politicians, but when it comes to the actual daily trench work, each building is on its own. No one else but your own staff, administration, and parents can make the decisions and set the directions that ultimately will determine the success of your program. That is true. At the same time, however, it would be a mistake to presume that each school functions in a vacuum, totally isolated from or immune to any outside influence. No matter how singular a building's efforts may be, for good or ill, they still are part of a larger governmental, political, and social context. For an individual building, national initiatives may seem remote and irrelevant, but as the rings of influence come closer to home we begin to take note. We noticed, for example, when the state created the Twenty-First Century program, and we would especially notice when the state proposed severe cuts in education spending later in the fall. Those special instances aside, outside of our own building, we are most attentive to the actions and policies of our own district and association. Both can have a significant, albeit often indirect, impact on any of our attempts at school restructuring.

The District

Given our experience at Jefferson, it is difficult to imagine any school initiating successful reform without substantial encouragement and help at the district level. Our own district provided a critical context of support in its philosophical and practical commitment to school renewal. Recognizing that virtually all elements within a school (e.g., curriculum, governance, instruction) are impossibly interrelated, the district developed a uniquely broad-based policy toward reform. Rather than focusing on a single program or area, such as technology, the district emphasizes five initiatives:

- Equity and excellence
- Empowerment
- Technology
- Site-based decision making
- Noninstructional support services

Implicit in these initiatives is the belief that in order to work, reform has to take place simultaneously in all strategic areas. Otherwise, change can be only temporary and half-hearted.

Lieberman and Miller (1990) point out that restructuring, as understood today, has produced a re-examination of the role of policy. Acknowledging that the actual processes involved in restructuring cannot be mandated, they note that policy becomes a matter of facilitating change, where "issues and visions . . . must be collectively created within a supportive environment that encourages people to learn about and to work through the change process" (p. 760). Our district has a long tradition of candid self-appraisal and willingness to advance in new directions. It is certainly not perfect, but I am convinced that it is better than most.

With its population shifting from a predominantly homogeneous, suburban community to a more urban environment with accompanying changes in family patterns, and given the increasingly complex demands of the workplace, the district purposely set forth on a broad course of school renewal and restructuring for all of its 16 elementary schools, 6 middle schools, and 5 high schools. Each of the five initiatives has engendered several of its own programs and policies to support change. Ensuring equity and academic excellence, for example, has included expanding and strengthening early childhood and primary programs, providing inservice multicultural training, allocating resources to schools based at least partially on student needs, support of mainstreaming and multiage grouping, and developing more effective means of assessing student progress.

The active involvement of the district is both comprehensive and thoughtful, reflecting a coherent philosophy about learning, instruction, and what schools should be doing for students and the community. This kind of self-definition of purpose and direction does not emerge overnight. A history of the district, written by a former district official, reveals substantial consistency in philosophical orientation in its schools for more than 40 years. It is pointed out that the five initiatives currently defining school renewal simply continue directions first established for the district in a 1952 outline. Subsequent years were marked by cycles of change and reversal familiar to those attempting large-scale reform in almost any district or organization. What seems important is that the district did not become complacent or mired in tradition but continued to move forward on the belief that it could always be better, do more. For an individual teacher in the district, that determination is real.

Professional Development. Before Jefferson set out to create its program for the twenty-first century, the district had already begun providing teachers with some interesting inservice opportunities. Not wedded to its textbooks, the district provided training in cooperative learning and problem-solving math. Like many teachers in the district, I took two summer "Math Solution" classes with Marilyn Burns and attended monthly follow-up workshops with our district math specialist. Cooperative learning was incorporated into these classes, but various buildings, including Jefferson, arranged for their own cooperative-learning sessions conducted by district personnel. Individual teachers also are encouraged to contact curriculum specialists directly if they have a problem requiring some specific expertise.

As with any district, teachers are at several different points in their own learning. To help teachers acquire new skills or extend proficiency, the district offers a variety of classes each year in a wide range of curricular areas, from literature to technology. In addition to the practical effect of such offerings, the implicit message is that there is an expectation of growing competence, that it is not acceptable to stand still professionally. For teachers who resist change, much of what the district has instituted through its policy shifts of the past several years is disconcerting and incomprehensible. A large percentage of the teachers in the district are at the high end of the salary schedule just by virtue of professional longevity. These teachers have become quite comfortable over the years, absorbing periodic minor changes in curriculum and instructional materials. More recent school renewal, however, has wrought an entirely different kind of change—change that is deep and systemic. This time I don't simply trade in one math textbook for another. This time I turn in all of my textbooks, eliminate my three ability math groups, and try to create an entirely new curriculum based on some broadly stated SLOs (student learning objectives) while using an assortment of brand-new materials. There is no manual. I am overwhelmed.

This kind of befuddling experience is repeated in our reading program as basals have been supplanted by whole language. Some teachers across the district are struggling and frustrated. At the same time, however, there are perhaps just as many, if not more, who are thriving and finding their own "renewal" in these instructional changes. In the same way that teachers have to differentially support students, in a single classroom, who have widely varying abilities and temperaments, the district has to provide similar help for its teachers. Teachers, no less than students, come in all ages, at various stages of development, and with diverse backgrounds, training, talents, and proclivities. The irony would be if we expected districts to accommodate the individual differences among teachers but did not apply the same notion to students and classrooms. Or vice versa.

Another key component in the district's support of teachers is the permeability of the decision-making process and the opportunities provided for teachers to assume leadership roles. Instead of staying in our classrooms and patiently waiting for deliveries of materials and instructional programs, teachers are included in the groups making major decisions affecting instruction. This includes committees for SLO revisions and development of curriculum materials. Each building has a "math leader" responsible for meeting monthly with the district math specialist and taking back new ideas and information. Math leaders also have been responsible for coordinating the expenditure of substantial funds allotted to each building specifically to support the new math program.

Much of the inservice training offered in the district is taught by regular classroom teachers. This has been especially true with technology. As more and more teachers have acquired their own expertise, the district has enlisted their services to teach courses on how to use computers, how to apply various software programs, how to coordinate technology with curriculum. A special two-week summer program brings teachers and students together to work with computers, video equipment, and a range of software. This program is run almost entirely by teachers.

Extended Governance. None of this may sound unusual in the context of current school reform efforts, but we should not forget that teachers historically have had about as much responsibility for curricular and building-governance decisions as the building custodian. "Top-down" was the operative term and was practiced as a matter of course, and still is in many areas of the country. Less hierarchical and significantly more open to teacher participation in decisions than most districts, ours has moved past any exploratory stage and now has difficulty finding teachers to take on broader responsibilities who are not already weighed down by other commitments. The point is that teachers are generally treated as professionals, expected to assume responsibility and contribute to decision making within and outside of their own buildings.

The district created a culture of change, emphasizing personal responsibility, excitement about learning and ideas, and willingness to institute and support new approaches to instruction. In the process it established its own image as a district in the forefront of reform, which it cannot maintain by relying solely on bodies in the central office and outside consultants. First-hand knowledge and experience aside, the cost of external advice is usually prohibitive. Thus, schools that initiate significant change, and actually achieve some palpable success, serve not just their own immediate constituents, but augment the larger district's depth and resources. When the conversations about change are sustained throughout the district, at all levels, with appropriate and judicious contributions from the outside, districts should be in a better position to maintain clarity and coherence in overall purpose.

Each fall, the School Councils (SCs) from all of the district schools meet for an extended inservice on various issues of school governance. Sessions are conducted by a mixture of staff, parents, and central office members. The effect is to provide SC members with a sense of the overall direction of the district, the various ways individual schools organize and establish the scope of their councils, and different ways buildings manage and resolve particular issues. While individuals from each school go home knowing a bit more than they knew before the meetings, the district acquires its own huge dollop of information about how the SCs are functioning and where they may need some additional support. This could not happen without the direct participation of school staff members and parents.

The Association

In most cases, "restructuring" refers to schools, but the more useful application might be to the entire education conglomerate of schools, districts, state offices, federal offices, and the professional associations. Loosening up the bureaucratic tethers on schools and teachers so that they can have more control over their own instructional programs, ideally, should be the result of significant rethinking within each tier of education policy making. This especially includes the unions. How effectively they can move beyond traditional issues of wages and working conditions to issues supporting the involvement of teachers in decision making is indeed critical in sustaining any expanded role for teachers.

Watts and McClure (1990) point out that current emphasis on extending the role of teachers to decisions related to professional, curricular, and pedagogical concerns is not new, that these issues were already prominent by the 1950s. Early attempts to bring such issues to the bargaining table, however, were successfully resisted by the very bureaucratic structures that teachers wanted to replace. Thus, by the 1970s, when collective bargaining became an established and effective tool for the unions, its success was confined primarily to issues of salary and working conditions. Watts and McClure assert that only more recently has there been serious acknowledgment of how school renewal depends on the direct participation of teachers, that the old "top-down bureaucratic models" of school decision making are inadequate to facilitate restructuring. The National Educational Association itself, they note, supports policies that include "vesting authority in the faculties of local schools; advocating high standards for teacher preparation and practice . . . ; establishing mastery of what is taught as the standard of student excellence; and providing full learning opportunities for all students" (Watts & McClure, 1990, p. 767).

While the associations may be moving forward at the national level, my sense is that the commitment at the local and even state levels may be less consistent. I have read and heard enough about "unhelpful" associations that I can fully appreciate how our own local and the district have created a special relationship that simultaneously meets members' interests while providing the district with enough flexibility to accommodate the needs of a shifting community population and to establish conditions for increased decision making at the building level. The partnership between the Association and the district produced a contractual agreement that specifically stipulates guidelines for consensual decision making, including provisions for "intervention" (involving district and association personnel) when conflict cannot be resolved. All of this would become strikingly relevant to our own school lives in the spring of 1991.

While the influence of the Association may not be tangibly present in the daily functioning of our building, its willing participation in and support of school reform and, especially, expanded decision-making responsibilities for teachers, add a certain validation to our own restructuring efforts. Knowing, too, that your district and association share a relationship that is collaborative rather than adversarial does much to provide a sense of stability and unambiguous direction.

GATHERING TOGETHER—AUGUST 1990

After two years of implementing our Twenty-First Century program we believed that the more laborious and stressful groundwork was behind us, and we looked forward to refining and extending what we had begun. We anticipated another challenging year, but we hoped we could begin to leave school a little earlier at the end of each day, enjoy our newly achieved camaraderie, and have fewer parents asking us to explain the disappearance of worksheets and textbooks.

All was rosy during the week of inservice meetings in late August; it was an auspicious beginning to the 1990–91 school year. We met at the nearby Grandview Tennis Club, a more modest establishment as these places go, but compared with our school facilities, it was a suite at the Hyatt! We gathered together, happy to see each other, all the old faces but several new ones as well. Over the previous years our staff had been gradually changing, sorting itself out. Some retired, while others not comfortable with the changes occurring in our building asked for transfers. There was enough time, latitude, and tolerance for each individual to work out his or her own decision.

New Staff

This particular year, with three retirements and the addition of two teaching positions, we could hire five new classroom teachers—one kindergarten, two third/fourth-grade teachers, and two straight third grades. This entering class of teachers was about as mixed a group as you could find.

Judy, with teaching experience in Maine and Alaska, and some years in advertising, was taking on a third grade. She would later take on much more, for which we would all be grateful. Pam, with a middle-school daughter and a college-aged son, had a lot of experience in schools, but this was her first regular classroom assignment. Exuberant, warmly nurturing, Pam would weather through some rocky times with her third/fourth-grade class, but end the year excited about starting all over again. Our other new third/fourth-grade teacher was Neil, newly married, looking a little overwhelmed by the flow of events, but happy to be where he was. Neil would face his own special difficulties during the year, but always with sensitivity, patience, and an ability to step back and analyze what was going on. Emily was entering her kindergarten class with many years as a preschool and Montessori teacher in her pocket.

Unable to attend this week of inservice because of family concerns, Fran was to be our other new third-grade teacher. Originally from Taiwan, Fran had spent at least 10 years teaching in the United States. Missing our initial inservice, which was not only an inservice program but also a special opportunity for the staff to get to know and work with each other, would later assume special significance.

Working the Program

Our attention that week was directed to major pieces of our program: how to use technology in our classrooms, different ways to assess student progress, positive discipline, special needs children, and team planning of curriculum. The topics and each day's events had been selected and planned over the summer by the School Improvement Team (SIT).

The SIT is the offspring of the original teacher/parent group that developed the "Schools for the Twenty-First Century" proposal. It has since become what Anne calls "the keeper of the vision," responsible for disbursement of the Twenty-First Century monies and larger policy recommendations and decisions such as whether to pursue having a daycare on site. The SIT is also responsible for program evaluation each year, providing information to the state education department on our Twenty-First Century program. Four teachers, four parents, the principal, and a representative of the classified staff meet once a month. In contrast to the sometimes jaw-tightening sessions of the School Council, the SIT's meetings are conducted within a distinctly informal and amiable atmosphere. The team members often meet at someone's home, sitting on the living-room floor with chocolate chip cookies and coffee.

While we heard from an outside speaker and the district language arts specialist during our August inservice week, most of the sessions were conducted by teachers and other staff. Technology is an especially good example of an area in which we are developing in-house expertise. If you have a problem with a computer, you don't have to wait six weeks for help from the district specialist. Our librarian is an excellent starting point, but more and more teachers in our building know what to do with a tangle of cables, keyboards that stick, programs that won't run. We have come a long way from the single Apple computer in the office to the workstations that now casually rest on every teacher's desk. We also have a few students who know more about computers than do the teachers.

Assessment was another inservice topic; it will always be an issue. It is an especially sensitive and crucial concern for our building, partly because of our selection as a School for the Twenty-First Century, but especially because so much of our program is outside parental experience and expectations. Many parents are not comfortable with change: "It worked for me; it should work for my child." They are nervous without a steady stream of skillsheets coming home, without weekly spelling tests, without timed multiplication tests. They are uncomfortable with classrooms where children freely move about, where small groups confer noisily on projects, and where the teacher rarely conducts formal lessons standing in front of the chalkboard.

For all of our parents, the community, the legislature, and whomever else is concerned, we know that at some point we have to demonstrate the merit of what we are doing. The problem is that we aren't willing to let standardized tests be the final measure. As teachers who see their students everyday, we *know* they're learning; we *know* they're making progress. Just how do we know? By watching them work, talking with them, looking at their work, listening to them. Instead of scores on a computer printout, it is our own best judgment at work. Of course, we also know that this is not enough.

Our own struggle with assessment mirrors what is going on at the national level. That is, what is the place, purpose, and validity of standardized tests? If you decide that these tests are not an accurate reflection of what your students learn or do not learn, what do you use to augment or replace them? While we may not want to judge Carla's reading skills solely by her ability to tell a blend from a digraph, neither is it enough to say, "Carla sure loves to read!" How does a classroom teacher determine if Carla is learning to make inferences from what she is reading, is able to interpret and analyze? What books does she read? How much time does she spend reading independently? All of this and more should be factored into an assessment of Carla's reading progress so that we can determine not only how to help Carla improve her reading skills but also how to evaluate the overall instructional program, in the classroom and as a total school. We tackle this issue anew each year, not just for reading but for every other major academic area for which we are responsible.

An additional, major part of our August inservice week was an annual report from Marty M., a graduate assistant at a nearby college. Marty was a valuable resource as we began to implement our program. He served as our outside evaluator each year, providing us with a kind of overall portrait of how we were implementing change and the effects of our efforts on such areas as the role of the teacher, student performance/behavior, parent and staff attitudes, and interactions within the school community. Marty based his evaluation on an accumulation of diverse material gathered over a given year—parent surveys, action research reports, district profiles, committee reports, SIT and SC minutes, and a year-end written reflection in which each staff member responded to a specific set of questions designed by Marty and Anne. In a sense, Marty's role went beyond that of formal evaluator. Well-acquainted with the staff and school, he could also be at once encouraging and supportive while tactfully pointing out the loose ends and gaps we overlooked.

One of the more persistent gaps is assessment. Although, as a staff, we don't question the critical need for solid assessment of our program, we have not adequately answered Marty's annual question: "How do you know your program is working?" We can offer all kinds of subjective, broad indicators, such as number of books checked out of the library or student responses on individual surveys ("When I'm at school I feel _____."), but we have not yet found the Rosetta Stone for revealing exactly what our students are learning. As we run to the battlements each year to grapple with assessment, our only consolation is that no one else has yet found a completely legitimate and accurate way to measure performance within an instructional approach that has burst the boundaries of what was once defined by standardized tests. So we continue each year, open to and trying each new evaluation tool—portfolios, performance assessments, anecdotal records—and hoping we are at least getting closer.

Togetherness

Although we were fully engrossed in the planned discussions, it may have been that the most important reason for our 5 days of meetings was simply to be together. In many if not most schools in this country teachers can teach right next door to each other for 10 years and never do anything more than share daily pleasantries and some Elmer's Glue. In contrast, we have become an incredibly gregarious, mutually supportive staff.

During one lunch period, several of us were huddled next to the pop machine laughing and chattering about some event or another. Neil suddenly turned up in the middle of the group, asking in his most earnest fashion, "Are we bonding now?" He may have been teasing, but he was acknowledging something we had been working at for several years.

In addition to $50,000 a year, the Twenty-First Century program allotted each selected school 10 additional days for each teacher. Five of these days were used for our August inservice week; the other five were used at the discretion of each teacher. For the first 3 years of our Twenty-First Century program, half of our allotted $50,000 was used to pay substitute teachers, releasing the regular staff for the equivalent of 2 full inservice days each month. These provisions gave us increased access to one of the most vital commodities in education: *time*. Because of this additional time, we had wonderful opportunities for extended inservice in such areas as cooperative learning, whole language, assessment, and technology. In addition, we used the extra time for team planning, sharing of ideas, developing units and lessons together, creating materials, and, at crucial moments, thrashing over questions related to the larger program.

Over the years we have dealt with some truly formidable issues: our special needs model (leading to mainstreaming), multiage grouping, whether to move the school to another building, and the school discipline plan. When we first began dealing with these matters (versus which new copy machine to order), the tension was almost unbearable. People would walk out of meetings; tears would flow; backs would go rigid. For some who had taught for many years, this was a new experience. Confrontation, dissent, compromise, being honest about feelings, taking risks—none of this was part of their familiar work world.

In this respect, it is probably impossible to overestimate the role Anne assumed in helping to initiate and support the extraordinary changes in our building. Few of these changes are as important as how we work together as a staff and where we direct our energy. In her first year at Jefferson, Anne shifted all routine decisions to the School Council, leaving staff (teachers, school counselor, and other support people) meetings for inservice topics. Before we could do anything about professional matters, however, we had to learn how to behave as professionals. We were certainly professional in our classrooms working with students, but with each other things easily fell apart.

With time and practice, however, we gradually learned to function as a group. Tears became rare, and now they usually flow over something unabashedly sentimental. During a spring meeting, one of the new teachers quietly and spontaneously thanked her team members for their support and willingness to help her during the year. Only the worst cynic would not have been touched; each of us could identify with the difficulties she experienced in her first year and how much we each have relied at some time or other on "a little help from our friends." Staff members frequently acknowledge each other verbally and even with notes back and forth. This seems corny, but it is a conspicuous symptom of colleagues trying not to take each other for granted.

We often disagree, but no one leaves the room; we still speak to each other after a meeting, and there is a minimum of mumbling behind doors. It has not been easy, and we have all had our strained moments. However, given the time to talk to each other, listen, wrestle with problems and misunderstandings, and simply be together, we are now able to survive the most sensitive issues, including teacher room assignments. Actually, working through room assignments later in the spring almost set us back a year. Nothing raises the hackles quite so much as suggesting to a teacher that she or he has to move a professional lifetime of accumulated teaching materials 30 yards to a different classroom.

In any case, that August inservice week was used by most of us to renew ties, be reminded of how we work together and communicate. We used up a lot of butcher paper for planning curriculum and brainstorming theme ideas. The primary team (teachers of the first/second-grade multiage classes) were their usual selves, all seeming to talk at the same time, but somehow ending up with specific and clear plans. The rest of us are always amazed; I think they are too.

The intermediate team, on the other hand, was really two teams. The first consisted of the third/fourth-grade teachers (Neil, Pam, and myself) plus the two third-grade teachers (Judy and Fran). Out of the five teachers, four were new. With just six years at Jefferson, I was the veteran in the group. The second intermediate team was made up of the two fourth/fifth-grade teachers (Jane and Clare), one fourth-grade teacher (Shirley), and two fifth-grade teachers (Grace and Edith). While the primary teachers were eager to try multiage grouping a year previously, the intermediates needed more time to think about it. Some were so close to retirement that it seemed understandable that they might not want to add any new wrinkles to their last years.

MARY

Lest anyone think that age is a barrier to change, meet Mary, 65 years old, with a cloud of white hair and a laugh like a stevedore's. She moves as rapidly as her tongue. I think several of us want to grow up to be just like Mary. She's a wonderful teacher; she expects her students (and the adults) to mind their manners, take care of business, work hard and think hard. Mary has taught for more than 35 years, has probably seen every kind of teaching method come and go, and yet she will tell anyone who asks that these last few years have been the most exciting of her professional life.

Mary says what she thinks, whether to another teacher, a parent, or an administrator. (Strangers don't intimidate her either. She has been known to follow someone into a store, scolding them for illegally parking in a handicapped spot.) Most of the time, this is a trait that benefits all of us—Mary often will give voice to what some of us are thinking but are too hesitant to express. Periodically, however, Mary can be brusque and sharp. For those not used to Mary, feelings can be hurt or umbrage taken. Mary realizes this, and she has actually tried to temper her comments during SC meetings, where parents, especially, often do not know how to react to Mary's remarks. Regardless of all this, Mary is a steady presence and model for the staff. If she could make it this long and still be enthusiastic, perhaps a few years of rolling change should not be so difficult for the rest of us to manage.

Because everyone on the first intermediate team, except myself, was new to the school and to each other, we spent these meetings mainly talking about how we could work together during the year, ways we could share, and who might share what with whom. In the process of these talks the four of us attending the August session discovered, probably with some relief, that we enjoyed each other's company, that we seemed to be able to listen to each other and were already willing to risk sharing our honest thoughts. I felt fairly confident that eventually we would be able to develop a collaborative arrangement as effective as that of the primary team.

Each of the newly hired teachers came in knowing that we were a staff moving toward teaching without basals and without reliance on textbooks and workbooks, that we were pursuing whole language, cooperative learning, and an integrated curriculum. It meant that during the year our conversations would become open-ended, searching dialogues on teaching and learning. It did seem a promising beginning, and in many important, often touching ways the year fulfilled the promise.

2

1990–1991, The First Half

We teachers were ready. We had completed our annual papering rites of covering the bulletin boards, making up perky signs for the classroom, setting up activity centers, shoving desks and tables into every possible configuration. Our bodies were stiff, hands scraped, and fingers band-aided. High school teachers don't know what they're missing in all of this, but they probably begin each year like the rest of us elementary folk—energetic and hopeful. We mentally recite some version of the "This Year Will be Different" speech: "This year I will be better organized. This year I will really challenge the bright students; I will get all my low students up to grade level in reading; I won't grumble as much. I'll cover all of the math strands. Everyone will be able to keyboard at least 30 words per minute. Come flood or fire, I'll read aloud to the class everyday." Considering how exhausted we are by the end of a school year, I often feel like some kind of Phoenix rising out of the ashes each September.

For a beginning teacher, little in life matches the combination of anxiety and joy in anticipating that first day of school. It is impossible to describe adequately the sense of awesome responsibility and wrenching uncertainty when it is you alone facing a classroom of smallish bodies patiently waiting for their first direction, waiting to find out if you are going to be funny, strict, mean, nice, "cool," or boring. After a couple of years, however, the first-day rigors are simply to be waded through so that everyone can move on to the real stuff of which school days are made.

I think most teachers tend to observe the familiar first-day rituals—review classroom rules and expectations, practice routines, distribute materials, and have some kind of get-acquainted activity. Then we begin. This year some of us began with a unit on whales in anticipation of a field trip to the Science Museum later in the fall. A somewhat new addition to several classrooms was a Middle East map, as both teachers and students struggled to learn relevant geography and thoughtfully deal with events in the Persian Gulf. The seven primary classes were working on a camping unit, which would culminate two weeks later in a giant sleepover in the neighborhood park, with parents, teachers, and children rolled into sleeping bags and looking like refugees from a natural disaster.

Most children quickly start to feel at home in their classrooms. This has become especially true as we have moved into multiage grouping, allowing students to spend two years with the same teacher. The previous year had been the first outing for our primary (first/second-grade) classes. These teachers had been eager to take on multiage classes, but serious reservations among some parents and staff kept us from instituting combination classes in the upper grades. At the end of the year, however, the primary teachers' enthusiasm for multiage classes had not diminished a whit, and enough parents with second graders were comfortable with if not committed to having their children move into another multiage class. Following through, this year we added three third/fourth-grade classes and two fourth/fifth-grades. I had had a straight third for three years and was a little hesitant about moving to a third/fourth-grade, but I needed some kind of change to shake up my incipient inertia. As it turned out, I now can't imagine teaching any other way.

This year was not typical. I had only 24 students (13 boys and 11 girls, 12 third graders and 12 fourth graders). I had never had fewer than 27 children in a class. The 24 this year presented the usual broad spectrum of personalities and abilities, quirks and giggles. Half of my third graders from the previous year had moved on to other teachers. The half that stayed with me as fourth graders were a mixture of students—a few very bright, a few needing much more help, a couple who routinely chewed up substitute teachers but who had made their separate peace with me. The new third graders were a jolly, although shy, lot. In this group were two in the REACH (gifted) program, two identified as special education students, and a whole bunch in-between. The younger children may have come in feeling a little intimidated, but if they did, it did not last very long. By the time I had mixed them in their seating and into different project groups, I think they saw themselves simply as Room 32.

Cooperative learning has become a more natural part of our classrooms each year, and most of us now automatically arrange desks in clusters, shifting students' seats regularly during the year. With six clusters of four desks in a cluster, I did as much mixing as I could—boys and girls, older and younger, quiet and outspoken, focused and distracted, adult-level readers and barely first-grade readers. I shifted seats at the beginning of each month, trying for compatibility as well as contrast. There was a lot of contrast to use, and age was not a predictor. Jake, for example, was a third-grade REACH student, a whiz in math, reading virtually every kind of material except fantasy, which he hated. Kenny, a fourth grader, read well enough but struggled with basic math, and writing more than two sentences was a morning's effort. Tom, another fourth grader, had been living with his grandmother since his mother had left him a few years earlier; he rarely saw his father. Despite all of this, Tom was a social wonder, enjoying his classmates, loving to work in groups, playful but always considerate. He was my everyday reminder that we cannot assume limits on any child's possibilities.

This was a class not unlike any other class in the school. I had deep thinkers and reluctant thinkers, leaders and shy followers. I had the quiet "yes" children who would rather eat school lunches for a year than break a rule. I had dark-haired Danny, too fast with a quip, and still learning that his fists were not an acceptable means of persuasion in an argument. There was Christie, quick as a whip, who loved to write but also to throw a football with the guys out on the playfield. Sharon, in contrast, usually stayed on the edge of the playfield, wandering around by herself, both socially and physically awkward, representing for the second year one of the more frustrating challenges to my abilities as a teacher.

This was my class, and I, along with my gentle building cohorts, would spend the year emotionally and intellectually immersed in one of the most intense experiences any individual can have in a lifetime. We would be teaching. The exquisite irony of being a teacher is that you become a better teacher when you understand that you can "never get it right." In a kind of Sisyphus fate, you realize that no matter how long you teach or how hard you try, there will always be something more to do, something else to do better. So why do we continue to stay with that rock and start up the hill again? I think it has something to do with hope. Each time you start up that hill, you believe that you will get farther, that it will be easier, that you will learn something new. In the process, you will reach a few children and help them to lead lives graced by quiet learning, passion, and humaneness.

So, we picked up where we had left off the previous June. Routines were in place, the year-long conversations had begun. We talked about Kuwait, whales, the Berlin Wall, what was in the daily newspaper, how to make up a bar graph. As the children moved through various small working groups for math and research, they talked about listening to each other, taking turns, and sharing the work. Sharon would have difficulty all year fitting into the flow of any group, but there were enough calm days when she could stay with an activity and forget about teasing and complaining. Danny, too, had his own lessons to learn about not giving up even when frustrated and temporarily unable to follow the thinking of his group. We talked about the stories the class wrote, about castles and underground caves, about quotation marks and sequence, about descriptions and plots. Everyday there were books to share, books the children read on their own, books they read in small groups, books that I read aloud to the class.

We were speaking in the "language" of our school. Visitors and newcomers to the building have to spend some time listening to understand. They have to listen to the students as they talk about their work, the problems posed, their ideas and solutions—"I know what, we can put a bushing on the axle!"; "Wait, I'll show you another triangle."; "Look in the atlas. Where's Bangladesh?"

They have to listen to the teachers. Is the talk a litany of complaints and trivia or matters of instruction and children's learning?—"What do you think of this paper? Should I have asked Tricia to add more?"; "What a dumb assignment! I should never have assigned that report on their kitchens!"; "I need another way to get the kids to learn their times tables. Any ideas?"; "I tried literature circles, but it just doesn't work for me. Maybe if I modify it."; "How about webbing out the unit?"

Then they have to observe the interactions, children with children, children and adults, adults and other adults. It is not just what they talk about, but how they speak to each other. Do they speak kindly? Do they laugh often? The children did seem to spend the year, for the most part, with good humor, cheerfulness, sensitivity, openness, and remarkable balance. The adults, however, were not always as blessed.

THE SCHOOL COUNCIL MEETS (AND MEETS, AND MEETS . . .)

The adults got down to business. The SC held its first meeting at 8:00 A.M. on Tuesday, September 11, 1991 (subsequent regular meetings convened every other Tuesday in the library). This decision-making body consisted of the principal, Anne; four parents, Kathy, John, Sandy, and Wendy; a specialist representative, Rose, our music teacher; the special education teacher, Dee; a member of the classified staff, Kerry (office manager); and a teacher from each wing (Clare,

Mary, Barbara, Edith, and Ellen). Jo, the librarian, served as chairperson for the year.

JO

Jo may have been exactly the right person to head the SC this year. With her basic sense of fairness and good judgment, she would give a steady hand to the helm. There are few people quite like Jo. There are moments when you want to throttle her right there in her meticulously organized library, and other days you can't believe you could ever live without her organizing some part of your life. Jo is proprietor, custodian, caretaker, and ever-watchful guardian of a glorious library collection of some 11,000 items, not including all of the building's audiovisual equipment, computers, software, and math and science materials. She is the quintessential librarian when it comes to organizing and tracking every item, no matter how minute, from atlases and wall maps to compasses and protractors. It is a joy on earth for a teacher to go into the library and not only know exactly what should be on the shelves, but where everything should be, and, if something is not where it should be, Jo will tell you where it is.

To maintain this extraordinary organization, Jo is ruthless when it comes to following library procedures. With her sergeant-major's voice and clipped speech, shoulders held back, eyes boring through you, Jo easily intimidates, and it takes a brave teacher to admit to misplacing a book. But, she has the soul of a true librarian and loves to be of service—there is nothing that quite pleases her more than finding some obscure fact for a child, coming up with just the right book for you to read to your class, helping you get all your computers linked to the printer, and making sure the library acquires books for every unit being taught.

Jo had a long elementary teaching career before becoming a librarian. She could probably retire in a few years, if she ever decided to make her summer travels a full-time pursuit. For now, we listen in the morning for her double-time steps clicking down the hallway or her bursts of throaty laughter, and we make sure we have signed the cards in our books.

The staff always received a copy of the SC agenda the day before each meeting, giving us an opportunity to buttonhole our rep and offer an opinion. It was always a loaded agenda; in fact, toward the end of the year several extra meetings were held to deal with all of the unresolved issues. Volunteering to serve on the SC involves a substantial investment of time, for which no one receives any formal compensation. Parents have to deal with childcare and juggle their work schedules. Staff has to cope with their own regular school and teaching responsibilities in addition to this particular role.

ELLEN

Ellen had agreed to serve as SC rep from our wing. This was just her second year as a classroom teacher in our building, or anywhere. She had completed her student teaching the year before with Nan, one of the other primary teachers in our wing. Ellen came to teaching later than most. I suspect that for every year that Ellen did not teach she stored up a little more energy to be applied when she was handed her classroom keys. A tall, attractive woman, saved by just a few pounds from being called "skinny," Ellen not only moves constantly, but is always thinking about her class. Some of this comes from the self-doubt that all of us experience, but for Ellen the introspection seems more constant and passionate. As a result, she provides me with some of the more provocative and stimulating discussions during the school year. "Okay," she says, as she sits on a desk in my room, "now tell me what you think about these two stories," and she sets out two pieces of writing by one of her students. We spend the next 15 minutes talking about appropriate expectations for children's writing at each level, about how to stimulate genuine writing, about what constitutes genuine writing itself. I don't think Ellen's curiosity is a temporary symptom of new-teacher enthusiasm; rather, she is doing what teachers should do: analyze their own instruction. I wonder at times if this is a propensity that comes best with age.

Ellen and her teammate, Kay, are tough to have as neighbors. They arrive early, stay late, and never seem to think anything is impossible. Chickens? Why not. Tadpoles? Sure, just create a makeshift pond in the room. As the year ended they were talking about salmon. Given all that they do in their classrooms, it amazed me how Ellen could work so conscientiously on her SC responsibilities (the effort was similar for each of the other teachers, staff, and parents). Also, I do think that over the course of the year Ellen extended herself in professional and personal ways that teachers traditionally have not had an opportunity to do before site-based decision making. She would be SC chairperson for 1991-92.

Tackling the Issues

As the year wore on, it was not just the burden of time that stood out, but certain issues led to extraordinary stress for all of the SC members. The minutes indicate that the first SC meeting, however, began benignly enough. Someone suggested that the Pledge of Allegiance and announcements be given over the PA system each morning. There must not have been a lot of enthusiasm for this idea, since we were still saying the Pledge on our own in June. One of the parents asked about a science fair, and there was discussion of extra P.E. time.

The science fair never materialized during the year (it would come up again the next year as well), mainly due to staff resistance. We felt, I think, that we were already doing so much in our classrooms that we didn't need something more added to our lists. We were reluctant to encourage something as openly competitive as a science fair (we are one of a few elementary schools in our district without a spelling bee), which often ends up with parents doing more than their children, and where children without interested parents are at a decided disadvantage. I also think there was a small additional piece. Some of us were beginning to bristle when parents made "suggestions." Why? I'm not sure. In retrospect it seems to have been not always the suggestion per se but a matter of who was making the suggestion. It definitely appears overly sensitive, but we had already become familiar with a small group of parents who, to our minds, were not happy with the program we were developing and were trying to find ways of leading us back to more traditional and familiar school experiences.

Also on the SC agenda was Becky's announcement that she would be starting a school newspaper that would involve as many children as possible. Becky had been hired the previous year to coordinate our building's REACH program. The intent of this program was to provide families with children identified by the district as "gifted" the alternative of staying in their home school rather than transferring to an all-day or pull-out program based at another school. The underlying notion was that Becky would provide regular classroom teachers with teaching support and materials so that they could appropriately challenge these identified students. Consistent with our larger special needs model, this was not to be a pull-out program, but rather Becky and the teachers would work to include other students in all of the activities. Hence, the school newspaper.

There were two additional issues on the SC agenda. One would move in and out of consideration all year; the other would lead all of us into a thicket of controversy that would last until mid-December.

The first had to do with our inservice meeting days. In the initial year of our Twenty-First Century program, we met as a staff every Wednesday morning, using half of our allotted $50,000 to pay for half-day substitutes. Parents were extremely unhappy with that arrangement; and we weren't thrilled ourselves. On those half-days students did not function well, and it was difficult for the teachers to go back to their rooms and smoothly pick up the afternoon. For the next two years, we tried full-day inservice meetings every other Wednesday, approximately twice a month, still with substitutes. This worked better, but it still seemed to add a difficult "blip" to the week, especially when we were not always able to have the same substitutes each week.

In the spring of the previous school year, someone had suggested a 4-1/2 day week. Contact time would remain the same, with a schedule adjustment (i.e., earlier start time each day), and students simply would be released to go home at midday on Wednesday. Staff could then use Wednesday afternoons for inservice and planning, without having to rely on substitute teachers. The major difficulty with this plan was how it would affect families dependent on childcare. The SC formed a committee of parents and teachers to study this proposal, specifically looking at the childcare issue. The 4-1/2 Day Committee, as it came to be called, would meet periodically all year and even into the next summer.

BUT *WHY* DO YOU WANT TO MOVE?

The second issue on the SC's agenda concerned the "Emerson Move." Jefferson Elementary serves the community of Grandview. Until 1984 there was a second school, Emerson Elementary, just over a mile from Jefferson. When enrollments dropped, the district chose to close Emerson, transferring its students and several teachers to Jefferson Elementary. As the story goes, Emerson rather than Jefferson was selected for closure because the district believed Emerson, being a more attractive, convenient facility, would be easier to lease (apparently schools do not need "attractive, convenient" facilities). As it turned out, it did attract the Boys and Girls Club, a preschool, and some other smaller enterprises. The Emerson teachers who came to Jefferson never stopped heaving great sighs of regret when describing their old classrooms and what they had left behind.

Also important to know is that our Twenty-First Century proposal stressed the importance of reaching children long before they enter kindergarten. Given this belief, we established the Parents as Teachers (PAT) program, coordinated by Chris. For two years PAT had been helping expectant parents and parents of preschoolers provide the early experiences that would lead to success in school. The PAT program also provides a support group for young parents, who meet regularly in a portable that, until recently, was plopped on one side of the school parking lot. (It now meets in another, more attractive portable placed under the trees next to the kindergarten/first-grade rooms.)

More recent history begins in the spring of 1990 when SIT met to discuss the status of PAT and plans for a daycare. Most of the SIT members had been with the group for at least two years, and several were part of the proposal-writing team. We had come to know and trust each other, and we worked together exceedingly well. At this particular meeting I'm sure we were in the library after school, munching on Jody's coconut-chocolate bars, and dutifully working through our agenda. At some point as we discussed the problem of space for a daycare and the limitations of the portable for PAT, Chris raised her hand and, in her soft-spoken manner, almost whispered, "What about Emerson?"

Once we realized that Chris's suggestion meant moving the whole school to the Emerson building in order to have an on-campus daycare and facilities for PAT, we agreed that this was a grand idea and asked when we could pack up. Pausing long enough for some discussion, we decided that the proposal should be studied and presented to the SC in September. As much as I believe in our democratic system of school governance, there are moments when there is the urge to make a unilateral decision. This was such a moment.

I have always disliked the Jefferson facility for its shabby appearance and awkward arrangement of space. A drab, almost ugly school, as only 1950s economizing could have produced, Jefferson consists of six boxy, single-story buildings plus a gym/lunchroom, all painted a fading yellow with brown and blue trim. The main office building includes the clinic, library, counselor's office, and conference room. Regular classrooms are spread through five separate wings (four classrooms to a wing), connected by outside walkways. The kindergarten and primary classrooms tend to remain in the wings closest to the main building, while the intermediate classes are in the other wings; the actual configuration has shifted each year (I moved four times in six years). The classrooms may be a bit larger than in most other schools, but we pay with leaky roofs, lack of storage space, poor ventilation, and unreliable heating.

Most of us did not agonize much over whether we wanted to take up residence in a building with more usable space, cedar walls, large indoor carpeted hallways, five classrooms (versus four) to a wing, more wall storage and built-in bookcases, and a campus that actually looked like a campus instead of a temporary holding facility. To many people this doesn't seem sufficient reason to move an entire school up the road. There were, in fact, many other reasons that we eventually—and too late—described in detail in a November staff letter to the parents.

What was important was that we strongly felt that the Emerson facility would be significantly more conducive than our present building to our approach to instruction. If students were still sitting at their desks for most of the day, passively filling in worksheets, we wouldn't need much more than an empty room to hold some desks. Instruction, how children learn, and our own role as teachers had changed so dramatically over the years, that we needed much more. We needed space for small groups to work comfortably without disrupting each other. We needed storage space to house all of the manipulatives we were using in math, and bookcases to hold the overflow of books the children were reading. We wanted the expanse of cedar walls to serve as bulletin boards to display student work. We wanted more ready access to each other so that we could collaborate and team teach. And, yes, as demanding and frivolous as it seemed, we wanted an attractive, warm environment that would be comfortable and support the family atmosphere of our classrooms. Over the next two months, however, our arguments often would be glibly dismissed as simply a desire for nicer "ambience."

As principal, Anne presented the Emerson proposal to the SC at its first meeting on September 11. Subsequent events would constitute perhaps the first major test of the staff unity we had been building for five years and of the site-based decision-making process that gradually had been coming of age over this period. For that first meeting, the decision was basically to look into the idea further, generate questions, and meet with Bill, the assistant superintendent for facilities, to determine what kind of upgrades would be required for such a move and whether they would be feasible. The "process" was being followed.

TEACHERS—TEAMS AND INDIVIDUALS

Otherwise, that month was a fairly normal September. Our Wednesday inservice meetings were launched in the middle of the month, and the usual "Back-to-School" night was held for the parents. I have not yet figured out how to make this a useful event. For a couple of years I tried describing curriculum and philosophy, but compressing all of that into 45 minutes is simply impossible. I think the parents get more from periodic letters that teachers send home, in which we explain what we are doing as we do it. This night seems to be mainly a time for parents to observe the teacher. Can he string more than three words together? Does she sound relatively intelligent, have a modicum of personality? I think often parents just look for reassurance that their child's teacher is not an idiot, that the school is functioning well, and that their child is behaving appropriately and coming along at least as well as most of the other children.

The team of third-grade and third/fourth-grade teachers had begun meeting, now with Fran. I must say, the five of us were wonderful. The new teachers raised numerous questions about forms, procedures, and budgets, but we also had ample time to talk about teaching. We shared ideas on classroom organization, how to handle writer's workshop, and, especially, math. The district had just developed new math student learning objectives (SLOs), which set out the specific strands (logic, geometry, number, probability, measurement, patterning) that would guide our math program. These revised SLOs were the result of a long process of research and discussion involving teachers, parents, and curriculum specialists. They also were coming to many teachers who had attended several district-sponsored workshops and received cartons of new materials to get them started. Each elementary school selected a math leader, who was responsible for attending regular district-level meetings, bringing back new ideas, and coordinating disbursement of building math funds to support the revised math program. In other words, the new SLOs were not a surprise, and we were not unprepared.

Pam, Judy, and Neil came in committed to whole language and with a variety of classroom experiences using this approach. Fran had been teaching for many years in the Southwest, but following a traditional basal and skills-sheet approach. Still, she noted that she had been taking whole language workshops during the summer and would continue to do so during the year. She indicated that she wanted to change her teaching methods, and everyone was ready to provide whatever help she might ask for. I will introduce Fran here, because her later situation would substantially complicate our year, lead to much personal anguish for different individuals, and eventually suggest how changes related to school restructuring are presenting some new issues and emphasizing old gaps in the way schools and districts usually have been organized.

FRAN

Pretty, with short, curly black hair, Fran was soft-spoken and always attractively, even stylishly dressed. In our initial team meetings she seemed shy, restrained. It may have been that she felt overwhelmed by the exuberant flow of conversation and easy bantering. She was also beginning at a distinctly different point in her approach to teaching. While the other four of us were standing waist-deep in whole language and all it represented for instruction, Fran had only begun to consider the possibilities of moving away from the traditional teaching she had been doing for so many years. At least in these early months, she never indicated anything but a desire to move forward, and while no one tried to pressure her, everyone was encouraging and sympathetic. The most commonly repeated advice was: "Start where you are comfortable, then gradually make changes." For Fran, starting where she was comfortable meant ordering full-class sets of basals, textbooks, and workbooks from the district warehouse. I thought then that sometimes we need familiar material trappings to feel in control, and that later in the year Fran would feel safer about "letting go."

Because Fran had been out of town during August inservice and had not had enough time to get her room in order, Anne arranged for some extra assistance. Helen, one of our former third-grade teachers, had retired the previous year but was a few months shy of a full 25 years. Rather than start with a new class, she would spend the time helping in various capacities in the building, including assisting Fran. Helen taught for many years, probably as what we would describe as a traditional teacher. Being a "traditional" teacher does not mean, however, that one cannot be an effective teacher. I taught across the hall from Helen for a year, and I know that she was exceptionally well-organized, conscientious, and tireless. She demanded a lot from her students, kept them accountable and on task. She was never anything less than genuine, professional, and caring about her students and colleagues.

While our intermediate team didn't reach the level of collaboration characteristic of the primary team, we talked a lot all year. We made a conscious effort each inservice Wednesday to get together and discuss problems we were having, share classroom activities and materials, and generally provide each other with support and encouragement. A distinctive element in all this was that no one pushed anyone to do anything; each respected the other's need to find his or her own pace in change. For the most part we seemed to share a certain philosophy about teaching, but we were also very different in our styles, interests, and the way we analyzed our instruction.

NEIL

While this team was enthusiastically studying whales in the fall, Neil one day announced he would not be taking the plunge. It just wasn't something he was interested in pursuing. He wisely decided to begin his teaching career with a topic closer to his heart—simple machines and inventions. Not many elementary school teachers invent toys. Neil even has a couple of patents, one for a brightly packaged spinner toy actually found on store shelves. Obviously, Neil added a refreshingly different quality to our staff. We knew he would be different when we walked into his classroom the day before school began and almost gasped to see bare bulletin boards, no colorful signs of welcome, no cute cubbies for materials. Instead, there was a genuine pink hairdresser's chair in the reading area, one of those old-style chairs with a large metal dryer that comes down over your head. The rest of the reading center contained piles of books and magazines in no particular order and was not particularly orderly. The desks were there, although Neil was still fiddling with how he wanted them arranged. He had one center: a workbench, complete with tools of all sorts and sizes. Neil was helping the rest of us to rethink what was most important about a classroom, not just in its physical makeup but also in content and method.

Over the course of the year our team would share much and make good use of Twenty-First Century days to get together. We talked often about how our writing programs were progressing and exchanged ideas on how to handle such things as peer conferences, revision, mechanics, and publishing. There were demonstrations of activities, such as a math menu on multiplication, which Judy had greatly simplified from the original version. I got a substantial boost listening to Pam describe her "literature circles" program, which she shared even more fully with Fran. Neil and I struggled to find a manageable, concrete way of teaching long division, and most of us passed math materials around accompanied by helpful advice.

So, while we may have been making decisions based on what was comfortable for us and our students, we were open to new ideas, more effective ways of doing things. In this respect, we were not unique; it is what teachers do in our building. I think the teaming of the primary teachers had a great deal to do with making sharing a part of the school culture. They met often to plan whole units, evaluate materials they would purchase as a team, and coordinate activities they would do together (e.g., field trips, enrichment activities). Within the primary team were subteams: Carol and Barb, Betty and Mary, Kay and Ellen. Nan lacked her own consistent partner, but she worked alternately with different members of the primary group. These seven teachers not only have opened their doors, but generously offer each other what they know, and no one hesitates to ask for help. We are learning that teachers don't have to know everything.

Other factors contribute to how we communicate as a staff. Inservice Wednesdays give us extended time to process issues, and in the course of doing so we become more comfortable and open with each other. Parts of Wednesdays also focus on instruction (e.g., cooperative learning, technology), so we routinely talk about instruction, assess what we are doing, reflect, and revise. We have become a staff that truly thinks about instruction, based on the belief that we are responsible for what goes on in our classrooms and are not simply caretakers walking through preset directives.

As cohesive a group as we are, however, we do not all teach in precisely the same way. Some teachers are more immersed in whole language than others; some like to teach math more traditionally; some are ready for technology, while others want no more than two computers in their rooms. Some teachers love science; several still avoid it. Writer's workshop is run differently in every classroom. There are spelling tests in some rooms, none in others (we struggle with spelling). It is a continuum of experience and professional growth. What we do have in common as teachers is an absolute commitment to providing learning that is meaningful, that leads children to thinking hard about questions, to producing work that is thorough, skillful, and authentic. In other words, quoting from the Nine Common Principles of the Coalition of Essential Schools, helping them "to use their minds well."

LEARNING AND CHANGING

We zipped through September and tumbled into October, Halloween pumpkins replacing fall leaves on the bulletin boards. Kay and Ellen, Betty and Mary started a whale unit but also sandwiched in "families and traditions" as they studied the Alaskan Inuits. Our first field trip for the year came in mid-October, about the same time that the school nurse decided it was time for eye tests. A major event was to change the traffic patterns in the school parking lot so that parents no longer could pretend they were driving the Indy 500 when picking up their kids after school. In other words, the familiar business of school continued without pause, belying the persistent if erratic effects of change that had begun to reshape almost every facet of our school lives.

So many school-change studies and articles focus either on the classroom or on the organization; but the two breathe together, or they should. If you talk about students using their minds well, you have to assume you want teachers and other staff to use their minds well too; and to support that you have to provide the adults with the same kind of latitude and opportunities for choice and problem solving as you do the students. That then leads to healthy discussions about and experiments with new forms of building governance. Or, if you believe that teaching and learning should be personalized, you expect that relationships among administrators, staff, and parents should also be personalized. So then you have to rethink the way you conduct evaluation of staff and how you communicate with parents. Cursory observations and brief written comments twice a year are no longer acceptable in evaluating teacher performance; and breezy monthly newsletters to parents are not enough to keep them fully involved and informed about their children's progress and activities at school.

As Jefferson began to institute program changes, we were cautious but I don't think timid. To the consternation and confusion of several individuals, change became a kind of way of life for many of us. As the mechanisms and dynamics of decision making for the building began to evolve and redefine themselves, so did our instruction and the way children were learning and interacting with each other in the classrooms. Ellen might be struggling to make sense of a discussion in a 7:30 SC meeting, but two hours later she was trying to figure out how to get her students to write a fully plotted story. In a Wednesday morning staff meeting we might be wondering how to involve more teachers in various committees; later in the day we would return to our classrooms and wonder about the best way to provide more alternatives and decision-making opportunities for our students.

My own issues, while specific to my particular classroom, illustrated the self-questioning that most of the staff was experiencing. In the middle of my first year of teaching (second/third grade) I shelved the six or seven levels of basal readers that I had inherited from the previous teacher. The next year I shipped them all back to the district warehouse. I was comfortably developing a reading program using a variety of tradebooks and literature. In my first years at Jefferson not all of the teachers had discovered the riches of our library, so I was joyfully free to roll one of our red wagons back and forth until my classroom shelves were full. It was a fairly fluid reading program of independent reading, teacher reading aloud every day (poetry, a chapter book, a picture book), small groups shifting in their membership, reading themes, and book extension activities.

This year, with the third and fourth graders, I thought I should consider a more structured reading program. All the anxious talk from parents about "getting the children ready for middle school" made me think that perhaps I needed to do more. (Parents should not believe that we do not hear them.) I thought that if we had a writer's workshop, why not a reader's workshop? Now totally dependent on my computer, I enthusiastically created a sheaf of activity sheets on which students would meticulously record books they read, their reading partners, summaries of discussions, descriptions of book projects, self-evaluations, and group evaluations. I let students form their own groups, following their buddies and based on what they wanted to read, but I scheduled set times everyday for groups to meet, have discussions, and work on projects, and we would have only reading activity during those times. It was an eminently organized program, and for many teachers this kind of program works well.

What I forgot is that I don't happen to be one of those teachers. I don't function well with set schedules and precise procedures. I fill in my planbook one day at a time, feeling at times inadequate as I see other teachers planning in detail for an entire week. Yet, two periods of silent reading continue to be the only sacred portions of each day in my planning. It is not that I am disorganized or random; in fact, parents have been known to request me for their children, citing my "structured" approach. And I believe that I *am* "structured," but mainly in the sense of trying to hold a clear framework of goals and curriculum inside my head as I plan instruction. Within this framework I allow myself the freedom to let each day's activities adapt to the rhythms of the students rather than stuffing students into a preset, highly structured schedule ("structured" in the traditional sense). If we are discussing the news and hands are still waving after a half-hour, I am more likely to let the discussion continue than to break off so that we can hew to scribbles in my planbook. I also think students need time and opportunity to make their own choices about what they work on. We usually spend some portion of our mornings in an open period in which students have a chance to complete unfinished work in math, reading, writing, or any of their ongoing projects, using their own judgments about priorities and time. They work individually, in pairs, and in small groups.

"Reader's workshop" was conceptually consistent with how I teach, but it was an artificial change in my instruction. I was always trying to work around the workshop period, nagging students about their record sheets, struggling to keep everyone "at the same place" in their reading or projects, all the while knowing in my heart of hearts that this was a goofy way for me to try to create authentic reading experiences. I had forgotten that reading should be a spontaneous, self-motivated, creative activity. Regimenting it with activity sheets and schedules, at least in my own classroom, transformed it into just another school subject and something to do to satisfy the teacher.

The most enduring instructional change seems to me to be the result of daily purposeful tinkering rather than sudden reconstruction. Assuming you are clear about where you want to go and are not caught up in random change "because everyone else is doing it," each day is an opportunity to come closer to your perceived ideal.

You add something here, drop something there, change a piece, move a piece; sometimes, when you are very lucky, revelations will occur, and you can turn instruction inside out. But, for the most part, instruction seems to evolve as a teacher's understanding and philosophy of learning and teaching evolve and become clearer and more responsive to his or her own style.

Unlike most other endeavors, teaching does require reinventing the wheel. The overarching concepts and principles about how children learn may be constant, but the everyday nuts and bolts of how to run a classroom, how to organize instruction, how to deal with children effectively—all of that is there to be learned, nearly from scratch, for each beginning teacher. Even the most senior teachers have to readjust each year to accommodate a new group of students replete with their own particular quirks. No two teachers are exactly alike in their temperaments, need for order, personalities, experiences, values, strengths, and weaknesses. A classroom is a highly personal reflection of all of these areas, and to feel comfortable and have students feel comfortable, a teacher spends years constantly pushing and tugging at virtually everything he or she does in the classroom.

What had changed over the years at Jefferson was that more of the staff had become engaged in this kind of constant tinkering with instruction, which, at one time, we believed had been permanently defined and limited by teacher manuals, textbook guides, and district guidelines. Released from this perception, we now were gamely coping with the glorious self-doubt and ambiguity that accompany the freedom to make one's own decisions. And, while we were fully cognizant of SLOs and curriculum guidelines, our decisions focused on instruction and children's learning. It was a quiet moment of grace before the nation's schools would be overtaken by standards and outcomes.

MENTORSHIP AND NEW TEACHERS

Somewhere in late September or early October, I became Fran's mentor at her request. The district has a mentoring program for first-year teachers coming in with no previous experience. Fran came into the district with a decade of teaching experience in the Southwest, but because she was stepping into a program that seemed drastically different from what she had experienced, Anne suggested that she join the district's mentoring program. This involves funded release time for school visits, meetings, and virtually anything else supportive of the new teacher. Mentors also receive some compensation for this activity. When individuals take full advantage of the program, it can be remarkably instructive for both the new teacher and mentor.

At our first meeting, Fran came with a list of nine areas in which she felt she needed assistance. After some discussion, she settled on development of positive relationships, student self-esteem, and whole language as the focus of her goals for the year. In the meantime, Pam would be receiving advice and counsel from Betty, and Neil would be looking to Clare, a fourth/fifth-grade teacher, for support.

I think all the mentors looked forward to working with the new teachers, but we also appreciated the challenges they were to confront—whole language, cooperative learning, mainstreaming, hands-on problem-solving math, multiage grouping, and all the other strands of our program. In September everything is possible. Each new teacher, including Judy and Emily, would have small but wondrous epiphanies in the classroom throughout the year, with a strong dose of frustration and bone-deep realization of how overwhelming daily teaching can be, especially when you are in the middle of a strong staff that is well-launched into so many different avenues of innovation and new professional responsibilities. The pressure is constant but not necessarily competitive. Still, when you notice that over an hour after the children have gone home every teacher in your wing is still correcting papers, creating and setting out materials, or planning for the next day, you don't feel especially comfortable strolling to your car 15 minutes after the final bell. When your team talks about how to improve writer's workshop or a reading program, you cannot help thinking about your own procedures and begin to self-analyze and evaluate. No one criticizes, but the tacit expectation is that "you *are* working hard, aren't you?" Each year we tried to set specific goals for relaxing and finding occasions for informal, fun gatherings; but we never seemed to do more than an occasional Friday after-school gathering at a local pub.

A district survey conducted during the previous year showed that 61% of the elementary certificated staff responding from 16 schools agreed that "there is too much change going on in [the district]. It is too much, too fast." In contrast, this statement found only 33% agreement at the five middle schools and 19% at the five high schools. Sixty-two percent of the elementary respondents also agreed that "I am under extreme stress trying to cope with all of the changes coming at me in my job." Again, this contrasts with 48% agreement at the middle school and 42% at the high school. This survey confirmed what we all observed every day in our individual buildings: that change had struck, not in polite, unobtrusive little jabs, but in some relatively grand-scale thrusts across the district, particularly at the elementary level. The stress is indeed palpable, and any teacher new to our district generally has much more to absorb and get used to than in other, less adventuresome districts.

MEANWHILE, BACK AT THE SCHOOL COUNCIL . . .

As we were immersed in all the usual school doings, the Emerson issue was following its own path toward confusion; but at least through October everyone was staying within the system, content to take a step at a time. In fact, the staff was probably too complacent at this point. Our own feelings had not entirely coalesced on the issue, and I think we were functioning as we traditionally had. That is, we acted as if someone else somewhere (i.e., administration or the SC) would take care of everything for us. We were too distracted by classroom demands to have been willing to take a more active interest in the proceedings. Also, I don't think we had any idea that the community reaction would become so intensely negative. When we finally did lift our heads out of our planbooks, it would be too late. But we would learn some pointed lessons.

When SIT met at the beginning of October, the parent reps indicated that more information should be going out to the community regarding the Emerson proposal. They said that other parents were expressing concern and asking why this move was being considered. On October 3, staff and SC members had another tour of Emerson.

During that tour, Betty happened to be following Wendy, one of the parent SC reps. Betty recalls that Wendy "had keys to everything." Betty asked her about it. A counselor with her own practice, Wendy explained that she kept an office in the Emerson building. This seemed only coincidental at the time, but later, as Wendy's position on the Emerson issue became clearer, this fact acquired greater significance.

WENDY

Wendy was not new to Jefferson. Her younger son, Carl, had been with me the previous year as a third grader and was with me again as a fourth grader. I also had Wendy's older daughter, who was now in middle school, a few years previously. Wendy and her husband both always made it a point to attend parent/teacher conferences. They demonstrated exceptional interest in their children's progress and were very alert to whatever was going on in the classroom. I often received notes from Wendy commenting on various activities. For example, the year Carl was a third grader I decided not to conduct keyboarding practice using what I called "disembodied" keyboards. The children hated the drills, which seemed to benefit only a handful of students. It seemed too much time for too little and too few. Nevertheless, Wendy wrote me several pages expressing her disappointment that Carl would not be having the same practice that her daughter had had. I received other such notes from Wendy through the years, and during the peak of the controversies regarding Emerson and multiage grouping, I received less gentle notes chastising me for various failings.

Wendy seemed the model caring parent, but I also found her quick to judge and unable to deal with any perspectives other than her own. She was not a stupid woman, but she seemed at times to become distracted by extraneous matters. In meetings, she frequently made comments that seemed irrelevant or that made no real sense. She had a difficult time relating to the other members of the SC, including the parents, and she eventually would estrange herself from the full group.

The SC met on October 9, and Sandy, a parent rep, said she had been receiving phone calls from parents. Wendy announced that she had summarized information from a study of the two facilities conducted five years previously, and this would be available in the office. The SC discussed a deadline for the final decision, suggesting that a date be set early enough to give the Boys and Girls Club sufficient notice to vacate if that became necessary. It should be noted that there was never a time during the deliberations that the SC stopped being sensitive to the position of the Boys and Girls Club and the other Emerson residents. The Club operates a daycare that is critically important to the community, and if a decision were made to move we wanted to be certain there would be little if no break in services, and that the Boys and Girls Club would be assured of an appropriate new location, which, it seemed logical, would be the Jefferson facility.

In addition to meeting on October 9, the four SC parents sent out an *SC Parent Newsline*, acknowledging the notes and phone calls they had received up to that point. They also described what they had been doing to gather more information and how they fully appreciated the difficult position of the Emerson tenants. This letter reminded parents that the SC would be meeting on October 26 to assess the situation and determine if they should continue to consider a move to Emerson. The emphasis was on trying to get parents to express their views on the issue:

> WE WANT TO HEAR FROM MORE OF YOU. . . . LET US KNOW YOUR ENTHUSIASMS AND CONCERNS. We are working hard to try to consider all aspects of the issue, but only with your response can we be sure we're getting at the right issues. . . . Don't assume that other parents with similar views are less busy than you and will surely respond. If you have an opinion, question or concern, we need to hear from you before Oct. 26. (*SC Parent Newsline*, October 9, 1990)

The staff had its own major Emerson discussion at its inservice meeting on October 24. The discussion was lengthy and thoughtful. As was typical, SC staff reps and other teachers, not Anne alone, brought up virtually every question and concern relevant to the issue. Staff meetings had definitely progressed from the early indifferent days of people dozing off, correcting papers, cutting out construction-paper teddy bears. In her first or second meeting with the staff, Anne directly but discreetly indicated that we should give our full attention to the business at hand. After some brief negotiating, it was agreed that needlework would be exempt. Thus, someone knitted, someone stitched, all of us listened. In the end, we reached consensus to move forward with the proposal.

CONSENSUS?

Consensus is a key part of site-based decision making, not just in our building but throughout the district. The collective bargaining agreement between the district and the Association, in fact, establishes guidelines for the decision-making process. Within this context, "consensus" implies more than simple ostensible agreement of all parties. It assumes that there has been extended, sufficient time for discussion and deliberation. All parties have had a fair opportunity to express their ideas and opinions. It is not enough to say, "The meeting was open to everyone, but since you didn't come we assume you agree." On controversial issues, such as multiage grouping, our staff will meet more than once, with everyone in attendance and opportunity provided everyone to express a view. We even take the time to go around the room, giving every individual a chance to voice an opinion.

Consensus also does not necessarily mean that all parties are at the same point of agreement. Most may "strongly agree," while others will simply "agree," having somewhat less commitment. There may even be a few who are not in agreement, but they "can live with the decision" and would not subvert it. Anne often sets up a scale (strongly agree, agree, can live with it, disagree but would not subvert) on the chalkboard, and we then each indicate our positions. There are no strict guidelines for what constitutes consensus. If everyone falls somewhere between "strongly agree" and "can live with it," the decision is made; but if there are too many sticking their yellow "Post-its" under "disagree," we have to stop and reconsider the issue. Would further discussion be pointless, or should we keep talking? How we proceed will depend on the nature of the issue, its perceived importance, the general atmosphere in the room, and any number of factors pertinent to the moment.

There is definitely a time to stop, to realize that a given proposal is not going to receive sufficient support, at least not for the near future. Then we move on. "You can't just keep battering us down," I once heard a high school teacher say in reference to the several faculty meetings his principal continued to hold on block scheduling. A small core of faculty opposed the proposal, and they obviously felt that the administration was simply trying to wear them down until "consensus" was obtained.

Consensus may be a group decision, but individual responsibility is at its heart. While it is incumbent upon the total group to provide every individual with an opportunity to express his or her ideas "safely," it is also each individual's own responsibility to speak up, to maintain a position reasonably, even in the face of substantial disagreement. If any individual claims to have been intimidated or manipulated into consensus, the process may have faltered somewhere, but it could also be that the individual was not able or willing to assume personal responsibility for expressing his or her differences.

In site-based decision making, as in most democratic decision making, a set of established procedures provides us with a systematic way of dealing with issues, working through questions and concerns, weighing the pros and cons, and giving all participants a fair chance to express their views. In the end, if we conscientiously have worked through the process, the final decision should be the best possible decision for that given time and for the given situation. Not all may agree to the same degree, but all will have been fairly heard.

This sounds wonderful, but it takes a lot of practice to learn and, I believe, a certain emotional disposition to be willing to accept the possibility that one's own truths and personal interests may not always predominate. I know that I was not the only person on the staff or in the community to spend the year learning how to follow and trust the process. Unfortunately, there were a few who did not try.

THE SCHOOL COUNCIL: INFORMED AND INFORMING

The teachers' decision recommending that the Emerson proposal continue to be studied was reported at a special SC meeting on October 26. (The staff and SIT can only recommend; the final decision on these kinds of issues comes from the School Council.) The SC also heard from Dave, district director of facilities/real estate, that in the event of a move the district could actually arrange what in effect would be "building swapping." Dave felt that it would be fairly easy to work with the Boys and Girls Club to develop a plan and schedule a move. The SC agreed that it would continue to look at a possible move and if that was eventually decided, "it would make the process work and would continue to address concerns" (October 26 minutes). Two committees were appointed, both with parents and teachers represented, one to write a letter from the SC to go home to parents, and the other to plan the November 7 community meeting. The process was holding.

October 31, Halloween. Another *SC Parent Newsline* was sent home summarizing some of what had been learned about the major structural differences between the two facilities, what would require repair at Emerson, cost issues, how a move might affect the district's long-term schedule for building modernization, and questions about interruption of services in the Emerson programs. This letter emphasized that no decision had been made and again asked for community input. It was a straightforward letter, offering information, but also, I think, reassuring parents that "the process" would be honored:

> We, the School Council, cannot make our decision until we have heard from the community. That is why it is VERY IMPORTANT that you attend the meetings on November 7 and November 28. At these

meetings, we will try to address the specific concerns but if significant problems cannot be overcome, we will not move. (*SC Parent Newsline*, October 31, 1990)

The SC parents agreed that they would not send out anything else until the teachers had had a chance to write their own letter to the community.

During Halloween week there is enough candy around the school to meet the annual sugar needs of Vermont. The children are less interested in number patterns than they are in their costumes and what time the party will start. Most of the classrooms have Halloween parties. Parents, usually moms (dads should be required to attend at least once in their child's school life), come in the afternoon to hang crepe paper and set up games and treats. Some teachers love all of this to-do as much as the kids. They dress up in their own clever costumes, bring treats to the staffroom and the students, and proudly troop through the classrooms in the annual school parade.

The day following Halloween can be a little sluggish as some children come in bleary-eyed and working off their sugar highs. I think we still had our giant skeleton on the chalkboard when one of the parents brought in a stack of fliers "to go home today," she said. I usually don't read these notices. After hundreds of such notices over the years I simply hand them to a student to distribute. This flier invited attention—it was too long (eight pages of single-spaced typing) and did not look like what usually came out of our office (unfamiliar type, no school letterhead). So I read. Then I balked.

Titled "Parent SC Representatives Questions and Concerns Noted by Parents," this document set out 59 such "concerns." There were three "Positives for Emerson" written in six lines, and 14 "Positives for Jefferson" that took two full pages of single-spaced type. The "positive" points given for Emerson reduced the argument to superficiality: "lovely music room . . . nicer-looking administration building."

A few of the 59 "concerns" were legitimate and objectively phrased, for example, "What are the number of walkers for whom Jefferson is the closest school?" or "What specific help will the district provide to find new homes for the Emerson tenants?" These kind of questions, however, were outweighed by a less positive tone ("sarcasm," one parent called it):

Are the benefits of a move to Emerson sufficiently compelling to justify expelling the 427 children currently housed there in daily programs, the other 650 in sports programs, and the expense of a move to the taxpayers/school district budget at a time when finances are limited?

It turned out that the move would have been of minimal cost to the district, as the labor simply would have been included in the existing work crew's routine functions.

To counter arguments that had been offered in support of a move, some of the comments stretched rather far:

> Teachers complain that the radiators at Jefferson are noisy, but they are handy for drying gloves or shoes wet from playing outside.

> The playground and field at Emerson is bordered on all sides by streets. . . . Police report that drug dealers and abductors often look for obvious schools on main roads.

During recess I discovered that not all of the classrooms had received copies of this letter. I used that as an excuse to let my stack sit on my desk overnight, small antidote to my irritation. Apparently, Wendy was waiting at home for her copy. When it did not arrive in her son's backpack (her son was one of my students), she and her husband sent me a letter the next morning. I passed the letter on to Anne for her own information; I wish I had retained a copy. Still, a teacher does not easily forget being called a "poor role model" for suppressing information that the community had "a right to know." As with previous notes from Wendy, I did not send a response. Eventually, the other classes received their copies of Wendy's letter. I sent home my stack.

BREACHING THE PROCESS

Decision making is, at best, arduous. It is often a complex process requiring much time and an instinctive understanding of what is civil and appropriate. Our own decision-making process over the years has been both difficult and fragile. Lacking any compatible examples of site-based decision making (SBDM), and unfettered by district directives about how to implement SBDM, we have been, in a sense, gradually creating our own precedents and traditions. Thus, many, if not most, of the staff (and parents) were still sufficiently inexperienced and perhaps even naive when the Emerson issue arose that we did not know how to respond effectively to events and actions that abruptly deviated from the process that we had been following. The appearance of the November 1 letter was a deviation.

Wendy had pulled together parent concerns, questions, and comments received by the SC over the prior two months, then shaped these to support her own biases. The contents of the letter would prove disruptive to the final decision, but perhaps even more damaging was that Wendy chose to breach the decision-making process as it had been proceeding. Although its title referred to "Parent SC Representatives," the letter was written and distributed without the "advice and consent" of the other SC parent representatives, and contrary to their agreement not to send out further communication until the teachers made their own written statement.

A year later, at an informal gathering, John, one of the SC parents, was still expressing bafflement and leftover anger at Wendy's disregard for the parents' agreement. I don't think anyone at school involved in this issue ever fully understood why Wendy acted as she did. Was she simply concerned about losing her private office at the Emerson center? Was it just the fear of change? It is hard to imagine that everything she did was motivated solely by the prospect of her son having to be in another facility for his last year of elementary school. There also was too much manipulation and hasty action to support the notion that she was acting on behalf of the community. Wendy demonstrated for us how easily one individual can waylay the decision-making process. So difficult to construct, so easy to undo.

Rather than resting on her laurels, Wendy made another unilateral decision: She went to the local newspaper with her letter and "concerns." On November 6, the day before the first community meeting, the morning paper published a front-page article with the headline, "School Plans 6-Block Move." In fact, no decision had been made, but the impression left by both the headline and the text was that this move was proceeding in spite of "overwhelming" objections from parents. Not surprisingly, the article quoted Wendy: "Of the parents we have heard from, 99 percent don't like the idea." That was Wendy's own creative computation.

Anne and John wrote letters to the paper expressing their concern over its precipitous and misleading coverage. But the tone for subsequent discussions was now set, and an editorial appearing on the day of the first community meeting only aggravated the situation by wrongheadedly suggesting that this decision was being engineered without sufficient communication with the community.

As they had been doing since September, the parent SC representatives continued to solicit questions and concerns from other parents, and they stayed in constant contact with district representatives (Bill, assistant superintendent; Dave, facilities director; and Wayne, maintenance/operations manager) in order to obtain information and answers to their questions. The district was scrupulous in its efforts to provide all requested information as objectively and thoroughly as possible, making no attempt to influence the final decision. This was especially demonstrated at the first community meeting.

This community meeting was held on November 7 at 7 P.M. in our school gym. It was a chilly autumn night. About 70 people sat at the long lunch tables, most with their coats still on; obvious friends banded together in small groups, many clutching copies of Wendy's letter. Several teachers were also present and, I think, uncertain about what to expect but already sensing more resistance than support. Anne opened the meeting with a general welcome, giving some history behind the issue and emphasizing that no decision had yet been made. John added his own remarks, expressing his hope that everyone would be able to listen to each other, keep an open mind, and clarify all of the issues related to the proposal. Both were trying to set the stage for a respectful exchange of information. The possibility of a nasty evening probably was not far-fetched.

Dave and Wayne gave their reports, methodically responding to all of the questions that had been raised up to that point regarding the condition of the two sites, the implications for the current tenants of Emerson, and projected costs. They spoke evenly and calmly, providing answers but not hesitating to admit when they did not know something. Dave, especially, who had gone through the brouhaha over the closing of the Emerson school six years earlier and its merger with Jefferson, was able to defuse some provocative challenges from a few in the audience about "failure to provide adequate notice" of this current proposal, "just like the last time."

We then broke into smaller groups with teachers sitting at each table to answer additional questions and, presumably, to present their own case for this move. I ended up sitting at a table that included Wendy and her husband. My memory is that of an attractive couple, somewhere in their late 30s, pressed together shoulder-to-shoulder, leaning toward the center of the table and nodding with what seemed to be earnest understanding. At the same time, however, they continued to repeat the "concerns" described in Wendy's letter.

The staff's viewpoint up to this point had not been formally or thoroughly communicated to the community. I think this meeting was the first time that many parents were hearing directly from the teachers. While a few teachers such as Betty were making spirited arguments in support of the Emerson move, others of us were less effective. Making strong public arguments was difficult for many of us who, like most elementary teachers, were not accustomed to making a case for ourselves, being openly assertive about our opinions, explaining what is good for instruction and why. Elementary teachers, especially, often seem to be conditioned to mollifying parents, soft-pedaling difficult issues, diffidently looking for compromise rather than boldly stating a position. This was not the best time to carry on such a tradition.

After the groups had met for about a half-hour, Anne reconvened us as a whole group and asked for a report from each table. She was successful in diligently keeping this on an informational level and steering around the few individuals who clearly were ready to launch into speeches or angry denunciation of the proposal without being fully informed. The community had gone through a bitter battle with the district over the closure of the Emerson school, and prior to that event the staff at Jefferson had its own problems with the community (some parents sat in the parking lot in the morning clocking the arrival time of teachers).

Bits of animosity lingered, and it seemed difficult for some people to separate the confrontative nature of those prior experiences from the current efforts to work through a more inclusive, systematic process for decision making. What the small group of vocal naysayers actually seemed to be saying that evening was, "We don't trust you." That was verbalized as fear about children walking along streets that children had walked along for years when Emerson was a school, as fear that children would have to cross the street at a four-way stop (never mind the thousands of city schools in the country), and even as fear about tree limbs falling on children on the playground.

The larger, overriding fear seemed to be the fear of change. For the previous four years our staff had struggled with each new initiative—technology, whole language, multiage grouping—and it had not been easy for anyone. Some chose to leave and find more secure harbors. Some stayed and ventured out a bit, doing only as much as they felt was absolutely necessary but basically adhering to their old ways. And there were those who leapt in, minds open, with humor to help. Change can be stressful and, at times, even overwhelming. As a staff, however, I think we have become accustomed to change, have learned how to manage it and not let it become an end in itself. Some of us even thrive on change, finding it absolutely necessary to our continued intellectual and emotional survival as teachers. What is difficult is that as we have been learning our "lessons of change" in the building and in our classrooms, the same learning and growing has not been entirely true for the broader community. Thus, when faced with not just a small change, but something that could reshape a large physical chunk of their daily lives, many in the community grabbed onto the railing and refused to let go.

Most participants seemed to leave this first community meeting with loose ends still dangling. Some parents were not necessarily convinced that a move would be good for the students, but they at least had heard enough to shift them toward the center, to a "maybe"; and some even left enthusiastically supportive of moving. But we still had that small hard-core group that left the meeting as adamantly opposed as when they came in, and nothing short of Jefferson collapsing in an earthquake would convince them that we should move.

DECIDING TO PRESS ON

The first community meeting was held on November 7. The staff met on Friday, November 9, to determine where we were and whether sufficient reason remained to pursue the proposal. We congregated in the library before school started, feeling not especially encouraged but not totally defeated either. After some discussion we reached consensus that we would recommend to the SC that it continue to explore the proposal. We also agreed that now the staff would finally write its own informational letter to the parents and community to explain its reasons for supporting a move. I think at this point we still believed that if parents could hear about and see (tours of the Emerson facility were arranged for the community) the differences between the two sites and how they related to instruction, they would support the move.

On November 14, I met with Betty, Mary, and Pam to write the teachers' letter. Taking notes, suggestions, and comments from the rest of the staff, we composed a five-page document that attempted to explain our preference for the Emerson site in terms of our program goals—we stressed, for example, the need for greater flexibility in classroom configurations, and teachers having ready access to each other for multiage grouping and teaming; the additional space and increased comfort of classrooms (to accommodate all of the student movement and group activity); how much more conducive to expansion of technology the facility would be; the improved facilities a second gym provided for specialists (art and music, especially); and some general items such as a larger teachers' workroom and office area, and more usable property (if more portables were needed in the future).

Because they had taught at the Emerson facility when it was Emerson Elementary, Betty and Mary embued our task with some extra energy and inspiration. They had collaborated for several years before coming to Jefferson, and as our approach to teaching changed and teaming was encouraged, the two of them were eager to renew their partnership. Following Ellen and Kay's example, they boldly removed the partition between their two classrooms and settled in for some genuine collaborative planning. Given Mary's sometimes crusty outspokenness, Betty was about the only person on the staff who was able to work so closely with her and even affectionately accept Mary's particular manner and disposition.

BETTY

Betty is one of those people who seem always cheerful and able to get along with anyone. Rather than being nice to the point of blandness, however, Betty is what we tend to call "spunky." I think she simply is constitutionally incapable of grousing through a day, unlike some of the rest of us. The year was difficult enough at school, but Betty also struggled with some serious problems at home. She managed to maintain her balance through the months, not just attending to her job, but becoming one of the staff's stronger and more articulate voices as we dealt with each successive issue.

Betty is typical of so many teachers. She had her first classroom right after college, taking only a brief time-out to have two children. She is now passing through her mid-forties with only 6 years remaining of the requisite 30 for retirement. Some teachers in Betty's position choose to resist change, others come along with both feet dragging, and still others, such as Betty, stand first in line. Betty not only chose to change her teaching, but has also gradually taken on more and more professional leadership responsibilities. Co-chair of SIT for two years, Betty developed more self-confidence over the years, becoming increasingly outspoken, but with a knack for expressing differences without making others feel defensive or hostile. In her high-pitched but almost musical voice, Betty finds words to coax us gently toward change, repeating her own commitment to what we are doing and helping us to reconfirm our own.

As we wrote our letter we were extremely aware of the need to be specific and concrete in our arguments. The charge that we wanted to move strictly for ambience, served to sum up the whole issue for many people as an aesthetic rather than a substantive one. Rather than countering with a strong explanation of why ambience actually can have a significant effect on daily learning, and taking the lead in selling the proposal, we spent a lot of time reacting, and reacting not very well. Our letter was a good one—thorough and specific—but I believe it was simply too late. Anne had it distributed to the SC members for comments and ideas. Wendy requested a couple of changes. The final six-page letter went home to parents on November 16. An excerpt follows:

REASONS FOR SUPPORTING THE EXPLORATION OF A POSSIBLE MOVE
FROM THE JEFFERSON FACILITY TO THE EMERSON BUILDING.

A letter from the Jefferson staff, November 16, 1990,
approved by the members of the Jefferson SC.

A few weeks ago, the SC asked the staff for a recommendation regarding a possible move to the Emerson building. We returned with a recommendation that such a move be further explored, as we believed there were enough potential educational advantages to warrant such a study. Our decision to make this recommendation came only after the staff had visited the Emerson site and spent several hours discussing the pros and cons of such a move.
 The staff has worked extremely hard over the last two years to implement an instructional program that we feel is significantly more effective in meeting the needs of all of our students. It is a much different program than what had previously been in place. *Whole language, cooperative learning, team teaching, problem-solving math, multiage grouping, and technology* require a different kind of facility than one adequate for traditional methods of teaching.
 We are at a critical juncture in our program, especially as concerns the introduction of more technology into our classrooms. We feel that we have made significant progress thus far and that our future progress could be substantially supported and enhanced if we were to move to the Emerson facility, assuming the district determines next month that the building itself is structurally sound.

The letter then described how specific features of the Emerson facility would support Jefferson's instructional program. It closed by addressing two issues that had seemed of most concern:

We are not insensitive to the situation of the tenants now occupying the Emerson facility, and we are especially concerned about the daycare program. If these issues can be managed with minimal disruption, we believe the reasons we've described here more than warrant consideration of a site move.

Some of the reasons may sound superficial, but this is more than an issue of "ambience." Your children spend at least six hours a day in school, with the staff committing from 8 to 11 hours, often including weekends. Office buildings and factories are constructed to be as comfortable and attractive as possible for their workers. This is not done just for aesthetic reasons; people need to work in comfortable, pleasing surroundings for their mental and physical well-being. The other important result is greater productivity. We believe schools are no exception; the business and joy of education should, in fact, especially merit the environment that can most effectively contribute to children's daily learning experiences.

The SC had had its own meeting on November 13. The members agreed that they would address community concerns, but still continue to explore the proposal. They also agreed that they would *not* solicit parental comments until the teachers' letter had been distributed. The minutes of this particular meeting show that most of the discussion, however, was devoted to reflecting on the decision-making process:

It was agreed the process would be positive and objectively examine concerns. Our intent is to make it work if at all possible, while continuing to address concerns as they arise.

. . . We need to work in a cohesive atmosphere. It was mentioned that the SC parent "list of concerns" was not distributed uniformly to all students and teachers, nor was it an actual list sanctioned by all of the SC parents. This caused a great deal of concern, and we now need to build a base of trust again [within] the committee itself. (SC Minutes, November 13, 1990)

These comments specifically reflect a reaction to Wendy's earlier actions. There was a lengthy discussion clarifying procedures for distribution of materials (e.g., signatures of all parents). More salient seemed to be some reflection on the cohesiveness of the group; the November 13 minutes added: "It was felt the concept of 'team' was getting lost and that we were beginning to feel a 'camp' mentality." Someone suggested that a facilitator be invited to work on team building with the SC. A December half-day was scheduled.

"MAKING PROGRESS . . . NEEDS IMPROVEMENT"

The next community meeting on the Emerson proposal was scheduled for November 28. We did not have time to think about it, and we were probably grateful to be distracted. Parent conferences were scheduled for six half-days before Thanksgiving, and we had to get moving on student progress reports. For many teachers the week before conferences is a blur. It is always a struggle keeping up with instruction, organizing and creating materials, attending meetings, and following through on a variety of other commitments. Shuffle progress reports into the mix and your life abruptly lurches into fifth gear.

Every year for at least the previous three years, each grade-level team sat down with its progress report and grappled with improving it, especially to make it more consistent with our program. The district sets some general guidelines for progress reports, but it mandates no specific format for the schools or grade levels. Whenever our staff is given latitude and options we seem to be unable to resist making life more difficult for ourselves. In this case, every team believed its progress report required some kind of revision. I suspect the office staff has little tolerance left for revisions. One more teacher request to retype and draw in little boxes and columns could lead to open rebellion.

Neil and I spent several hours working on our progress report. We pulled out the third-grade and fourth-grade forms used the previous year and tried to blend them into a single form for our third/fourth-grade classes. We changed the wording of some items and simply deleted others, but we especially wanted to add items that reflected the skills that we valued more than "neat handwriting." We added, for example, a category called "Being a Learner," which included: "adjusts to change, takes risks, finds creative solutions, makes decisions." To the math section we added: "uses variety of problem-solving strategies" and "can explain or describe strategies and solutions." Most progress reports traditionally have been checklists of narrow discrete skills, which then often define instructional goals and how teachers will teach. We were trying, instead, to create something that would reflect rather than shape learning experiences, that would help shift the attention of both parents and teachers to the more profound and complex aspects of children's learning.

Just how do you give parents an accurate and specific picture of how their children are doing and what they *can* be doing? Still holding onto the basic form of the familiar progress report, we do not use letter grades. We use similar, probably euphemistic systems, each in effect saying "making progress," "satisfactory," "needs improvement." We know that most parents glance at these marks first; but we also want them to understand what each mark means. Some of us add anecdotal records to the formal progress reports. During conferences Ellen and Kay have shown videos of their students reading. Several teachers attach samples of student work as reference. Many of us simply have resorted to writing long "summaries" of student progress. I know that I am not the only one to have produced three single-spaced typewritten pages on more difficult children.

None of this seems to have made much difference in the reporting process. Parents still come in wanting to know "where their child is," while teachers want parents to know where their child *should be* and what they need to work on to get there. Several of our inservice meetings on student assessment have involved parents, and it was an important revelation for me to hear these parents talk about the anxiety they feel in attending conferences. Many worry that the teacher will point out some glaring deficiency in their child, which in effect would be saying the parent is somehow at fault, in other words, a "bad parent." I recall one particular conference with a parent where this anxiety seemed to be especially evident:

Conference day. A single, working mom, with an older child besides Randy, Ms. Stone is exactly on time for her 1:30 appointment. We exchange pleasantries and I ask her to sit across from me, with Randy's progress report and samples of work on the table between us. She immediately reads the checklist of skills, and not seeing any "needs improvement" marks, visibly relaxes. She leans back in her chair and smiles a bit. She is relieved. The rest of the conference will be almost perfunctory for her. I indicate the page of comments and additional anecdotal records attached, which she glances over, but is not going to read carefully. I ask if she has any specific questions or concerns, and she mentions Randy's spelling. I point out how his spelling has actually improved since the previous year but also describe how we will be working on spelling as a class and individually this year. She says she does not really have any other concerns.

I spend some time talking about goals for the remainder of the year, asking if Randy has regular quiet time in the evening for homework and reading. He is not the most avid reader and often has trouble concentrating during silent reading periods. I gradually bring up areas in which I think Randy needs more experience and additional help, which I try to balance with comments on what he has been doing well. By the end of our 25-minute conference Ms. Stone seems reassured about Randy's progress and we have set some goals for the next few months. However, I am doubtful as to how much of an impression that has made and how well Ms. Stone will be able to follow through at home.

Like perennial unfinished business, progress reports and the format of parent conferences emerge every year to be agonized over, fiddled with, discussed, and eventually changed just enough until the next year. It seems that the more we revise our instructional program and commit ourselves to more meaningful goals for children (e.g., cooperative behaviors, problem-solving skills), the more we also complicate assessment and reporting. But I don't think that any of us wants to revert to the old ways, and substantial inservice time has been spent talking about assessment and sharing different methods and ideas. As we have read about and tried various alternative forms of assessment such as portfolios and student exhibitions, we have learned that none of this is self-evident or easily implemented. Everyone tries things in his or her own way, a step here, a step there. We share failures probably more than successes, but we talk about what we learn from each. So, we just continue to look for answers.

LIFE GOES ON . . .

Life in the classroom continued at its own pace. For those 6 hours of daily contact with students, you really don't have much time to think of anything except who is doing what, why a group is not working well together, what other materials you can find on China, who hasn't finished what and why, and all of those hundreds of concerns crowding every minute of a teacher's classroom day. Ellen and I actually found some time in early November to coordinate schedules and plan a "reading buddies" program. Kay and Neil worked out a similar arrangement.

We paired the children, third and fourth graders with first and second graders, mostly by temperament and personality. At 12:10 each Monday, half of my class migrated over to Ellen's room, and half of her class crossed over to mine. They then had 20 quiet minutes to read together. It was a bit like arranged marriages, and in this case all seemed blissful. Bodies distributed themselves in various corners of the two rooms, each holding onto his or her special book for the day. At this relatively early point in the year, not all of Ellen's students were independent readers, so some of them brought in stories they had written themselves. Our buddies program lasted for the rest of the year, and both the older and younger children never seemed to lose interest.

As a staff we keep trying to find ways of mixing our intermediate and primary children, if only to enhance the sense of community within the school; several also would argue that learning receives its own special push when the children can come together in this way. Our educational system has successfully embedded the practice of separating children by age and grade, with the accompanying myth that such separation is instructionally sound rather than simply a matter of organizational convenience. If we consider the joys and emotional benefits derived from growing up within a large, extended family of siblings, cousins, second cousins, aunts, uncles, and grandparents, would it not be natural to believe that a school can provide children with the same kind of loving, nurturing environment? We were trying to fulfill our goal and, in a sense, our promise of becoming a *developmental community* school.

Fitting in the PTSA

Life was continuing both in and out of the classrooms. One of the more familiar of any school community is its PTSA. Our PTSA co-presidents were heading into the eleventh hour of planning for the big fund raiser of the year: an auction and pizza dinner. The PTSA presents an interesting question for schools that are moving to site-based decision making. If there is any kind of SC body making substantive decisions, where does the PTSA fit in? When there are major issues, such as with Emerson, what is the PTSA's role? Does it take a position? Does it serve as a liaison of some sort? Does it coordinate informational activity with the SC?

Complicating these questions is the fact that the PTSA still makes decisions following standard Robert's *Rules of Order*, which is significantly different in spirit as well as procedure from what has evolved into consensus decision making. Parliamentary procedure may ensure order, but it is, in essence, a linear process rather than one intended to be all-inclusive, constantly spiraling in upon itself to achieve consensus of the whole. Those accustomed to following their Robert's *Rules* may not share the same kind of orientation to group processing as would those used to the sometimes more personal, fluid, and often "messy" kind of processing that undergirds a consensus decision. If that is true, where would the PTSA fit within a building that is drastically revising its decision-making structures to accommodate a breadth of opinion and participation?

There are no fixed answers, no models. Each school determines its own changes and shapes its own kind of organization and culture. We may be at too early a stage in this kind of reform to have any really useful examples of what happens to traditional organizations such as the PTSA. The crucial factor then becomes how the individuals involved interpret the changes and go about changing their own roles. Some may decide no change is necessary, that the larger institution may change around them and it will be okay. That may work; or it may not. In our case I think the PTSA opted for the latter course, mainly due to lack of experience. Opinion on this probably varies considerably, but I think the PTSA ended up simply being there. It was neither a hindrance nor any visible help to the major issues with which we dealt that year.

SETTLING EMERSON

As we came back from our Thanksgiving break, I began to struggle with the Pacific Rim. Social studies is not my strength, mainly because I have not figured out how to present a topic without fragmenting it into a series of nonrelated cutesy activities ("Let's make origami birds!" "Do you know how to use chopsticks?"). I continue to listen to discussions on integrating curriculum, attend workshops, review new materials, try various ways of planning and conceptualizing, but I am still dissatisfied and hope that someday I may unravel the mystery of planning a truly provocative, authentic social studies curriculum.

We have been working on integrating our curriculum, and some teachers have made more progress than others. Jane, a fourth/fifth-grade teacher, and Shirley, a fourth-grade teacher, have both used simulations as one approach to this. The primary team plans several units, such as on frogs and tadpoles, systematically blocking in the different skill and curriculum areas. Because two of the third/fourth-grade teachers were new, and it was my first year with this combination, we were basically not ready to do the kind of full planning together that the primary team was doing. We met frequently, shared ideas, and found ways of doing short-term things together. Neil and Pam went so far as to switch classes, with Pam teaching a unit on maps and Neil doing a unit on simple machines. In retrospect they felt this was not satisfactory and preferred trying actually to plan together rather than just switching off in this way.

As the paper turkeys were coming down off the walls and snowflakes began to go up, my class was receiving index cards, which, I hoped, would be their entry into Pacific Rim research. Groups had chosen their countries, come up with questions they wanted to answer, and were thinking about ideas for their final projects and presentations. I was trying to blend some traditional research techniques with what I had been gleaning from Nancie Atwell's *Coming to Know* (1990). Across the hall, Kay and Ellen were starting to have their classes think about trees (following up on a teacher inservice workshop), and the PTSA was ready for its auction.

The SC met on November 27. The minutes show that Anne reported on her meeting with the county Building and Land Division (BALD). BALD was supportive and indicated a desire to facilitate the process; it had even prepared a detailed calendar. A Jefferson move apparently presented no entanglement with building codes.

John, an SC representative, expressed concern about the community feeling that it was being railroaded and that most parents seemed to be against the idea of the school moving. But he also felt that these people could be "sold," given more time. Time was what we did not have. We could not postpone this decision for a year because of our conversion to integrated technology classrooms (rooms had to be rewired) and because plans for major improvements to our playground had already been postponed. Clare expressed her own frustration at attempting to educate the public on the many changes being made in education itself and how this related to the proposed move.

CLARE

This was Clare's second year at Jefferson. Far from being a beginning teacher, however, she brought to our building many years of teaching experience, accumulated wisdom, and an unteacherly propensity to speak her mind. Perhaps it was Clare's many years at the middle-school level that contributed to her forthrightness and impatience with all the niceties that elementary teachers tend to observe in dealing with parents. She was never rude, just extremely direct.

Two years before coming to Jefferson, Clare decided she needed a break. Since sabbaticals generally are not part of a public school teacher's career, she obtained a leave of absence from the district, then set about establishing herself as a computer consultant to various businesses. Fortunately for education, she missed the ebb and flow of school life and especially missed working with students.

When Anne discovered that Clare planned to return to the classroom, Anne worked her administrative sleight-of-hand to hire and persuade Clare to take one of the fifth-grade positions in our building. Clare's arrival could not have been better timed. We were beginning to add computers to our classrooms, closing our eyes and plunging ahead, not knowing RAM from ROM or bit from byte. Clare knew a lot about computers, not just how to use them but all those arcane things too, such as when you need special cables, how to set up a Q-system, and how to troubleshoot various glitches. Clare also knew a good deal about software and how to organize a classroom to make use of computers. She gave several inservice sessions to help make everything less mysterious and actually feasible.

Clare served as a stabilizing presence on the SC and within the staff. She was a good role model in how to speak frankly and oblige other people to do the same. She was not one to back down, and we fondly remember her following one parent out to his car the night of the first community meeting on Emerson, politely explaining to him why he was wrong. With all of her teaching responsibilities, Clare also spent a couple of evenings a week in classes, working on her master's degree. (The next year Clare would assume the principalship of an alternative middle school in the district.)

The second community meeting was held on November 28. This one followed nearly the same format as the first one, except that the opening was handled by Betty, Mary, Pam, and myself presenting the gist of our November 17 letter. This for me, personally, provided some interesting insight about my own emotions. I stepped up to the mike with the other three teachers behind me; my intention was to try to explain that our desire to move was based on substantive instructional reasons and not just a whimsical desire for more attractive surroundings. Somewhere in the middle of my twelfth sentence I began to cry. I was embarrassed, especially since it took me by surprise. I suspect that it startled everyone as well as myself. Mary, of course, gave me a shoulder, and Betty valiantly picked up from where I had crumbled.

The Emerson issue was with us for almost three months. It took up substantial time and preoccupied our thoughts. I think it had a repressive effect on us as teachers. As Betty said at one point, parents "don't believe the way we teach." I think it was more. I think it was the sense that our professional judgment was not enough. Granted we needed to better communicate the educational reasons for wanting to move, but I believe a piece of us also felt that parents should have had more faith in our judgment of what we believed was educationally sound for their children. Thus we felt not only frustrated at being ineffective in communicating our message, but also angry and sad that our role as teachers seemed diminished. I think that is why I wept.

A Staff Decision

Two days later the staff once again met in the library. The mood definitely was not upbeat, but we agreed that we were not quite ready to raise the white flag. A few days later the SC sent home a survey to determine the extent of parent support. The combination of "strongly disagree" and "disagree" responses added up to over half of the total number responding. The staff met again. Faced with the reality of this survey, we agreed that we would withdraw our recommendation. The decision was neither painless nor clear-cut. I don't recall anger, only deep disappointment and, I think, some emptiness. For many of us, it was difficult giving up, or giving in. Some wanted to reserve the option of proposing the idea again the next year. Most, however, seemed to feel it would be fruitless, that it was better to let the idea simply drop and move on to new business. And so we did.

A bit of flotsam in the wake of this issue: The SC held a special half-day in December, essentially to bind up wounds. A facilitator was invited in to help the group assess its working relationships of the prior three months. They made lists and discussed "what we did that worked well," "what were some of the problems?" and "what's next?" It should be noted that their "what worked well" list was about as long as their "problems" list. This suggests that an aberration in one individual's behavior may skew results and complicate the process, but does not necessarily do irreparable harm to the full group; that, in fact, the group actually may choose to pull together and find some promising areas for growth.

The experiences with the Emerson issue still fresh, the SC group singled out some critical areas for improvement and discussion:

- Defining the role of SC members in dealing with outside groups
- Avoiding allowing "subgroup" actions to influence final decisions
- Ensuring that *all* concerns are thoroughly expressed during meetings
- Being sure that everyone speaks at the SC on issues
- Working on definitions of trust and cooperation
- Making conflict acceptable
- Continuing to work on the consensus process
- Having guidelines for press releases
- Knowing and following SC procedures
- Learning how to inform a large population
- Agreeing in advance on strategies
- Being clear about when to report to others
- Better informing the public about the process of decision making that is followed
- Having training for new SC people
- Building a sense of trust within the SC

Wendy did not attend this particular session.

TIME OUT

As December began, my class was immersed in the Pacific Rim. Small groups huddled in their favorite spots around the room, using their bundles of index-card notes to develop projects. Sporadic bickering would break out, but by this time of the year students were fairly adept at working things out by themselves. The New Zealand group would experience considerable difficulty early on in this project—a clash of too many steel wills and temperamental personalities. But they persevered. Erna began by working by herself; Marcy and Karen decided they could work together; and Danny and Peter encouraged each other's procrastination.

A teacher has much to learn, especially patience. Although I am still needy in this area, I have more of it now than I ever used to, and I have learned that children cannot be rushed, that they need time to "muck about" and to think and get used to new challenges. By the end of our unit, the New Zealand group would end up being the most cohesive. Their final presentation (a videotaped drama, "In the Library") was developed and executed with imagination and wit. Danny would demonstrate surprising dramatic talent, appearing in borrowed high-heels and curly wig to portray the school librarian. Not one for hard-core academics, Danny could learn in spite of himself when lured by some role playing or artwork. For finally coming together, for their sterling performance and exceptional effort, each group member received a Principal's Award, something probably every child in the school hopes for each year.

When Anne first came to Jefferson we were following "assertive discipline" and becoming, to my mind, more and more assertive with less and less discipline, specifically "self-discipline." I loathed the marble jar (drop in a marble for each "good" behavior exhibited), and I never did get the hang of putting names on the chalkboard with checks beside them. More problematic, however, was our use of detention after school for serious offenses. A child receiving a certain number of BCs (behavior citations) would be faced with time in detention. For the younger children, especially, the threat of a detention was sometimes almost terrifying.

Now focused on classroom matters rather than school colors, one of the first topics of our weekly staff meetings was to explore our schoolwide discipline plan. This was a ripe topic on which to test our collective abilities in group processes. As we struggled with the issue we also struggled with each other and our own inexperience in dealing with conflict. Our current discipline plan is not the result of that single first meeting. Rather, it is the product of several years and many meetings, the product of much self-examination and ongoing attempts to define clearly what we believe is the best environment for children. Although based on Jane Nelsen's book, *Positive Discipline* (1987), our actual discipline plan still shifts and changes, but I think now that it is less in terms of something like how long detention should be (we actually have no detention period) and more in the nature of how to make expectations clear to children, how to help them take responsibility for their own actions, and how to help them manage their own behavior. This is a system that relies heavily on emphasizing the positive over the negative. Hence, the Principal's Awards.

Any adult can recommend any child in the school for such an award. Children also have recommended adults, and adults have recommended other adults. Pam one day was summoned to Anne's office to receive a Principal's Award. Mary had nominated her for providing extra help in the lunchroom when Pam actually was not assigned to be on duty that day. You can give it for virtually any behavior that demonstrates caring, responsibility, special achievement, and effort.

How it works: Marcy is lunch helper and her assigned table is extra messy one day. Carol decides on her own to stay and give Marcy a hand. I happen to be watching, and I think that's truly fine. I take out one of my little Principal's Award forms, fill it in with Carol's name and her special behavior, and put it into Anne's box. A few days later, Anne calls over the P.A. system to ask that Carol be sent to the office. Upon arrival, she is invited into Anne's office. Anne shows her this gorgeous certificate, complete with blue ribbon, gold seal, and her name filled in. She and Anne get to talk together, just the two of them, with Anne letting her know what a wonderful thing she did for Marcy. Carol goes flying back to her room with certificate in hand, and Anne gets to have her own special glow for a few hours.

The middle of December. We had sloughed off much of the leftover itch of Emerson and were feeling more charitable toward our fellow adults. Our principal intern was doing some weekly physical education activities with my class and showing me how P.E. skills could be taught without the competitive fervor of the Dallas Cowboys. Our Pacific Rim projects were being presented and videotaped; I was reading aloud from Lynn Reid Bank's *Indian in the Cupboard*; and we attended an all-school assembly to hear the Emerald City Brass Quartet. Wendy was one of two "art helpers" assigned to our classroom. On December 20 she was scheduled to present an artwork to the class, but Mother Nature intervened and the students never did get to see what she had selected.

Tuesday, December 18. My class was heavily into multiplication, and I was feeling guilty about not adequately covering all of the math strands—geometry, logic, probability, number, pattern, and function. I was probably moaning about this as Ellen drove me to the car dealer so that I could pick up my car, which was being serviced. We had tried to leave immediately after school, because the weather reports were predicting a major snowfall. By the time we arrived at the car dealer (a 10-minute drive had taken almost an hour) cars were already lying abandoned along the road. I picked up my car at 5:00 P.M. and four hours later pulled into my driveway. Schools would be closed for the rest of the week, which meant heading right into winter break. We would be out until January 7. It was time to take a breath. The rest of the school year would be a breeze.

3

1990–1991, The Second Half

January 1991 began typically gray. The snow and ice held on until after New Year's Day, confining most of us to a one-mile radius from our homes. It was a welcome opportunity to forget about school and to repair some tattered perspective. When we began the year four months back in September, blissfully setting up our rooms and outlining curriculum for the year, we had no idea what lay ahead. Suddenly we were in the middle of the Emerson issue, and we were not prepared. We were not prepared to deal with the negative community reaction, not prepared to form our own response and then respond quickly and convincingly. So we lost. We lost on the particular issue, but we gained something rare in schools. We gained an identity as a staff. We learned that most of us indeed shared a coherent philosophy about teaching and learning, one that we gradually became better at articulating and justifying with conviction, not just among ourselves but to others as well. We learned that we were a staff willing and supremely able to work together, and listen to and support each other, and that there was grit among us. It was time to go back to work.

The children actually seemed relieved to be back in school. They returned, eager to share dramatic tales of winter survival. The staff was only slightly less wide-eyed, each person having his or her own version of "How I Survived My Winter Vacation." While most of us were trying to remember where we had left off, the two fourth/fifth-grade classes and two fifth-grade classes were merrily preparing for the "Medieval Faire," a culmination of their medieval study unit. For these intermediate teachers, this collaboration was a significant event during the year. When Jefferson began to shift to multiage classes and more teaming, the primary teachers jumped in with both feet, barely pausing on the shore. Teachers in the upper grades, for some reason, often seem to be more resistant to collaboration and change. In our case, the one fourth-grade and two fifth-grade teachers were among those closest to retirement in our building (the fourth-grade and one of the fifth-grade teachers did retire at the end of the year), so it was probably harder for them to give up their long personal habits of independence. Jane, a fourth/fifth-grade teacher, was also a veteran in the classroom but she seemed to seek out and thrive on change.

Jane had begun the medieval unit with her own classes a couple of years previously, as a substitute for the Christmas festivities that used to appear in classrooms before districts became more conscientious about religion in the public schools. Some of our older teachers still mutter nostalgically about the absent Santas, reindeer, decorated trees, and other familiar Christmas symbols that they now must keep stored in their cupboards. For myself, I find it a relief not to have to deal with one more ritual, one more reason for a classroom party. We have a more quiet, thoughtful December as we head into winter break, and, most important, no child feels awkward or uncomfortable during festivities that may not have anything to do with his or her own beliefs and culture.

Jane's inventive thought was that while each class was studying the medieval period on its own, they could at least come together for an all-class celebration. They did, and the children had a memorable time. As Jane recalls, "They were so excited, and they did such a good job." The teachers planned outlandish games, a medieval meal (use your fingers), and even some of ye olde music and dancing.

JANE

Jane is another of our mid-career teachers. She was at Jefferson before Emerson closed and has weathered through more than one cycle of community–school conflict. With almost 20 years of teaching behind her, Jane was working hard to leave teaching about three years earlier. She somehow managed to juggle night classes and regular teaching to complete a degree in business. As she started to send out resumes, we started to change the school. That caught some of her attention, especially since she was part of the group that worked on the Twenty-First Century proposal. We might still have lost this curly-haired dynamo, if not for the district's ITC (integrated technology classroom) program. This is a voluntary program, and Jane was among the first to step forward. She says that between the changes in our own building and the incredible challenges posed by the technology program, it would be impossible to be bored. That was at least two years before the Twenty-First Century program. No talk about resumes since then.

My own class by now had found its stride. Comfortable with me and each other, the students noisily came in each morning, burbling about this and that, and, I like to think, happy to be at school. The first five minutes in class seem like mild chaos as backpacks are stored, jackets hung, and students exchange a few last words with friends before taking their seats. The room gradually falls silent as the last student opens a book to read and four others sit down for keyboard practice on the computers. Sometimes I write directions on the overhead projector if I want the class to do something before starting their reading. For the most part, I do not have to address the class at all until the end of silent reading when I give them my, "Good morning." This year's group of third and fourth graders was particularly efficient in the way most of them took care of daily affairs and helped each other. I did not have to say very much very often.

AND WORD FROM THE GOVERNOR?

In early January most of us were paying scant attention to the little ruckus kicked up when the governor presented his education budget in late December. The particulars of the budget are not especially relevant here, except to say that he proposed major cuts in education expenditures and that there were several critical issues besides teacher salaries, including class sizes, block grants, funding for special programs and materials, health insurance contributions, as well as at least maintaining previous funding levels for the community colleges.

The state Education Association (EA) had not been sitting on its hands all fall. With the governor's budget announcement, the EA set into motion a series of carefully planned actions that eventually pulled even the most distracted of us into the center of the controversy. January through the first part of April provided a major civics lesson in how politics, government, Jane & John Q. Public, the media, and a union settle their differences. At this initial stage the EA focused on getting its position out to the public, organizing and educating its own members on the issues, and establishing parent–educator lobbying groups. I think the Association genuinely believed that, if sufficiently mobilized, public opinion could force the state into providing more funding for education and eliminate the need for a strike.

For the first few weeks, events moved slowly, mainly because everyone's attention was riveted on the Middle East.

STAYING CALM

While the adults tended to their own anxieties about the approaching United Nations deadline for Iraq's withdrawal from Kuwait, the children came to school seemingly more curious than afraid. Most of the younger primary children were not even aware of events and their implications. Even my own third and fourth graders did not seem to be especially concerned. We had a news report from two students each day, but they showed more interest in the boy who wouldn't cut his hair for school than in what was happening in Iraq. I wanted to be sure they had a chance to air their anxieties and questions, but I also didn't want to push them. The fifth graders had more extended and often fervent discussion than the younger children. Clare reported almost daily sessions with her own class, in which students engaged in energetic discussion of the issues and varying viewpoints.

In this kind of situation, the principal very much sets the tone for how a building will cope with difficult issues or crises. In her years at Jefferson, I have never seen Anne falter as a centrum of calm and humane understanding of people's needs. Typically, Anne's foremost concern was that the children feel safe, feel free to ask questions, to share any anxieties. SIT had planned a visit to an elementary school in a neighboring district on January 15. Anne canceled the observation, explaining that it was important that we all remained in the building to keep life as normal as possible for the children and to be there to deal with any difficulties.

On the morning after Operation Desert Storm was launched, we began the day with a staff meeting. Uncharacteristically subdued and quiet, we met in the library, I think, feeling exceptionally close to each other. Anne wanted us to talk not only about how we would deal with the event in our classrooms but also about our own feelings and anxieties. I recall how open staff members were, how tears came without embarrassment. Teachers expressed fears about their own military-eligible sons and daughters, as well as empathy for parents with sons and daughters already overseas. I couldn't help but think how remarkable Anne was for her seemingly instant understanding that the children would be all right if we were all right, that the adults in the building needed support and a safe place to express their own feelings as much as did the children.

DECISION MAKING CONTINUES

Part of maintaining normalcy in our building meant tending to daily affairs, both in and out of the classroom. Building issues for Jefferson were both typical and not-so-typical, and with our new governance structure they seemed to involve almost every adult's participation at some time or other.

The School Council Deliberates

Bruised but not incapacitated, the SC held its first 1991 meeting on January 22. The issues were routine—a proposal for some kind of all-school event; a request from the counselor for activity pay for her work with the Student Council; and a request for funds to send two teacher representatives to a regional technology conference (the SC approved the request but also channeled it to SIT to see if Twenty-First Century funds were available to help). Someone from the 4-1/2 Day Committee gave an update on its progress in studying a proposal to extend the regular school day to provide Wednesday afternoons as no-student, teacher inservice days.

Carol, one of our primary teachers, proposed a whole language inservice workshop for the entire staff, to be presented by a group of consultants and publishers of whole language materials. The workshop would be held either after school or during one of our Wednesday inservice meetings, with the $750 cost covered by the $1,000 remaining in our building's language arts fund. Yes, most buildings do not have a separate language arts fund, much less one as generous as this was. As part of its efforts to support on-site decision making over the last few years, the district apportioned its language arts and math monies among all of the buildings. Each was responsible for examining its own present and future curriculum needs, then deciding how to spend these funds. Buildings generally followed their own procedures, but for the most part they established teacher committees to make proposals and direct the allocation of funds. Often each teacher received a certain amount of discretionary money. Teachers sometimes pooled their individual funds to purchase materials for team use. Funds also were reserved for materials, equipment, and inservice activities that would benefit or be used by the whole school.

The School Improvement Team Deliberates

For its part, the School Improvement Team was working to carry out its charge as "keeper of the vision." We met on January 25, under the cheerful co-chairing auspices of Betty and Kay. The nitty-gritty business on our agenda was reviewing staff suggestions on how to use Twenty-First Century funds that had been added to the original budget. We followed up on the SC's request to help fund teacher attendance at the regional technology conference, in addition to approving requests for additional printers and software for our REACH program.

The rest of the agenda was more typical for this group, that is, issues that related to the overall direction and implementation of our program. This included a discussion of whether to apply to the district to have a preschool/childcare pilot facility on our campus (the school board earlier in the year had approved a proposal for eventually establishing such services at every elementary school site). I recall that this was an unusually difficult discussion for SIT. While most of us were enthusiastically in favor of this idea (especially since it would help meet one of our Twenty-First Century goals), one parent expressed deep personal opposition to this kind of preschool/daycare program. Essentially, June felt that such programs are detrimental to families, that they "make it too easy" for parents to leave their children in the care of others, and that parents (read "mothers") may do this to free up time for their own personal pursuits rather than for work.

Once established as the larger policy-guiding body for our building, SIT had not had to face many controversial issues. Consensus among parent and staff representatives had come almost too easily and amicably. This childcare issue, however, led to a different kind of exchange. I remember that the group was sitting around a large table at the back of the library. Instead of their usual relaxed postures and easy bantering, people were sitting rather stiffly in their chairs. Faces looked tight, and you truly could feel the tension gripping the group. I think almost every person expressed some opinion on the matter, with all except June indicating support. Another parent said she shared June's concerns but she also felt that for the many parents who could not afford private daycare, a school facility such as had been proposed would be a major help. While staff representatives were uniform in their support of the proposal, Joan, the school counselor, took time to make some comments that both recognized and validated June's feelings.

This was a situation that emphasized the significance of having sufficient parent representation. It was important that the contrasting opinions came from parents as well as staff, thus avoiding an "us and them" division. We were fortunate in having parents on SIT who understood our program, its origins, and its goals. Most of them were able to balance their own personal biases and values with the needs of the total school. The daycare issue was the first on which we had had to deal with a significant difference of opinion on SIT. It may have been telling that June was not part of the original SIT group that wrote the Twenty-First Century proposal (she would become a PTSA co-chairperson the next year). This particular experience was an especially vivid reminder of how the continued viability of our program depended not simply on staff support but also on those many parents who were willing to listen, learn, and grow along with the rest of us.

Finally, Anne went around the table, asking each of us to indicate if she could support, "live with," or "not live with" the proposal. June held to her position, while the rest of the group expressed its support for the proposal. We then worked on finding some compromise, which ended up as the following statement (which June accepted, albeit still with reservations):

> Though many on the committee believe that the best solution is early childcare at home, the need for childcare outside the home is recognized. Therefore, SIT recommends that the SC actively pursue our becoming part of the preschool/childcare pilot program. (SIT minutes, January 25, 1991)

I have given this meeting and this particular discussion some extended attention, because it is a good example of how we had learned to work through issues and develop consensus in our building. This issue required just one session. Other issues, especially those involving the full staff or the SC, often have involved discussions spanning several meetings and using literally hours of time.

The Staff Deliberates

Our Wednesday inservices essentially have allowed the staff to function as a committee-of-the-whole. Certain issues that come before the SC often are referred to the staff for its views. We usually hold separate discussions in our grade-level teams or building wings, but for serious issues, such as class configurations and the Emerson move, Wednesday meetings allow us to engage in more extended, careful discussions. The SC representatives then can be more confident that they are accurately representing staff views, and the staff feels reassured that final SC decisions truly have considered their own particular positions and concerns.

I have been in several gatherings with teachers and administrators from other schools. For many of these educators it is difficult enough coming to consensus within their SCs, or analogous bodies, but there is also the potential problem of staff members not "buying into" a decision because they often feel they have not been fully apprised of the situation and/or have not had sufficient opportunity to voice their own opinions. If there are individuals who feel in any way omitted from the decision-making process, virtually any effort to implement decisions is likely to fail, either through lack of participation or outright subversion.

I don't know if everyone in our building fully appreciates the exceptional access we have to the decision-making process, the incredibly effective way in which it operates, and the extended time we have for thoroughly thrashing through the issues. Each of these elements of building governance is absolutely vital to programs of reform envisioning complicated change. Lest anyone dismiss our experience as the singular and privileged outcome of a financial windfall from the state, I must emphasize that we are not the only elementary school in our district immersed in this kind of major structural and curricular change. Nested within a district formally committed to reform as a long-term policy, each of the other 15 elementary schools, 6 middle schools, and 5 high schools spends its own many hours mapping out and implementing change.

THE QUESTION OF "GOOD TEACHING"

Anne may be an administrator, but she still has chalkdust under her fingernails. Rather than being enamored with administrative detail, she is a principal who regards administration as important mainly to facilitate the more monumental task of improving instruction.

"Principal" is the shortened form of "principal teacher." Somewhere in our history we lost the key word in the title. The principal's role is a combination of both administrator and teacher. Over the years, the administrative functions have come to take precedence, until principals often assume their positions with only a few years of classroom experience, and not necessarily successful experience. We therefore may have principals who balance their budgets but lack any idea of how to fulfill the more important part of their jobs, that of instructional leader.

When I first came to Jefferson, Arnold was principal, but he would retire at the end of that year. Arnold had been with the district for many years and, like the other members of the "old guard," he probably viewed his role of principal as mainly administrative—make sure the buses leave on time, paperwork is completed, the lunchroom is orderly. Arnold's approach to teacher evaluation was well-intentioned and familiar, if not exceptionally helpful. Following district procedures, he would come into the classroom for about a half-hour, watch your prepared lesson, and then fill in a form with a series of complimentary comments. After reading his report and being confident your career was not in jeopardy, you went on about your business until the next observation. This is an experience that most teachers should recognize.

Anne demonstrated her interest in instruction in many ways, but few things seemed as delicious to her as revamping the teacher evaluation process. Whenever we saw her bustling down the walkway, armed with yellow legal pad and a videocamera, we knew that some kindred soul was at the other end nervously awaiting his or her observation. Anne and that teacher had probably had a preconference, with Anne asking what she should look for in the lesson. The teacher might have asked her to focus on certain students as well as on questioning skills, organization of an activity, some other specific area. It varies considerably from teacher to teacher. Anne usually videotapes, and the postconference consists of watching the tape together and discussing the lesson, ending with some clear goals to work on and recognition of what the teacher is doing well. The whole process takes more time than before, but you feel it has been time well spent and not simply a formality to satisfy district mandates.

Over the years we have become used to having the videocamera in our classroom, having learned how effective it can be in revealing some of the smallest but significant details of a lesson. At first, you may self-consciously see only yourself fumbling with the overhead projector; or you look at only a few students and believe everyone is right with you. Then you replay the tape, and this time you notice that Brian is carefully following his neighbor's example and hasn't a clue as to what he is supposed to be doing. So you have to ask yourself some hard questions. Is Brian the exception? Are you missing those quiet ones on the periphery? Did you explain clearly enough? How did you check that students were following? *Did* you check?

Anne does not always videotape, but her use of the technique illustrates how thorough she is and how much of an added effort she gives to the evaluation process. In tribute to Anne's willingness to haul around all of this equipment for our benefit, the school technology committee purchased a television and VCR at the end of the year expressly for Anne to use with teachers. One of the few occasions in which we saw Anne openly exasperated was when she was trying to hunt down a VCR in the building to view a teacher's lesson.

Everything is of a piece. Just as we hope to provide children with the skills and wherewithal to take charge of their own learning rather than having it served on a platter, we should be extending the same idea to ourselves. Anne treats evaluation as a way of helping teachers to improve their own instruction. While she may take the lead, the entire effort depends on the direct participation of and interaction with the teacher. As you analyze a given lesson, you can extend your insights about all of your teaching and how children are learning. Do this often enough, and you begin to be less dependent on external opinion, less vulnerable to uninformed judgment. It takes most teachers years to shed their sensitivity to the slightest criticism, whether from administrators, parents, or other teachers. Every comment is swallowed whole until you develop your own rational filters to evaluate what you are doing. You eventually become accustomed to evaluating, and you make it an ongoing personal habit rather than a twice-yearly brief interlude in your classroom. Without clear-eyed and ongoing self-evaluation it is too easy to fall asleep at the chalkboard. As long as no one is saying you're doing a bad job, you assume you are fine, and you lose that valuable sense of uncertainty that can give the edge to your teaching, ensuring change and improvement.

Supporting more teacher involvement in their own evaluation, our district and local association worked out, and the membership ratified, a contractual agreement for a new evaluation process. While some basic components of the familiar old model continue for beginning teachers, more seasoned teachers now have two years in a "growth cycle," in which they develop their own goals and means for implementation. Wide latitude is given to areas for "growth." A teacher could, for example, determine that she needs more experience using computers in her classroom. She would develop a plan that could include inservice classes, visits to other classrooms, reading, and her own action research. After the two years, she shifts to the performance cycle for a year, then moves back into the growth cycle.

Well before this new plan was adopted, Anne was creating opportunities for some of us to shape our evaluations to be more directly relevant to our individual instructional needs. My teaching style is such that I rarely conduct discrete formal lessons with the whole class. Planning such an activity for an observation began to feel a little like "pretend" or "dressing up" for the principal. Understanding this, Anne suggested that I take a half-day release. She recommended that Charlie, an outstanding teacher from another building, be invited to spend the morning in my classroom. Then we would spend the afternoon together discussing his observations and my concerns, and we could have extended time to mull over questions together. It turned out to be one of those rare moments of professional compatibility. I took pages and pages of notes, and the excitement of that discussion buoyed up my teaching life for a very long time.

Clearly, then, Anne's interest in and expertise with instructional evaluation is neither cursory nor perfunctory. She has many years both of her own diverse classroom experiences as well as of coordinating and evaluating instruction. I think if you asked her, she would not disagree that it is a passion.

A TEACHER STRUGGLES

For most of us, Anne's "passion" was responsible for personal and professional insight, reaffirmation of our growth, and recognition of our efforts. For Fran, however, Anne's meticulous attention to instruction probably engendered only frustration and anger.

Fran was hired late in August. Not having time to change plans for an out-of-town trip, she missed our pre–Labor Day week of inservice, which meant missing a critical overview of our program's history, philosophy, and instructional approach. Because Fran arrived at Jefferson with no orientation and little time to prepare for instruction, Anne asked Helen (who was completing four months of service so that she could retire in December) to assist Fran in the classroom. After a few weeks Helen withdrew from this assignment, indicating that she was not comfortable with the way Fran managed the class and that her presence and suggestions did not seem to be welcomed. With most of the staff unaware, Anne made unscheduled, and exceptionally frequent, visits to Fran's classroom throughout the first half of the school year, into January. Believing that Fran needed significant improvement in basic teaching and management skills, Anne attempted to work with her in these areas; they met often, Anne explaining where and why she perceived difficulties and offering ideas for improvement as well as suggesting that Fran observe teachers in other classrooms.

The obvious question is how Fran could have had almost a decade of prior classroom experience and come to our district with what Anne judged to be inadequate instructional skills. It does perhaps indicate how elusive a demon evaluation can be. How do districts determine what is "good teaching"? What are the criteria? Are they consistent from district to district? school to school? principal to principal? Should they be? Who evaluates? How do they evaluate? How stringent and responsible are districts and teachers willing to be in maintaining high standards for their profession? Whatever the case, Fran and Anne were not judging instructional competence through the same lens.

Fran began the year in our team meetings talking about her desire to move into new methods of teaching. In my role as Fran's mentor, I visited her classroom a few times and tried to make some suggestions as to how she could do this, especially with the writing process, since that was one of her stated goals. Rather than trying to grasp the conceptual rationale for writing workshops, she sought to collect specific activities, such as writing a poem about shoes, without grasping some general principles for introducing children to poetry. She did not seem ready to explore the context of how children learn to write, so that she could generate her own activities and relate them to the larger curriculum. Fran was used to a more piecemeal approach to teaching, a familiar approach that has been with us for years in the form of basals and "teacher-proof" manuals. Her teaching started with the method or activity rather than with the children.

None of this is to suggest that all of us on the staff have figured out to perfection how to develop curriculum based on children's interests, language, experiences, and abilities. Far from it; and that was perhaps a crucial factor holding us together. We were each, in our own way, struggling to shed old teaching behaviors while simultaneously creating new roles for ourselves, and we needed external support. We relied constantly on the empathy of fellow teachers and on their willingness to share ideas and insights.

Problem-solving math, for example, was a surprise package for most of us. It not only presents an entirely different teaching approach but requires that we give up our old, comfortable ideas of what constitutes elementary math. This kind of shifting and rethinking is tough, and virtually impossible to do alone, whether you're a novice or veteran teacher. Neil and I consumed a lot of potato chips over the year as we plopped down after school to try to integrate the math strands, find concrete applications for common denominators, and figure out how to use our pattern blocks, color cubes, and all those shiny new materials to make math alive and relevant for our students. Kay and Ellen were doing their own puzzling over subtraction with regrouping, how to teach it with hands-on materials, how to create meaningful, even fun situations for application.

I don't think Fran was ready to challenge or think about instruction in this way. I had supervised student teachers for several years, but had never acted as an in-school mentor before. Asked to be Fran's mentor back in the fall, my inclination was to provide her with as much help as possible and to be available, but I did not want to force her into anything, especially given her own extended teaching experience. I explicitly told her more than once that I hoped she would come to me when she needed help. She did from time to time, but almost never about instruction. I don't recall her asking for ideas or help with math, reading, or the content areas, except to request my teaching materials on Washington State. Instead, she asked me how to fill out preobservation forms (for evaluation), about the wording of parent letters, how to deal with parents who were dropping in after school without an appointment, where to find certain materials. Fran may have requested me as her mentor, and she genuinely may have wanted a mentor at the beginning of the year, but after a couple of months, I felt she was quietly trying to go her own way.

It is probably not fair for me to describe this situation without giving Fran's own views. This is not a formal study; so I felt that I needed to exercise special caution in not exaggerating issues that involved Fran. I also tried to avoid any personal criticism of Fran and instead to focus on how the institutional mechanisms appeared to work and not work over the ensuing months. My goal for this narrative was not to build cases for or against individual personalities but to provide a participant-observer's perspective on how the multiple facets of a school community responded to the issues, conflict, and stress engendered by radical change. There were indeed gaps, which, I hope, can serve as lessons and warning lights for other schools and districts.

MAINTAINING PERSPECTIVE

I think many of us often felt school consisted of two separate worlds. A large part of our attention and emotional exertion was given over to maintaining the integrity of our program, which meant confronting and dealing with parents who could not or would not understand what we were trying to achieve in our school for their children. This relatively small group of parents clung hard and fast to traditional images of school and education. Children moving around a classroom, lots of student talk, blocks and geoboards instead of worksheets, children selecting their own books instead of indentured to a basal, groups collaborating on projects versus only individual assignments—all of this shot right through the center of some lifelong assumptions about how children should be taught. And when your most deeply held assumptions about a highly personal institution seem threatened, you are not likely to go off meekly into the night. All of the resentment, frustration, and, probably, fear that these parents felt would eventually be manifested in specific issues: Anne's tenure as principal in our building, renewal of Fran's contract, and the staff's decision to move to all multiage classes in the next school year. An additional, but related, issue would be the statewide teachers' strike in April, which would be another lovely opportunity for staff and a few parents to realize they had some differing views.

Each year I have a handful of exceptionally difficult children, in classes that usually number more than 25 students. When someone asks how my day has been, I often groan about how tough it was to get Gil or Shelley or Pete to behave appropriately, follow directions, work with others. What I too often overlook is that the great majority of students actually do what I hope they'll do, and with unfailing graciousness and enthusiasm. During the year, as a staff, we too often allowed ourselves to be overwhelmed by the criticism and intransigence of a relatively small group of parents. They eventually did create problems for us that were genuinely infuriating and fully tested our resolve as a staff. But we also found consistent, reassuring support all year from parents who, while sometimes uncertain and not fully comprehending the direction of our program, were patient and willing to learn, trusted our judgment, and basically wanted to know, "Is my child learning? Does my child enjoy going to school?" These were the parents who were often the most active in the school, on committees, and as classroom volunteers, helpers in the office and library, field trip drivers, room parents, party planners, all-around assistance providers. On any given school day, at almost any given time during school hours, no matter where you are in the building, you can easily bump into a parent. You can tell who they are by the name tags stuck to their shoulders.

As in most schools, however, our largest group of parents is the one from which we rarely if ever hear a word, but we know they're out there. Notices go home for signing, and they come back signed. Surveys go home to be completed, and a surprising number come back completed. With a few exceptions, all of the parents conscientiously make time to attend fall and spring conferences, and we get Cecil B. DeMille turnouts for pancake breakfasts, art fairs, and school carnivals. Otherwise, this particular lot of parents seem to be our "happy campers," comfortable with their school just as long as their children seem happy and appear to be making progress. We don't always appreciate these parents enough.

Special Needs for All

The other part of our school world was in our classrooms. The children studied the Washington state pioneers, made up their own history books, worked through math menus on area and perimeter, wrote their stories, wrestled with long division (while their teachers continued to question its relevance), and still found energy to play hard and laugh well. The children's daily life remained intact and normal, complete with emotional and social problems. Every teacher has his or her share of "difficult" children. No matter how difficult the struggle with curriculum and instruction, I suspect that for most teachers the more agonizing task is in helping troubled children. Teachers have the privilege of learning, as they work with these children, that each child is more than a bundle of labels: "reading disabled," "behavior disabled," "unmotivated," "hyperactive," "overly aggressive," "dysfunctional." Instead, each one is a supremely complex and often confounding collection of unique traits. These are the children who can most remind teachers of where our own human frailties lie. When a child succeeds at constantly "pushing all of my buttons," I have to work hard to recognize what is hooked to each "button" that can make me react so strongly. Danny loved to jab at my buttons, and in my three years with him, from third through fifth grade, we would develop our own separate peace and mutual understanding.

DANNY

> Every few years a teacher has that one student. Danny took that role this year, as he had the year before. I have always had a special affinity for my quirky students, the ones standing off to the side, insistently tapping out their own odd

beats. Usually, they also tend to be the ones who drive a teacher crazy. This was Danny, freckles and rosy cheeks, playing Rocky in the ring one minute, and whining like a 2-year-old the next. A smart aleck with a fast-draw lip, Danny also could sit quietly for a long stretch then suddenly come up with the most perceptive insight in a discussion.

Danny did not fit in. Most of his classmates came from homes with middle-class norms. While they walked, Danny swaggered; while they argued, Danny threw a punch; while they brought in their homework, Danny always "forgot"; while they talked about Legos, Danny talked about motorcycles and guns. Also, while most of them felt fairly good about themselves, Danny felt unsure, awkward, and left out. His Mr. Tough Guy bravado was the only thing that kept him from disappearing into the woodwork. Much would change the next year, Danny's third year with me, but for this year we still had weekly skirmishes over any number of things—sloppy work, incomplete work, homework, rude behavior, teasing, brawling out on the playfield. At least we had reached the point where Danny functioned well in the classroom 99% of the time. He still could fall apart on the playfield where the expectations were not as stringent and there were too few adults to monitor problems.

Danny knows a lot about the world—snakes, birds, cars, space, the oceans. He is bright, verbal, and a demon reader. He can write with flair and wit, and has an ear for how words should sound. From a single-parent home with its own private history of disruption, he also knows more than most of his classmates about how, for some people, daily life is not always neat and pleasant.

We have too many "Dannys" in our school, some caught in even more serious problems. We keep trying to find effective ways to help all of them. From experience we have learned that punishments and threats do not work. Any changes in behavior derived this way are usually temporary, and, more important, little or nothing is learned about personal responsibility and how to manage one's own problems. Thus, during the year we continued to work on our "positive discipline" plan, which included class meetings. These are not casual gatherings to air problems. They follow a certain format and have specific goals of helping children to assume more responsibility for their own behavior.

Agendas for class meetings are set by the students, which include everything from whole-class issues to disagreements among individual students. Children learn how to present their problems and viewpoints objectively and how to deliberate and make fair judgments. When a class decides that consequences are in order, the students work through options to determine what would be most appropriate and fair. It can be a startlingly effective process in helping children to take responsibility for their own actions and learn how to analyze and work through sometimes intricate issues. Class meetings are not readily implemented, and not all of the teachers have instituted them in their classrooms. The meetings take practice, for both the teacher and the students. For teachers uncertain how to begin, valuable help is available from Joan, our school counselor.

JOAN

Unlike most school counselors who must divide their time among buildings, Joan is ssigned to our school only. This has not come without a price, most of it in the form of extra assignments for Joan. In addition to all of her regular duties, such as counseling and testing, Joan is also responsible for our ESL program and volunteered to act as advisor to our Student Council.

A tall, dark-haired woman with one of those ear-to-ear smiles, Joan is indispensable. Students and staff rely on her to untangle problems, find solutions, and provide understanding. Students sign a sheet posted outside of Joan's door when they want to talk with her, while staff will buttonhole her wherever we find her. I don't think she ever has an uninterrupted lunch or recess. It is not just that Joan is the counselor; we go to her because she is so remarkable in her ability to combine caring, sympathy, and forthrightness. She is especially effective talking to parents, some of whom are often hostile. She is supportive and understanding but also strikingly honest without being judgmental. Joan is even more effective with the students, working with many of them all year as they seek her out for talks and reassurance.

Joan's insight and analytical abilities have contributed greatly to most of the major decisions we have had to make as a staff over the past four years. Typically Joan sits in on our staff meetings, listening, listening. Then she begins: "Another piece to this is . . . " She is usually right; we have often overlooked a telling point in our discussions.

We committed ourselves to mainstreaming our special needs students (remedial reading, learning disabilities, "gifted," physically disadvantaged), because we believed it was consistent with our program philosophy and how we viewed children's development. This is a policy endorsed by our district and consistent with some national trends; nevertheless, we are not experienced in how to deal with some of these students. For most of the minutes of each day, our classes function wonderfully well and *all* of the students benefit from their consistent associations with each other. There are times, however, when we run into proverbial brick walls, when teacher, and student, will feel exasperated and helpless. Almost every teacher nods with understanding when I talk about "carrying students in my head" after school, on weekends, driving, pushing a cart down a grocery-store aisle. Without some sense of external support or hope for resolution, that kind of preoccupation easily leads to resentment and anger, which is not healthy for anyone.

In most schools teachers struggle alone with almost no outside help or support. We have tried to change this by creating some release valves. The fact that most of the staff talks to each other frequently is itself a help. Sometimes just venting a frustration is sufficient, but teachers are also good about providing advice and perspective. Joan acts as the fulcrum for our dialogues. She knows all of the children who have a history of problems, and usually knows their parents, too, and we constantly seek her out for suggestions and to help us better understand the students. Joan will listen patiently and offer her thoughts as some of us rattle out our frustration for the day. She frequently visits classrooms to observe children and give us ideas for how to deal with specific situations. When we have parent conferences, Joan sits in if requested. She often helps to defuse tension and clarify problems.

In some especially serious situations, Anne becomes involved. The few students who repeatedly fight and bully other children, usually end up in Anne's office. It also does not have to be just physical abuse. Small groups of fifth-grade girls from two different classes somehow got caught up in a brutal daily exchange of threats, epithets, and racial slurs. Even after numerous meetings with their teachers and with Joan, they continued their verbal assaults on each other. Anne met with them in her office. She not only laid out our school guidelines about expected and appropriate behavior, but also explained district guidelines regarding student conduct, its exclusion of verbal abuse and racial bias, and the consequences for violating those guidelines. Anne wrote a letter that was mailed to each of the girl's parents explaining the problem, emphasizing school standards of behavior, and requesting that they address this matter with their daughters. There were no further problems of this particular nature for the remainder of the year.

The point in all of this is that taking care of students goes beyond the individual classroom and the individual teacher. All of the adults are responsible for all of the children. Our recess and lunch aides seek out teachers when there are special or chronic problems, as do the specialists (art, music, library, P.E.). The problems children have today are frequently so complex, so entangled in so much of their own family histories, that teachers cannot be everything to every child. So we talk—students with students, students with adults, adults with each other. In that sense, it is a year-long conversation.

HEARTS, FLOWERS, AND BRICKBATS

February. The hunt was on for pink and red construction paper. At this time of year favorite colors are already scarce. I confess that some hoarding goes on starting in December, as a few of us can't get comfortable with yellow valentines. Talk in the workroom continues as it has all year—"Who has something quick and simple?" "Where did you get that idea?" "Ooh, can I have one of those?" Ellen and Kay were launched into geography units, discovering that most first and second graders may not be ready to deal with scale on a map but that they can create their own treasure maps. They were using stations for a math menu on money, while Jane was setting up more stations for her fourth/fifth graders, which were a sophisticated integration of different curriculum areas (math, reading, computers, etc.). Nancie Atwell's *Coming to Know* was my own constant and boon companion as I exposed my class to more note-taking experience as a prelude to writing reports on Honest Abe.

School Council Business

Working on its own learning, the SC began February with a second inservice meeting to deal with its processing and manner of working together. Given readings on cooperative learning, the group met with the same facilitator who had helped them back in December.

A regular meeting was held on February 12. This was an especially substantive meeting. The technology committee gave an update on its 5-year plan for the building; a proposal was made that a disaster plan be developed by a committee of parents and staff. The major item at this meeting, however, was a presentation by the 4-1/2 day committee. (The early work of this committee coincided almost exactly with the succession of events in the Emerson decision. We had learned a few things.)

The 4-1/2 day committee had emanated from a SIT discussion in the fall. The previous two years of inservice Wednesdays using substitute teachers seemed to be unsettling enough for the children that parents were complaining in noticeable numbers. The teachers themselves were not pleased with the arrangement. Working up a full day's lesson plans every two weeks is not part of the joy of teaching. These Wednesdays also broke the rhythm of the week (you don't always plan the same activities for a substitute as you would for yourself), and it was difficult for some of the students to cope with the midweek change. Our lunchroom and playground staff was especially testy about the midweek increase in disruptive behavior.

With this charge, the 4-1/2 day committee set out to explore the idea of lengthening each school day a few minutes in order to dismiss the children early on Wednesdays. The plan seemed simple when first proposed, but few ideas related to schools ever remain simple, and it soon became clear that this would be an extraordinarily difficult plan to work out. Especially daunting were the issues of transportation (which dictates the lives and fortunes of most districts in the country) and daycare for children who had no one at home in the afternoon. And, there was the specter of parent resistance. We seemed to be suffering from a kind of post-Emerson syndrome, overly sensitive to any hint of criticism and determined not to be put on the defensive again. If insufficient information to parents had been the problem in the fall, this time we would smother them with information and involve them up to their ear lobes in the decision-making process.

The 4-1/2 day committee was made up of an equal number of parents and staff. Its members methodically and thoroughly, almost compulsively, researched the proposal and alternatives: They conducted a phone survey to determine how various schools in the area used early release programs; a survey was sent to each Jefferson family to assess views on the idea; and a team of parents and staff visited a school that was already doing what had been proposed for our building. The committee then compiled a package summarizing the information it had amassed and presented it to the SC on February 12. Teacher SC representatives took the proposal and information back to their respective wings for comments and/or recommendations. The discussion and work on this issue continued for the rest of the school year. The plan would eventually be approved by the SC and implemented in October of the following year. Surprisingly, no significant opposition emerged from parents or the larger community.

ONE TEACHER'S ESTRANGEMENT

February was a critical month. I believed I wasn't doing anything useful as Fran's mentor and that the district was about to pay me for responsibilities not fulfilled. So I withdrew from the mentorship. There were no ill feelings, and I think Fran may have been relieved. I told her that I didn't think I was providing her with the kind of help she wanted, but that I would be available at anytime if she simply asked. At this point I and, I am quite sure, the rest of the staff were not aware of the substantial attention Anne had been giving Fran's teaching. Anne and I had brief exchanges during the fall, enough for me to discern that she was not necessarily satisfied with Fran's performance, but I did not realize the extent of intervention she was trying to provide. I did not find out until months later how often Anne had observed Fran and had had conferences with her, trying to help her to improve her performance. Anne always has scrupulously avoided discussions with staff about other staff members. In my position as mentor I was especially obligated not to discuss Fran's teaching with Anne.

In retrospect, I can only surmise how bewildered Fran may have felt, given her previously successful experience in other districts. But there were two issues. One had to do with our particular instructional approach, including taking on whole language and the rest of the curricular strands of our program. The other issue was simply basic teaching techniques and classroom management. As mentor, following the goals Fran had set for herself in the fall, I tried to deal with the former. Anne focused on the latter, but this more basic issue inevitably became entangled with approach to instruction. Fran's actions and reactions over the next few months indicated that she believed the problem was solely that she had not taken on whole language consistent with the rest of our program. I am not aware of whether she ever accepted, to even a slight extent, Anne's assessment of her teaching skills, separate from instructional approach.

At this stage, the staff basically was acting as if there were no problem. If you deny there is a tornado approaching, maybe it will skip over you. We had enough to deal with, given the increasing possibility of a teachers' strike. More important, over the past couple of years a kind of tacit agreement had developed that we would not intrude on each other's school affairs unless invited. This also meant trying to avoid rumor-mongering and behind-doors criticism. (Obviously, like most healthy human beings, we had our catty lapses from time to time, but on the issue of Fran we actually didn't have much to say until almost the end of the school year.) I don't recall Anne ever discussing Fran with the rest of the staff, and we hardly ever saw Fran herself. Some of us caught a glimpse of her early in the morning when she checked her mailbox and ran off copies, all with hardly a word to anyone. At noon she picked up her lunch, then went back to her room. She usually didn't stay late after school because she had to be home to take care of her two girls. The third/fourth-grade team often suggested meetings after school, on Saturday mornings, or early mornings, but citing demands from home or inservice workshops, Fran almost always found this impossible.

For a period early in the year Fran did attempt to join the larger staff in informal situations and participate in inservice and team meetings. She attended our team meetings through the fall, mainly listening, sometimes expressing concerns about expectations for change. In her naturally nurturing way, Pam was always especially supportive in repeating that the change would come, and that each person moved at his or her own pace.

At that time I think Fran was having more trouble with her students' parents than with the staff or with Anne. She talked to me several times about parents who were critical of assignments she made or who would stop in after school without an appointment to question her about different matters. I suggested that she stop apologizing and giving lengthy explanations, which she was doing. Trying to justify herself in this way only put her constantly on the defensive and invited more criticism. A particularly salient instance was when Fran received a parent letter scolding her for "unfair" bathroom rules. She had been having problems with children playing in the bathrooms (what elementary teacher hasn't?), so she told the children they would have to raise their hands whenever they wanted to go to the bathroom. She probably could have found a more workable system, but it was not a desperate issue. It didn't merit the excessive parent reaction about embarrassing students, or the lengthy letter Fran originally had planned to send. I suggested she simply send a short note acknowledging the concern. She did, and there was no further parent comment, at least on the bathroom issue.

It is not news that teacher training programs leave out a lot. One of the many survival skills they overlook is how to deal with and communicate with parents. Knowing how to cope with parents can determine whether you will expend your energy and emotion on instruction and on your students, or whether you will spend the year feeling besieged and demoralized. On the one hand you genuinely want parents to be involved and interested in their children's school life. And most parents are quite content receiving newsletters, talking at conference time, periodically helping out in the classroom, and calling if they have particular questions or concerns. On the other hand, you inevitably will have parents who express disagreement with what you are doing or how you are doing it. A teacher's effectiveness with her students, her sense of success and peace of mind for the year, can sometimes depend on how effective she is in responding to these concerns. If she is unable to offer parents adequate reassurance, she is likely to find them hovering over her shoulder all year.

I cannot speak for middle- and high school teachers, but I know that elementary teachers are not accustomed to having to justify or explain what they do in the classroom. For the most part, over the years as long as everyone was following the unwritten rules of "elementary teaching," that is, teaching in traditional ways familiar to earlier generations, no one had much to quibble about. Now that we are changing the rules some parents are not pleased, and they question anything that appears too different for their comfort. "Why don't you have weekly spelling tests?" "I don't see any homework coming home." "Will my child be ready for middle school?" "Where are the grades?" "My child doesn't do well working in a group." Often the issues underlying such questions are complex and cannot be answered in one or two sentences. Teachers need to be prepared to work with parents over the long term to build understanding. And whatever the question or problem, teachers have to be able to confront each one with candor, often bluntness, and, especially, with their own full understanding of why they are doing what they are doing.

Think of yourself as a first-year teacher, eager to apply all those whole language ideas you learned about in your education courses.

Two weeks into the school year, and Mrs. Skinner happens to stop by. "Um, I was just wondering about Brad's reading," she says. "I mean his sister learned to read with basals and phonics, and I think she's a really good reader. Aren't you going to use those same books? Phonics, what about that? I've been hearing about whole language. What's that all about? Is that what you're using?" Mrs. Skinner utters her last question as a challenge.

How do you respond? Will you be able to respond in 25 words or less and satisfy Mrs. Skinner? It's a delicate situation. Like any other parent, Mrs. Skinner is anxious that her child learn to read. You have to be able to respond to that concern with sympathy and convincing reassurance, in your tone, manner, and actual explanation. All of this requires that a teacher be both professional and appropriately personal. I think most teachers have no difficulty demonstrating understanding and patience, but they are less successful explaining what they are doing, because they are not always clear themselves as to why they are following a certain approach. "This is what my district/principal tells me to do," "This is what I learned in my ed course," or "This is how everyone else teaches" is not enough; also, none of these answers suggests personal responsibility.

A teacher who feels confident about his or her teaching is someone who has thought a good deal about instruction and learning. This is a teacher who has spent time and continues to spend time reading about and discussing instruction, who thinks about it constantly, and who also has gradually developed a set of principles and core of ideas that guide his everyday teaching. When you can plant your instruction firmly in some clear rationale, you can feel more professionally self-confident. Too often teachers immediately take the defensive when questioned or even mildly challenged. A parent note about anything can trigger undue anxiety and self-doubt. So, you learn how to take a breath, weigh the actual gravity of the parent's concern, then respond appropriately. Sometimes you don't respond at all. A few years ago I received a long, typewritten letter from a parent chastising me for not adequately challenging her "gifted" son. This came after a series of notes in a similar vein, each of which I had tried to answer. Finally, I went to Anne and asked how she thought I should respond to the latest letter. "Did they ask you to answer?" she asked. Glancing through the letter again, "No," I said. "Well?" Anne said. I filed the letter away, continued to do the best I could for this child, and did not receive any other letters. Sometimes parents simply want to vent some frustration, and teachers need to learn to listen with understanding and not feel their professional reputations are at risk.

During Fran's first months at Jefferson a few parents were unhappy enough that they registered their concerns with Anne. By February, however, the situation somehow had reversed itself—Fran seemed to be firmly allied with most of the parents in her room. This does seem an odd turn of events, and the staff was as surprised as anyone. Our only explanation was that, as a new teacher, Fran had to go through the kind of testing many beginning teachers experience when they are new to a school and not familiar to the community. Once Fran had settled in, and parents saw that she was going to be a more traditional teacher than most of the rest of us, they may have been pleased and perhaps relieved to have this option.

Although Fran's relations with parents improved, she was not regularly interacting with staff. She missed more than one of our Wednesday inservices because of workshops and seminars, and we were seeing less and less of her during the day. I can only surmise that this coincided with her difficulties with Anne and her displeasure with Anne's ongoing observation of her teaching. Ellen later commented that Fran had come to her room a couple of times in tears, saying that Anne "was not being nice to her and telling her she was a terrible teacher." Judy's classroom was right next to Fran's, and she said that Fran spent considerable time with her, voicing similar complaints as well as sharing some personal home problems. I admit that except for one spontaneous comment, I never heard from Fran in this way. Perhaps she felt I was too close to Anne or that I would not be as sympathetic as the other staff members. I don't know.

A Cohesive Staff

Another factor in Fran's gradual estrangement from the larger staff may actually have been the staff's own closeness. Visitors to our building often comment on the openness and general camaraderie. Staff members talk a lot with each other. Banter is ongoing, good-natured, and caring. Five years earlier, however, staffroom talk was typical: empty chatter and a lot of complaining, especially criticism of specific students. That has changed as drastically as almost anything else. Teachers still endlessly talk about their diets, but we also talk a lot about instruction, sharing our successes, problems, plans, interests. We often talk about specific students, but the tone is considerably different. Very often teachers exchange warm, funny experiences and those precious "aha!" moments. If they are having problems with individual children, teachers generally ask for ideas on how to help, what to do next.

I don't want to leave the impression that our staff spent the year in unbridled collegial bliss. As with any group of human beings, everyone did not always get along with everyone else. We had our spats and petty moments, blurted out a sharp comment from time to time. Jo and I had a falling out over who was going to have a certain substitute teacher. Jo prevailed, but we exchanged only a glare and silence for weeks. No, we were and are far from living an idyllic staff life. What seems to save us, however, is that we can usually distinguish the trivial from the important. You may grumble at someone for taking all of the watercolors from the art room, but you then sit down with your team members and amicably negotiate how language arts funds will be spent.

Most of us tend to follow a hodgepodge of teaching styles, but we seem to share a similar approach to instruction, and this allows for considerable interaction. Each year additional cartons of textbooks that teachers in our building have decided they will no longer be using are returned to the district warehouse. For the most recent three years, math materials essentially have become team orders, with some supplements for individual interests. Carol, the building's language arts leader, can propose a whole language literature workshop for the entire staff, feeling assured that most of us will find it useful and consistent with the way we are teaching. Inservice Wednesdays have given us several opportunities over the past few years for shared experiences in such areas as cooperative learning, technology, and action research. Given this common ground, it is conceivable that a new teacher might feel uncomfortable if she or he does not hold similar views on instruction and learning. Fran joined our staff expressing a desire to work in this direction, but I think somewhere along the way she changed her mind. Whatever happened, by February it was clear that she had begun to withdraw.

It is difficult to imagine that this was an issue of exclusion. Whether you come to our building to do the wiring, substitute for the regular custodian, observe in the classrooms, or whatever, visitors and newcomers are always welcome. This is an outgoing, curious staff that goes out of its way each year to help new teachers and a raft of student teachers feel comfortable. New staff members only have to ask and they generally will find something stuffed into their mailboxes the next day. Except for the last couple of months of school,

Fran was treated no differently. Teachers were encouraging and generous with materials and ideas. Even in the most difficult final weeks when some of us found relations with Fran were, at best, awkward, most of the staff was still polite and often even sympathetic.

In early February Anne suggested to Fran different ways in which she could get additional help. One suggestion was that Fran take a brief leave from the classroom and spend the time with another teacher. Anne recalled that Fran did not respond well to that idea, so Anne suggested instead that another teacher come into Fran's classroom to provide help with management and model some different activities and ways of planning. When Fran didn't express any preferences as to who this person would be, Anne approached Gail, who had been working as Ellen's Wednesday substitute for the previous two years. Gail agreed to work with Fran from February 11 until April 5, the beginning of spring break.

By this time relations between Fran and Anne had become mutually distrustful enough that Fran's husband attended one of the meetings she had with Anne, and the office manager was always in attendance to take notes. Fran also had begun talking to her students and their parents. She apparently made enough of a case that a letter signed by at least two dozen parents (including one of the PTSA co-chairpersons) was sent to the superintendent urging that Fran's contract be renewed. They contended that Fran had done an excellent job with their children, especially in math and reading.

The question that lingers, of course, is how parents' concepts of "good teaching" and "meaningful" learning can differ so substantially from those defined by a district, a school, or even a single teacher or principal. As events erratically unfolded during the spring, it became apparent that the parents supporting Fran were parents who believed their children needed predictable, daily classroom diets of worksheets, workbooks, basals, drills, and isolated skills practice. That is exactly what Fran was providing. She was also providing letters home to parents discussing her situation with Anne; hence, the letter of support from the parents.

As a teacher new to the district, but with previous experience, and because she was a minority, Fran was hired on a provisional contract rather than the noncontinuing contract generally given to new teachers. Unlike a noncontinuing contract, which provides no assurance of continuation, a provisional contract carries the understanding that if the candidate meets district criteria of competent teaching, she or he will receive a continuing contract at the end of the school year. In this case, the catch phrase was "competent teaching."

IF IT'S CONFERENCES, IT MUST BE SPRING

Spring conferences seem to be easier than those in the fall. Perhaps it's the warmer weather, or perhaps it's a tendency on the part of both parents and teachers to feel the year is almost over. It's not so much a sense of giving up as saying "we'll try again next year." I think many parents simply are relieved that their children have completed the year and will move on to the next grade. This seems to be true in spite of the fact that our school has a no-retention policy.

In the classrooms, the tale is somewhat different. Most of us seem to pick up speed in the spring, realizing there is still so much we haven't been able to cover. In Room 32, we were emerging from long weeks in early state history to run headlong into "energy and simple machines." After a couple of frenzied first years, I finally figured out that I have to alternate science and social studies units; to do them simultaneously is almost chaotic. Like other teachers, I was struggling to figure out how division with two-digit divisors was consistent with hands-on work in measurement and geometry. I'm sure Einstein just picked up his slide rule. We were also doing a mini-unit on folktales, tying them into our previous work on the Pacific Rim.

Trusting Students, Trusting Teachers

Erna and her classmates were spending part of each morning rehearsing a play she had labored over for weeks. When Erna first asked about "producing" the play I was up to my ears in pulleys and levers. So much was going on in the classroom that I first said that there was no time. What I actually was saying was, "If I have to keep track of one more activity I'm leaving for the Bahamas." Erna, to her credit, persisted. Finally I told her that she could select her cast and practice in the small open area right outside our back door, and they should let me know if they had any problems—"Just keep the door open so I can hear you." Erna never did come seeking my Solomonic wisdom. A couple of times as we were walking to the lunchroom I asked how things were going and she said they were fine, just a few problems but they had worked them out. It would end up that before I had ever watched a rehearsal, they were inviting the class to a performance. Quite a performance it was! At least a dozen children were involved as both actors and stagehands, feverishly creating sets, taking care of props, all madly whispering to each other about who should be where and doing what. The class and I genuinely enjoyed watching this rousing tale of kidnap, ransom, detectives, and innocent victims. My own private enjoyment and wonder came from realizing how Erna and her group had done this all without me.

I had similar but smaller moments like this all year, but one of the more memorable and raucous instances occurred earlier in the fall while we were studying whales. I had received some material from a whale research center in New England, which explained that for $15 individuals or groups could "adopt a whale." This meant that once you sent in your contribution you could select a whale that the center had been tracking, and they would send you pictures and periodic reports of recent sightings, which you could chart on a map. The class thought this sounded great. The only question was the $15. If I had pulled it out of my wallet, asked parents for a small donation, or even just used part of my building budget, we could have had our whale in no time at all. The class agreed, however, that they wanted to earn the $15 themselves. Did they want each student to earn 50 cents at home or should the class as a whole do something? They opted for the latter choice, and so began a 3-week project.

As their homework, I asked the students to research fund-raising ideas and told them we would choose a project later in the week. They came in with some predictable ideas, such as a car wash or bake sale. They also came in with other, more interesting ideas, including Mollie's idea of a magic show for the school and Jimmy's idea of doing chores for the staff. Considerable time was spent hearing the pros and cons of each of the ideas. I tried not to give an opinion. It took us at least two half-hour sessions to whittle through the list of ideas and end up with a final four or five. I don't remember the exact vote, but the magic show and chores were close enough that we seemed to be at a stalemate, no one budging. I suggested that an advocate for each of the two proposals meet with Anne and see if there would be any school restrictions on each idea. Jimmy and Mollie were equally impassioned about their respective ideas and each had won over half of the class. I was not about to be the final arbiter.

When the two students returned to the room after their meeting, Jimmy looked positively dazzled while Mollie was working on holding a stiff upper lip. Anne had listened to the two proposals and apparently explained that it would not be appropriate for students to charge other students admission, but that they could ask teachers for "donations" for chores. An eminently good sport, Mollie worked on the publicity (letters to put into staff members' mailboxes); others worked on the forms teachers and other staff would fill out to indicate the chores they wanted to have performed. While I stepped in to set a 50-cent maximum fee, the students figured out the scale for the various chores. I also had to become involved in maintaining the intricate logistics of students' comings and goings, and setting up a large chart that they filled in with their assignments.

The staff was happily obliging, often requesting three students for a task—cleaning, moving materials, even doing some extra tutoring. Everyone had a chance to do something over the course of a week. A treasurer was selected to keep track of the funds, and at the end of the week she reported that the class had earned $15 with close to $5 left over, which the class voted to add to its party fund. I agreed that they had worked hard enough that some of their earnings rightfully should be enjoyed. This fund-raising project took a lot of regular class time, but the students were significantly more enthusiastic about this activity than anything else we were doing at the time. I gave them as much independence and room for self-direction as I could, and they were able to handle virtually every detail on their own, loudly coordinating with each other as they went along. They made great decisions, had much fun, and adopted a whale.

In the self-help literature it is called "letting go." In education literature it is called "empowerment." In my classroom, it was called "the teacher has come to her senses enough to trust Erna and her classmates to take care of themselves, work out their problems, and make their own decisions." This kind of learning for a teacher takes not only time and experience, but a certain amount of honest introspection. I still have a tendency to want to control every minute activity in my classroom, but as we have changed our approach to instruction over the years, it is impossible to hold on to all of the reins. As I have shifted decisions to my students, I have had to come to terms with my own need for control. Teachers have been accustomed for so many years to having their classrooms as little fiefdoms within a school. If we could not significantly influence state, district, and building decisions affecting our professional lives, we could at least hold onto the inner sanctums of our classrooms and maintain our professional self-esteem that way.

However, when staff is invited to take their seats at the decision-making table, and they begin to make a profound impact on curriculum, instruction, inservice, discipline, and a myriad of other areas of school life, they can begin to rethink not just their own roles in a school but the roles of their students as well. How perverse it would be to legitimize expanded decision making for teachers and parents, but not for students! Jefferson Elementary set out to be a *developmental community* school—committed to the notion that both adults and children could come together as a community of learners, learning how to assume responsibility as well as how to share responsibility. The learning had taken hold, and it would continue.

Across the hall, Kay and Ellen were tending to tanks of tadpoles. Their children were finding out firsthand about the wonders of metamorphosis in nature and recording the details in their observation notebooks. They also were making decisions. On Fridays, they relaxed with some "Plan, Do, and Review" time. Every first and second grader filled in a half-sheet with a description of what he or she planned to do for 45 minutes. They would turn those in, then proceed to follow their plans. At the end of the period there was a review session in which the two classes met together. Four children from each class shared what they had done, and the rest of the class asked them questions guided by Mr. Bloom's venerable taxonomy.

KAY

> For a long period, our district hired few new teachers. As such, its teaching population sort of grew up together, until one day someone noticed that there weren't very many wide-eyed young freshmen entering our ranks. That has begun to change, and when a school is lucky and discerning, it gets someone like Kay. Kay is a 25-year-old with the wisdom and instincts of a seasoned teacher. After one year in her own classroom, she and Ellen decided to team the next year. Watching Kay makes one think about the old question of whether great teachers are made or born. There are some ineffable elements in being a teacher that one cannot teach, let alone package in any methods course. Kay brings to her students keen perception, zest for learning, natural spontaneity, and an ability to self-analyze and revise. She is co-chair of SIT, which would be intimidating for most young teachers, but Kay takes it all on with good cheer and aplomb.

Working together, Kay and Ellen were managing to combine enrichment, independent work, choice, and practice in higher-level questioning. Seemingly heady stuff for 6- and 7-year-olds, but they took it enough in stride that it had become comfortable routine. Thank goodness for children and daily routines. Whatever the vagaries of life outside the classroom, these routines provided ballast to the days, and the children helped us to maintain perspective and a sense of humor.

EARLY WARNINGS

One of Anne's more helpful skills is her ability to look ahead. Much like a driver who habitually glances a mile down the road checking for obstacles, Anne was acutely aware of the decision we soon would have to make on classroom configurations for the next year. More multiage classes? Fewer? Keep the straight grades? Some parents were already lobbying for "more choices," meaning more straight-grade classes. In anticipation of the expected dissension and travail we eventually might confront, Anne wrote a letter, dated April 2, to the parent community. One purpose seemed to be to educate parents further on the reasons for multiage grouping:

> As we prepare our children for this very different future, and as we look at the changing needs of students who come to us, it is apparent that we need to change the structure and management styles of our classrooms. We have many students who, for one reason or another, are not able to concentrate or to focus on academic studies until they feel accepted, wanted, and good about themselves. Multiage grouping does support the developmental levels and individual needs of students.

She wanted parents to understand that multiage grouping was not something radical and specific only to our school:

> Multiage grouping is not a new concept. Deliberate mixing of age and grade levels in elementary classrooms has been common for many years across the country. . . . [Our district] has a commitment to implement the organization throughout the district. Several schools have begun the process and all schools are involved in the discussion. This is not an experiment. It is based on a tremendous amount of research conducted . . . over the last 10 to 15 years.

Anne especially wanted to stress, I think, that no decision had been made, that we were, as ever, working to keep faith with the decision-making process in our building. She encouraged parents to keep themselves informed and to contact the SC parents if they had questions or "wanted [to give] further input." We were not yet ready to deal with the classroom configuration issue, but Anne had already begun to protect the process.

HEADING FOR THE STATE CAPITOL

The possibility of a strike had reared its gruesome little head back in the fall as the state legislature began to haggle over the budget, and the governor, to many points of view, was not exactly fulfilling expectations of an "education governor," as he had been dubbed earlier. I think our staff, like most elementary school staffs, was trying to ignore the issue during most of the fall. Even when the state Education Association (EA) began to sound heavy warnings through the media and its own network of representatives and publications, we were still looking the other way. By March, however, unless you had lain in a coma for weeks, deep in your heart you knew that a strike was a real possibility.

Of course, much talk burbled down the hallways, in the workroom, and over the doughnuts in the staffroom. It was apparent that some of the older staff members still carried scars from the strike taken against the district about seven years earlier. During that strike, Mary had chosen to continue teaching, and she received some overt resentment for that action. She at first kept her own counsel about this strike, but later there would be no question as to where she stood. Most of us were still trying to make up our minds. We had few doubts as to the legitimacy of the issues, the compelling reasons for the EA's position; but we didn't want to leave our classrooms. The year had already presented enough disruptions. Some staff members, such as our librarian, were absolutely opposed to a strike, regardless of their sympathy with the issues. What was important was that people talked. They expressed their reservations and their fears. But they also talked a lot about the issues. This is a staff that was now profiting from all the years of talk, of working through problems openly, expressing personal points of view without fear of reprisal from peers. You could say what you felt you had to say.

The strike did not come overnight. Once the governor submitted his budget to the legislature back in late December, the EA began to implement its own campaign, which was basically to educate the public as well as its own constituents. The media coverage began slowly. An article here, an article there, two minutes on the 11 o'clock news. By March the momentum had built to front-page coverage, in-depth analysis, interviews with a broad range of parties, and special reports from the broadcast media. By March the gross ignorance of public and teachers had changed into detailed familiarity with not just the issues but all of the major political players in this drama. By March we knew just which legislators were sympathetic, which ones were in the middle, and which ones were out there nailing planks to the barricades.

While most of us were devouring the daily newspapers, our best information was coming from our own local union office. The newsletters were helpful, but the most effective conduit for information was one of our new third-grade teachers. Back in September when we were assigning ourselves various responsibilities (SC, SIT, Language Arts Council, Math Council, social committee, etc.), Judy volunteered to be our union rep. We have always had trouble finding someone willing to do this, but Judy said she thought it would be interesting and there were only a few meetings to attend during the year. She was actually enthusiastic.

JUDY

> Judy is a woman of clear voice, definite opinions, and a hearty laugh. She was new to our school this year, but she had taught for two years in Maine and worked in an early education program in Alaska. A career in advertising behind her, Judy now had her sneakers-clad feet firmly planted in a classroom of third graders. Having Judy in our building provided a healthy boost to our morale and attitude; and she became an instant source of new ideas and practical ways of implementing an integrated curriculum. It may have been something broad, such as how a genealogy unit could lead to a study of state history, or something concrete, such as how to organize materials in the classroom. Judy is also the resident "neatnik" on the staff. Whenever I walk through her room I go back to my own room and compulsively dust and wipe.

After the staff met for the umpteenth time to hear Judy's umpteenth report from the latest union meeting, we had no illusions about the possibilities for breaking the impasse with the state. The governor was adamant in his opposition to EA proposals for additional education funding (his proposed budget in fact decreased funding); the Republicans were offering their own budget that added to education funding at the expense of social services; and the Democrats were trying to do everything.

The presidents of the local associations met on April 13 and voted to strike against the state legislature. Members of our own local met on the evening of April 17 at one of the high schools to decide whether we would join in the state strike. Teachers from our building were clumped together in the bleachers of the school's gym. There were several subissues to discuss prior to the final strike vote. I don't think I was the only one wishing for some antacids.

Someone once asked me why we were so anguished by the prospect of a strike. Strikes are not, after all, a novel or new way for unions to make a point. It was a good question. Just why were we so wrought over this strike? Actually, it could have been any strike. I think there were two main reasons for the turmoil we were feeling. First, implicit in a strike is conflict. Various factions disagree and cannot come to terms. We elementary teachers generally do not deal well with conflict, whether it is with each other, parents, our own communities, the district, or the state. We like everyone to get along, even if only superficially. If people admit they are not getting along, then you usually have to deal with confrontation, and that is another unpleasant problem. Second, I think we truly felt torn in our professional responsibilities. We believed that the issues at stake were crucial to the future of education in our state, but we also felt that we should be in our classrooms. Many believed that certain employees such as teachers, nurses, and firefighters should not be allowed to strike. Perhaps. I think to some extent that we did feel we were neglecting our immediate responsibilities, but our belief in the validity of the EA proposals eventually proved to be the more compelling factor.

Speakers that night came and went, each holding onto the standing mikes scattered up and down the bleacher steps. We listened, whispered, nibbled chocolates, nodded when we agreed, groaned our disagreement. We had a chance to warm up for the final vote by voting on smaller, mainly procedural questions. I was sitting above the main cluster of our staff, and I could see that we were voting with more than one voice, actually several; we were voting our own minds. Closeness sometimes demands loss of individual voice; but there is closeness that provides the reassurance that can liberate the individual voice.

When it was finally time to vote yes or no on the strike, people seemed to pull themselves together, resolve whatever indecision they had been nursing, and quickly mark ballots. We streamed down the stands, dropped our ballots into the boxes, then headed out to the lobby to wait. No one asked others how they had voted.

It did not take long for the ballots to be counted. We walked back to our cars in rare silence. There was nothing to say. I don't know if we were all thinking similar thoughts; but I couldn't help thinking the others were, like myself, hoping we had done the right thing.

STAY CLOSE. . . . "WHO HAS THE PICKET SIGNS?"

For many of us, this was our first strike experience. For teachers who had gone through other strikes, I think this may have been the first time they found one that was not internally divisive and rancorous. After all, we were a staff that already felt close and supportive of each other. We had spent the last few months talking about the strike, the issues, the what-ifs. Also, we had a principal who understood our position. Anne never assumed an adversarial stance before, during, or after the strike. In her administrative role she could not demonstrate open support, but she did make clear her sympathy with the issues and, especially, her appreciation of how torn we all felt. Because we were technically on strike against the legislature, we were not picketing individual buildings. We also were not locked out of our own building. We kept our room keys, and Anne indicated no objections to our coming and going to pick up and drop off classroom materials. She in fact let us know that "it was lonely in the front office" and that she wouldn't mind if we dropped in periodically. Anne also specifically advised us to keep in touch with each other. She felt it was important that we find ways to meet and to talk with each other every day. It was her usual message: The integrity of the group and the well-being of each individual depend on words exchanged and time spent listening.

Just by carpooling, I probably spent more time with Pam and Betty in one week than I had all year. Our first carpooling took us to the state capitol. It is one thing to sit in the bleachers with a few hundred of your own district's school employees, and quite another experience to be knee-to-knee with about 14,000 other individuals carrying signs, backpacks, children, and a big message. When you spend most of your days in a single building with the same relatively small group of people, it is rather exhilarating suddenly to be in an intimate crush with thousands of other people focused on a common goal. For several of us it all was so obviously reminiscent of the '60s. To be sure, this group was somewhat neater and less colorful in appearance, but no one could deny its zeal and commitment.

I recall Judy standing in the workroom at school one day just before the strike. Running off some hand-outs for us, she exuberantly declared how "thrilled" she was to be able to participate in this strike. "I missed out on the '60s, so this is my chance," she said.

Others in our building were far from thrilled, but they came through. Jo was never in favor of the strike, but once the decision was made she was always there. She was at the state capitol, marching sedately without a sign; and she came to our informal daily meetings. Each person made his or her decision about how to participate, but I think everyone participated. Mary physically could not do a march, but she passed out leaflets and hung fliers on doorknobs. Judy never faltered in her own enthusiasm and ability to keep us all not only informed but also exceptionally organized.

Fran did not participate in any of the strike activities. My understanding is that she felt that such involvement could threaten her position with the district and provide grounds for nonrenewal of her contract. This seems an absolutely valid concern; however, it was unfortunate that she could not join the staff in an event that served to draw us even closer together and strengthen our respect for mutual differences.

The strike lasted 12 days. In between the two major rallies at the state capitol were daily events organized by each local and each school. Most of the effort was directed at educating the media and the public. With 21,000 state school employees on strike, it was impossible to ignore the issue. The EA had prepared well. For the length of the strike, thousands of supporters took up leafletting, picketing, and door-to-door canvassing; there were local rallies, people on phone banks, and community forums.

Each building was encouraged to contact its PTSA and arrange a community informational meeting. Judy talked to the co-chairpersons of our PTSA, but they said such a meeting was not necessary. The support from our own community was, at best, measured and subdued. But there was also our trusty core of highly committed parents who actually formed their own small group to call other parents to provide information and muster support. The majority, however, was simply quiet, as if waiting to see what eventually would happen.

One of the beneficial sidebars to the strike was how it forced us to look beyond the relative comfort of our own district. Besides what we learned from the media and material from the Association, we experienced huge revelations just listening to the idle chatter on the picket lines circling the state capitol. Prior to the strike, I don't think any of the teachers in our building were fully aware of some of the conditions being faced by other districts in the state. While our own district always faces the threat of major financial pruning, it is not in the least comparable to that of some other less well-off districts. Relatively speaking, we have enough desks, materials, texts, personnel, and classrooms. Because of a special levy we have a wondrous budget to support the installation of technology in our K–12 classrooms, and we have received generous building allowances for new language arts and math materials. So it was very easy to believe that this rosy world belonged to everyone.

The strike quickly brought home the realities so that we could be somewhat less ignorant of what was at stake around the state. Given our own ignorance, it was not surprising that most of the parents in our community seemed to have little conception of how critical the issues of this strike were for schools outside of their own fairly comfortable suburban setting, nor did they seem that interested. Even if they could not appreciate the desperate straits of other districts around the state, I hope our parents eventually realized that the gradual cutbacks being made in their own district would have a severe impact on teacher/pupil ratios and on facilities and services. As a staff we did not succeed in adequately communicating that message, but it was also the responsibility of the district to do so, and the responsibility of the community to inform itself. I hope some of that happened.

The legislative session was scheduled to end on April 28. Rather than extending the session to reach a compromise on the budget, the governor gave the legislature a cooling-off period, adjourning the body to reconvene on June 10 ("uninspired leadership," the EA called it). Each of the striking locals then had to decide whether it would continue the strike or return to work. No one was happy with the situation, but we felt we had made our case. It was especially important that we had significantly broadened and deepened public support and, in so doing, arrested the attention of the legislators.

At 7:00 on the evening of April 28, we again climbed up to our bleacher seats. The mood this time was wholly different. It was almost elation. No state budget had been passed, and we were still uncertain about the prospects for education funding. However, I believe we felt we not only had found our voices, but could harmonize as well. Traditionally, teachers, especially elementary teachers, are less than militant. But in just over a week we had created a giant ruckus throughout the state, noisy enough that it forced people to listen, and clear enough that it convinced a good portion of the public and the legislature that we had not left our classrooms on a whim, that education in this state was deeply at risk.

Much occurred that evening. It was warm; people were fanning themselves with their paper ballots. The president of our local called the meeting to order, asking that media representatives leave the room and the doors be locked. Although there were reports from members of the bargaining team, someone in the general audience asked for a report from the executive director of our own association.

JACK

A former high school science teacher, Jack has been with the EA for about eight years. Gracefully in the midst of middle age, not too tall, with graying curly hair, Jack serves as a sturdy fulcrum between the Association and the district. A soft-spoken and mild manner can belie Jack's no-nonsense, realistic approach to negotiations and meetings. He is one of the most direct, utterly clear individuals I have ever met, and he listens. It is in great part due to Jack that the relationship between our association and the district usually has managed to remain mutually respectful, constructive, and progressive.

Jack slowly shuffled up to the center microphone at the bottom of the bleachers. Everyone waited, expecting one of his typically straightforward, solid statements. That's how he began, a methodical report of the Association's lobbying and bargaining activities at the state capitol. He then went further. In a still steady voice he began talking about how proud he felt not just of the extraordinary efforts of the past week, but because the membership had conducted itself in a manner befitting the profession, that we had worked together as unions have always believed they should, in unison. At some point, unexpectedly, his voice cracked, and several hundred people sat absolutely still, cherishing the moment.

The gist of the evening is that we voted by a large majority to go back to our classrooms, as did the other locals. Local presidents agreed that while the strike was suspended, strike activities would continue until the final budget was passed. They were, and when the budget was passed in June, the final $7.2 billion for education was $195 million more than what the governor's original proposal had requested. While the EA did not get everything it sought, it won substantially more than had been offered back in December.

In many individual buildings we also gained a few things that could not be toted up with dollar signs. Jack's moment on the floor of that high school gym was a celebration for all of us. He was saying what most of us probably wanted to say to each other but had not yet found the words. The strike had indeed been stressful; the anxiety and doubt never quit. But teachers in almost every building stayed in touch. Teachers at Jefferson actually met every day and talked every day. The effect of the strike was to reaffirm our ability to work together, but I think it did something more. Over the years we had been learning that we could control our daily teaching lives, that we did not have to rely on a central curriculum office to tell us what to teach tomorrow. The strike took this emerging sense of autonomy and pushed it beyond our school walls. We realized that we could be a profession with viable power, capable of exerting tangible influence over all of those outside decision-making tiers (district administration, school boards, state education offices, legislature, governor's office, the media) that too often have defined and locked in the limits of our responsibilities.

An interesting, albeit ironic, capstone to the strike was the annual "Teacher Appreciation Week," which happened to fall in the same week that we returned to school. The intentions are sincere, and it is amazing how much time and work PTSA parents invest in this annual spring event, an indication of the high level of parent participation we enjoy in our building. Fresh muffins with orange juice in the staffroom, little apple pins and favors in our mailboxes, secret meetings with our classes to ensure flowers and notes every day, salad lunch in the library. Most teachers seem to enjoy this week, but I have always seen it as an in-house version of all the teacher awards that bloom in the spring.

These days it seems that every television station, major corporation, newspaper, and even the Oval Office has some kind of "Teacher of the Year" award. I personally find these awards collectively patronizing, and they seem to be an easy vehicle for various groups to demonstrate their public interest. Somehow it seems inappropriate for teachers, along with actors, singers, and athletes, to be, in a sense, competing for such awards. The main issue, I think, is that such awards seem a poor substitute for the public respect that used to be accorded teachers; and they temporarily distract us from the issue of fairly compensating all teachers for the work they do and the responsibility they take for young people's lives and learning.

We had just completed perhaps the most successful teachers' strike in the state's history, in which we demonstrated and felt enormous professional pride and independence. We knowingly and even willfully antagonized many people, probably not a few of our own parents, on behalf of some profoundly important issues. And yet there we were, a few days later, receiving some self-conscious, pre-planned gestures of recognition. Most of the teachers did not sense any awkwardness in the situation. Elementary teachers seem to become accustomed to and enjoy these somewhat sentimental school events. They glide through the rituals as well as anyone else. Even if teachers disagree, the norm is to be compliant, to get along. No matter how much our roles are extended and changed, how much we assume responsibility and leadership in our building, we are, in most ways, still acquiescent to traditional expectations.

THE CLASSROOM—AGE GROUP OR FAMILY?

Compared with all of its previous meetings, the last SC meeting, held on April 16, the day before the strike vote, was a mundane affair: a review of the proposal for renovating the parking lot, an update from the 4-1/2 day committee, and introduction of Susan, who would serve as coordinator for the 4-1/2 day proposal. There was also a report from Anne that we might lose two teaching positions the coming year due to funding cutbacks. In looking ahead to that next year, Anne presented four different classroom configurations that the staff had come up with, each representing different combinations of straight-grade and multiage classrooms. She noted that an evening meeting would be planned for parents to discuss the different configurations for multiage classes and the SC decision-making process.

During inservice Wednesdays, we spent considerable time as a whole staff and in small groups talking about the options for class configurations for the next year. Would we have a mixture of straight classes and multiage classes again? If so, how many of each? Would there be more intermediate multiage classes this time? What were the pros and cons of each plan? We did not make any decisions in these early meetings; instead, as with other issues, we used the time to prowl through ideas, flesh out arguments and different viewpoints. And, as with those other issues, energetic discussions in our meetings spilled over into conversations in the hallways, over coffee at recess, a quick comment on the way to class. Because we could work through issues in this prolonged way, we usually were ready to reach consensus when a final decision was required.

Our processing is atypical in the sense that we do have some additional time; however, the processing itself and the issues with which we grapple are not unique. Other schools in our district and across the country are making the same tough trek to effect substantive change in education. Our experience illustrates the compelling necessity for finding some radically new ways of restructuring time and adding resources so that schools will be able to continue their efforts without having everyone—teachers, staff, parents, administrators—give up out of sheer exhaustion.

Decisions on class configurations are normally the province of the principal. In most cases, there isn't much to decide. "Split classes" often are forced administrative decisions. When there aren't quite enough students for a full class of each grade, they are combined into one class, hence the "2-3 split," for example. These classes literally are taught as side-by-side curricula—separate textbooks, workbooks, often even content, for each grade. In contrast, multiage classes represent an entirely different view of children's development and the kind of classroom environment most beneficial to learning and growth. In brief, the idea is that children's abilities are not precisely defined by age. No specific set of skills appears at one age and not earlier or later for each child. Schools are the only place in which we are grouped by age, and this historically has been true primarily because it has been so convenient and efficient, neatly conforming to the old factory model of school organization.

Way back at the inception of our Twenty-First Century proposal, the writing committee spent a good deal of time discussing and researching multiage grouping. The result was that we believed it would be more consistent with the overarching theme of a *developmental community* school than would traditional grouping by age. Thus, for the almost three years of the program's life, multiage grouping was an ongoing goal for our building. It began with the primary teachers excitedly shifting to first/second-grade classes. The intermediates cautiously followed this year with two third/fourths and two fourth/fifths. Based on these experiences, and looking ahead to subsequent years, we arrived at some shared conclusions.

Multiage classes work, in our situation, because they more naturally accommodate the way we teach and organize our classrooms. In addition, they clearly reflect our view of children and the goals we share for their learning and development. What does this mean in real-life terms? It means that our classrooms become "family" groups rather than age groups. When my third and fourth graders spend their 180 days together, working on shared projects, solving common problems, listening to and helping each other, they have a better chance of becoming inquiring, tolerant, caring individuals able to collaborate with others having a wide range of personalities, skills, backgrounds, and even personal eccentricities.

The multiage classroom acknowledges that age does not circumscribe level of skills, talent, or ability. Considerable spillover occurs at each end of the spectrum. No regular classroom teacher should find it surprising to hear me say that my previous class of third graders (8-year-olds) included children who could barely read a primer as well as children who perused encyclopedias for pleasure, or children who were still in the dark about place value as well as children who loved to tinker with complex number patterns. I had an 8-year-old who often spoke and acted like a somber judge, and an 8-year-old who instantly lapsed into tears if she forgot her lunch money. Combining two age groups tends to level out such wide gaps and make differences less acute.

There is an entire body of research on multiage grouping. Our own reading seemed to say that, at the least, multiage grouping produces no differences, and, at its best, can lead to significant improvement in learning and personal/social adjustment. Attending to this literature, but relying primarily on our own experiences, most of the staff gradually became convinced that multiage grouping would be more beneficial to our students than straight-grade classes, and it would prove more satisfying for teachers.

Two additional arguments were the logistics argument and the parent argument. Frankly, for a couple of our older teachers, these were more compelling than anything based on actual classroom or learning benefits. Almost two years with a mixture of straight and multiage classes had played havoc with our curriculum sequence. This was especially true for the intermediate grades, which looked like a string of pop-beads—some of the fourths were with thirds, some fourths with fifths, and other fourths clustered in one straight-grade classroom. Trying to figure out some kind of rolling spiral that would avoid children repeating science and social studies topics seemed incredibly cumbersome, if not impossible.

The parent argument had to do with the perceived issue of "choice." Some parents insisted they wanted to have a choice of the kind of classroom in which their child was placed (one staff member wryly noted that we heard no such argument when single-grade classrooms were the sole choice). Meeting this request for choice led to a couple of difficult situations.

Shirley, a fourth-grade teacher for many years, was adamant the year before that she wanted to remain a fourth-grade teacher, so her classroom became the one straight fourth grade in the building. Children whose parents insisted they be in a straight fourth grade were placed in Shirley's class. She consequently ended up with not only a relatively large class, but a class with an exceptional number of special needs children. In addition, at the beginning of the year, some of Shirley's students, along with children from the fourth/fifth-grade classes, were telling the fourth graders from the third/fourth-grade classes that the latter were not bright enough to be in the other classes. It was something we were able to work through with the children, but the idea had been voiced, and it would hang darkly for any child in a multiage class as long as there were straight-grade classes alongside of them.

SHIRLEY

Shirley had been a successful elementary teacher for more than 20 years, nested for almost 10 years in the same classroom at Jefferson. Well-established in the community as an effective teacher and obviously self-confident about her teaching, Shirley understandably might question the need for making significant changes in the existing school program.

Some of Jefferson's veteran teachers chose to transfer or retire soon after we began implementing our Twenty-First Century program. In contrast, Shirley seemed determined to stay at Jefferson, nimbly dodging change while appearing supportive and collaborative. This was not as difficult as it sounds, since Shirley had an outgoing personality and natural tendency to nurture. She was always available to listen to anyone's personal problems and was generous about helping other teachers, especially beginning ones. Kind and genuinely caring about her students, Shirley was devoted to her own family—husband and daughter (also teachers), and a college-age son.

After all of her years of teaching, Shirley still came to school each day wearing a nice dress and high heels. In her late 50s, slim and physically fit, she was almost perennially cheerful, full of amiable greetings—"Good morning! It's Monday!" "How is everyone!?" Unlike the stereotypic image of the teacher isolated in the classroom, Shirley sought out company and enjoyed the full community of the school. She volunteered every year for a role in the school play, and seemed never to miss a fund raiser, field day, or band concert. However, this kind of outgoing bahavior was primarily social; it was difficult for Shirley to collaborate in more professional capacities, such as planning curriculum. I think she basically had her own instructional program in place and saw no reason to start tampering with it.

Shirley was uncomfortable with many of our program changes, particularly the multiage grouping, the discipline plan, and mainstreaming of special needs children. Her way of coping was not unfamiliar. Having had little professional experience with open dissent, Shirley tended to wait until after our meetings to express her feelings, dropping a comment here, a comment there. Oddly enough, for all of Shirley's cheerful demeanor and personal warmth, she was one of the more negative voices on the staff, almost predictably pessimistic about any proposed change.

I suspect that Shirley stayed on as long as she did because Jefferson had become too much her home, the place outside of her own home where she felt most comfortable and secure. Eventually, however, the changes became too much; Shirley seemed increasingly unhappy with her old school but unable to leave for a new school. She would retire the next year.

AS WE WERE SAYING . . .

The SC's first meeting after the strike was on April 30. A new administrative intern was introduced; Becky gave a report on the results of a "Needs Assessment Survey" that would determine the focus and format of our Learning Assistance Program (LAP) the next year; and Clare reviewed recommendations from the technology committee. This latter proposal covered such areas as equipment and software inventory, distribution and support, maintenance and troubleshooting, technology leadership and coordination. For the following year every classroom teacher would have a Macintosh computer; each classroom would have at least two other computers, while each technology (ITC) classroom would have four. It was noted that there was still some confusion regarding the kinds of technology the specialists (e.g., art, music, P.E.) would receive. As in so many other instances, our specialists were at the bottom of the receiving list when initial allocation plans were being developed. Our REACH coordinator, for example, would not have her own computer for 2 more years. Providing equity for specialists was an issue we obviously had not yet resolved; but we likely were not the first or last to face this problem.

School reform focuses so intensely on the regular classroom that the role of itinerant specialists can easily emerge as an afterthought and be resolved with an ad hoc arrangement.

Rolling along, the 4-1/2 day committee reported that its parent survey would be sent home later in the week. Another survey was being developed to obtain ideas and opinions from the students. A flier explaining the 4-1/2 day concept would be distributed to local merchants, whose views were considered important since the children would be released early from school on Wednesdays. Previous feedback from the merchants indicated that they wanted to be informed of when children might be frequenting their establishments (e.g., grocery store, pharmacy, deli). No one's views would be overlooked. Plans were made for the staff to spend May 15 discussing the 4-1/2 day proposal.

A parent informational meeting was scheduled for the evening of May 6 regarding the outlook for staffing for the next year as well as information on the various class configurations that had been proposed. Parents and staff formed a subcommittee to plan the meeting.

AGAIN, THE MATTER OF "GOOD TEACHING"

Gail completed her assignment with Fran on April 5, just before spring break. The strike almost immediately intruded, and the issue of Fran's teaching competence was suspended for a couple of weeks. Gail's work with Fran led to no significant changes and actually may have exacerbated the situation. Gail was supposed to provide Fran with model lesson plans, help with class management, and generally demonstrate how to teach more effectively. Gail felt that Fran was unable to accept such assistance and interpreted Gail's efforts as criticism rather than help. None of us having been with the two of them, it is difficult to know what actually happened. Whatever the reasons for this unsuccessful intervention, by May 1 Anne had not seen enough improvement to preclude her from writing a formal letter to Ted O., the superintendent, recommending nonrenewal of Fran's contract.

Thus, while we were working through our own building-level processes to deal with multiage grouping and the 4-1/2 day proposal, other procedural/legal actions began to grind forward. Fran retained a lawyer, whose legal services would be required for the remainder of the school year and for part of the summer. Fran began to further involve the parents in her classroom. She continued to send them letters giving her version of the situation and explaining it as a "philosophical difference." According to Anne, Fran urged her parents to question what was going on in the school, implying that we were engaged in something unsound and detrimental to the students.

After Anne submitted her recommendation to Ted, Fran wrote a letter to him claiming discrimination, a difference in philosophy, and mismanagement and incompetence on Anne's part. Fran then had a meeting with Ted to discuss and appeal the recommendation. Based on the information he had received up to that point, Ted decided to sustain Anne's recommendation, which he then submitted to the district's board of education, which in turn accepted his recommendation. The issue continued through the next several weeks and became entangled with parent dissension over multiage decisions.

Was Anne's recommendation capricious, biased, or in any way lacking in professional judgment? Fran obviously believed the answer was yes, and several of her parents would soon demonstrate the intensity of their agreement. Anne, however, is a highly skilled administrator. While she may love giving out Principal's Awards and chatting with first graders, she also is in touch with the administrative nuances and details of her job. She knows about instruction; she knows how to evaluate instruction and how to help teachers improve their teaching. Anne knows how to observe and follow up with clear and precise suggestions. She also knows how important it is to document, in specific detail, every aspect and step of this evaluative process; and with Fran, she did exactly that. If our routine twice-yearly evaluations are written up as three-page, single-spaced descriptions and explanations, then it would be difficult to expect anything less for something so much more serious and with so many potential legal entanglements.

Anne did not rely simply on her own evaluations. At her request, the district's director of elementary education made an observation in Fran's classroom prior to May 1. Apparently the director found nothing to justify abrogating Anne's conclusions. All of the steps Anne took, including the in-class teacher assistant and the frequent and extended classroom observations, were not specifically mandated under the terms of Fran's provisional contract or by our collective bargaining agreement. Anne could have based her spring recommendation to the superintendent solely on two standard classroom observations.

Fran had also claimed discrimination as part of her response to Anne's recommendation that her contract not be renewed. This claim, even on the broadest definition of discrimination, would seem difficult to justify. Although the district's teaching staff is predominantly white, it still includes enough Asian teachers, such as myself, that I don't believe our presence in a building is particularly unusual to anyone. Throughout this narrative, I have tried to describe the several forms of support Fran received, first as a teacher new to our building, and then as a teacher requiring additional teaching assistance. Of course, Fran's own perceptions may have been quite different. When one's professional competence is being questioned it is probably extremely difficult separating that from impressions of personal criticism or bias.

Fran had the option of resigning at the end of the school year. If she had followed this suggestion her contract with the district would not have been renewed, but Anne's letter recommending nonrenewal, with its supporting comments, also would not have gone into Fran's permanent file. This is the kind of career nexus none of us would want to face.

A PRINCIPAL

Principal, school, kids! It's Anne Mays, our principal of (Jefferson) Elementary School! She taught all over in Africa. She's a wonderful principal. She gives out 200 Principal's Awards every year! We really like her. Her favorite plant is evergreen trees. She also likes some opera, but she's choosy. Her favorite movie is *The African Queen*.

She looks a lot like her daughter. They both have pointed noses. She is not married now. She's very nice and has a keep-cool attitude. I hope she becomes principal at all the schools, all the years I go. She has a lot of black, gray, white, colored clothes. Her hair is like an old T.V., some's black, some's white. I would say she's about 5 ft. 11 inches in height, but that's my guess. She doesn't have glasses, I don't think.

She has large tuck-in shirts that look good on her. It's usually white. She has a lot of necklaces. She has thin lips and a thick chin.

She's the best principal a person could have! (Written by Randy, age 8, after Anne visited and was interviewed by my class)

Anne has played a central role in the recent life and times of Jefferson. She has been catalyst, navigator, counselor, and the one most willing to look at our program with a sharp, unjaundiced eye. She is a strong personality with definite opinions and high expectations. Anne is pragmatic yet visionary, both intelligent and compassionate, and sentimental but clear-eyed. Not one to waste time on small talk, she also can seem sharp, distant, unapproachable. For those of us who have been at Jefferson since Anne arrived, it took some time to feel comfortable with her, and for her to feel comfortable with us. Establishing trust has required many shared experiences, both the setbacks and the successes. Heaven knows we each have had more than one moment of pique with Anne, but gradually most of us also have learned to knock on her door, say our piece, and get on about our business. This is more unusual than it sounds.

For earlier generations the image of the principal was probably the stern schoolmarm or the genial but authoritarian paternal figure patroling the halls. Anne breaks both molds. An incredibly energetic, multifaceted woman in her late 40s, Anne is helping to create a new image and job description for an elementary school principal. There is the Anne who fulfills familiar functions: attending weekly principal meetings, puzzling out the building budget, negotiating with the electricians, attending PTSA meetings, having heart-to-heart talks with errant students, calming anxious parents, and dutifully completing district paperwork. There is also Anne as a spokesperson for school reform, who sits with business leaders, university folk, and state department officials, and tells them exactly what she thinks, usually with measured tact. There is the human relations expert who artfully keeps at least four different decision-making bodies in the school working harmoniously and productively. There is the encourager and supporter who does not forget to recognize daily contributions of the staff (custodian, aide, secretary, teacher) as well as of the many parents who are a constant presence in the school. There is Anne as instructional leader, who wanders through classrooms whenever she has time, "just to visit," she says, who stops for a hug from a tiny person returning to class. And there is the Anne who keeps a rocking chair in her office reserved for any staff member who needs "an ear" and a bit of advice.

Anne, without question, is an administrator. She has a desk calendar highlighted in three different colors, which helps her keep track of and quickly handle every detail that befalls a principal. We have never stopped expecting her to be in charge of the daily operations of the school. When we walk into our classrooms each day, we have to be able to focus entirely on what will happen for the 6 hours that the children are there. We can do this only if we feel assured that everything is in place and running smoothly, knowing that someone else is arranging to have our walkways repaired or finagling additional hours for an instructional assistant.

A Front Office Team

Anne manages to keep most of the balls in the air, helped immeasurably by an indispensable, unflappable office staff. I think we have all benefited from the feeling of teamwork that Anne has established in the front office. She expects the same level of competence and responsibility from the office staff as she does from the teachers, and she treats them with similar respect and appreciation.

Office staffs are part of school change. In addition to handling the multiple daily demands of a school—from cut knees to copy-machine breakdowns to counting the absences—they are often the first line of defense in responding to parent questions and concerns, and thus must be fully knowledgeable about what is going on in the school at any moment. Because the office staff seems to handle every detail with equanimity and lightning efficiency, we tend not to notice how difficult their jobs are; and we take for granted the fact that we can send down a sick child at any time, that our emergency supply orders will be filled, that substitute teachers will show up at the right time, and that somewhere in the dark innards of the office computers every teacher's budget will be tracked.

Recognizing how integral the office staff and other supporting positions are to the efficient and effective operation of the school, Anne made sure that classified staff is represented on both the SC and SIT. Somewhere along the way, we also stopped referring to "the faculty" and began simply to say "the staff," which served to recognize the importance of all of the adults providing services in our building. (There is, in addition, that horde of faithful parents regularly swooping through the school to provide various kinds of assistance.)

A Listener

Although she is an effective administrator, Anne is more interested in people, adults as well as children. Not a naturally gregarious person, Anne works best one-on-one or with small groups. She does not mingle easily at school pancake breakfasts and PTSA meetings, and parents are not always completely comfortable with her. What Anne does so successfully, however, is quietly and sympathetically work with individuals, one at a time, keenly cognizant of their particular strengths and limitations. She is able to look past the most grating qualities in a person and ferret out something positive. "Every challenge is an opportunity," she keeps repeating. That sounds contrived, but I think she believes it. Anne has the ability to find the common center in each person, that part in each of us that is vulnerable and insecure, wanting assurance that we are appreciated. Anne is profoundly tuned into people's emotions and feelings; but she is not a maternal or doting figure. I think her great skill is that she can listen; and she instinctively knows what it takes to help different individuals feel secure enough to express their feelings and find ways of helping themselves.

I am sure that most of us have had at least one occasion when we have sought Anne's advice. Sometimes we have requested time simply to talk and air a frustration or concern. One of the new teachers in the building was staying after school until almost 6:00 P.M. each day (school gets out at 3:30 P.M.). The physical toll was one thing, but more than that was the guilt she was feeling over not spending more time with her family. When she finally went in to talk to Anne, Anne's advice was that she make Monday her family night, that no matter what the perceived demands of the next day, this teacher would walk out of her classroom by 4:30, with nothing in hand, go home, and do something with her family. It worked, and the teacher ended up feeling successful about her first year without having sacrificed her need to be with her family.

Sharing Responsibility

Anne has demonstrated and expressed her belief that we each need opportunities to grow and to change, to learn to use our minds well, work comfortably with others, become more self-confident and able to deal with problems. To let this happen, she has been willing to give up some of her traditional venues of power in order that others can venture out into new arenas and learn more than they knew the day before.

One of the first things Anne did when she arrived at Jefferson in 1986 was to give each teacher his or her own budget. This is revolutionary; school people are astounded when they discover that I have my own annual budget, which I actually spend according to my own discretion. It took the staff a while to learn how to handle their own monies (I went into the red the first year and underspent the second). However, we have become quite astute about how to apportion our funds during the year, how to look ahead, how to combine funds with other staff for larger projects. If there's anything that said to us in 1986 that a new order had arrived, this was it. We no longer had the sense that there was some big pot of money sitting under the principal's desk, into which only he could dip and dispense funds as some kind of charitable largesse.

Providing individual budgets seems a small gesture, but it does so much both practically and symbolically. Practically speaking, teachers learn about school financing; we have to become more responsible about how we spend money and we become more attentive to the actual priorities for our building. At the beginning of the year, Anne reviews the entire budget with the whole staff as well as with the SC; we see how funds are being allocated (although with such a small budget there usually isn't much wiggle room) and we have an opportunity to ask questions and make suggestions. SIT works with Anne in allocating the funds we receive from the Twenty-First Century project. Money symbolizes power. When it is confined to the purview of one person, so is power. Open up access to money and how it is spent, and you begin to share power and responsibility. A point of interest: After six years of teachers managing their own individual budgets, Jefferson is still the only one of 16 elementary schools in the district to have this policy.

In a school such as ours, we not only share responsibility; we now actually *expect* to be included in major program plans and decisions, including hiring of new staff. During the previous summer several teachers were involved, with Anne and Joan, in interviewing applicants for openings on their respective teams. For the intermediates, there was no question about our enthusiasm for Neil, Pam, and Judy. Our fourth choice decided to take a position elsewhere. Then, through a combination of administrative circumstances involving the district personnel office, Anne hired Fran for that fourth position. We had no problem with that selection, recognizing that there are still many situations in a building that will require a principal's executive decision. To be candid, however, I think that when we begin working with teachers whom we help to hire, we feel some enhanced sense of responsibility for their success.

Sometimes the assumption is that if you distribute responsibility in these kinds of ways, you somehow diminish the importance of the principal. On the contrary, restructuring schools today involves a more complex form of organization than the simple top-down, authoritarian arrangement of the past. Responsibility is now diffused in a way that there are many easy roads to confusion, divisiveness, and, finally, paralysis. It is therefore critical that, as a school begins its own renewal efforts, it have a principal who will be able to mediate the various interests, recognize and validate individual concerns, maintain direction, and help keep us from taking everything too seriously. For all of Anne's openness and encouragement of staff and parent leadership, she unquestionably remains "the principal," and most of us, parents and staff, rely on her doing her job so that we can do ours. Perhaps most important is that she is the individual who sets a tone of consideration and respect in the building, who helps us keep our backs to the wind, and who is passionate about how we tend to children's learning and their daily well-being.

STRUGGLING TOWARD CONSENSUS

An inservice meeting in our building is probably more convivial and relaxed than anyone would expect, especially anyone who has attended many school staff meetings. Routines have evolved over the three years of our program. Prior to the start of a meeting, little groups snatch a few minutes together, huddled by the mailboxes, in the staffroom, in the workroom. Generally wearing something extra casual, such as jeans and their gray Jefferson sweatshirts, teachers hold onto their coffee mugs ("to the greatest teacher"; "thanks for helping us grow"), sip and share bits of information on class doings, a bit about one's spouse, sympathy for a cold, and, yes, whether the field trip forms were sent in.

A few souls who wander into the library too early get to help Anne move the tables into a horseshoe arrangement. We later have to move all the tables back, literally, as they were—in her never-ending quest for order, Jo has sewn little ties into the carpet to indicate where the tables must sit. The rest of the staff dribbles in, and usually we begin on time, comfortably nested around the tables. Snacks are passed along as the discussion gets underway; there are final whispered comments here and there, with muffled laughter as we settle down. As relaxed as we are, we are usually attentive and involved. As much as some of us may grumble about the time it takes to process so many issues during the year, we realize what the alternative is, and so we refill our mugs and take our seats.

Sometimes, at the end of a meeting, Anne comes up with a "warm fuzzy," such as drawing names then making an "I appreciate" comment about the person whose name you've drawn. Anne is usually aware of the sentimental pitfalls in this kind of activity, so we keep it brief and don't indulge too often. For a staff as busy as ours, even the more crusty among us appreciate this periodic pause in our workweek to express some personal thought about each other. This kind of moment also allows the more quiet, usually unrecognized staff members to receive a verbal pat on the back—"Thanks to Jody [recess aide] for staying with my class until I could get back to the room"; "I really appreciate Barbara [school nurse] helping with our lice problem"; "Brenda [office aide] has been terrific getting all my laminating finished"; "I have really appreciated Ray's [art specialist] efforts to coordinate his projects with our social studies units."

Pursuing the Multiage Issue

Prior to the community meeting on May 6, the staff spent considerable time during one particular inservice Wednesday discussing the various classroom configurations for the next year. At that stage opinion was still in flux. Most of us were trying to accommodate parent requests for several different combinations (kindergarten/first grade, first/second, second/third, third/fourth, fourth/fifth, plus straight grades for the third, fourth, and fifth grades). It was mind-boggling simply trying to get the class sizes fairly even and also figure out some methodical, workable way of rotating curriculum topics. As before, we met in teams, developed lists of pros and cons for each plan, reconvened as a whole group, tried to combine all the viewpoints, then come to some consensus. After struggling for most of the morning, we settled on three configurations: Plans A, B, and C. Plans A and B included mixtures of straight grades and multiage classes, while Plan C was an all-multiage configuration. With these plans, we realized the final decision would require more thinking and discussion, not in any formal gathering, but simply squeezed into moments after school, waiting one's turn at the copy machines, perhaps across the table at our local pub.

In contrast to the meetings on Emerson, the community meeting on May 6 was a fairly benign affair. We still heard some adamantly negative voices, but nothing approaching the vein-popping outbursts in the fall. Again, there was a general introduction and overview of the proposed configurations. Then parents and teachers together met in small groups to discuss the merits of each plan. By the end of the meeting, a few parents were still unyielding about wanting straight-grade classes, but many parents seemed comfortable with the other options. Special concern seemed to be coming from the kindergarten and first-grade parents. The former worried about their children being intimidated by older children; the latter worried that their children would not be sufficiently challenged if grouped with the younger ones.

Between May 6 and the next staff meeting, we had considerable time to think about the various configurations and the outlook for the coming year, which was very much based on our classroom experiences. By this time the multiage intermediates were far enough along in the year to feel confident about their positive reactions to working with the mixed groups. That, combined with the continued good feeling from the primary team, the research we had been reading, and our concern about a coherent curriculum and consistent long-term experience for the children, all served as context for our May 15 staff meeting.

We gathered again in the library. And again we laboriously evaluated Plans A, B, and C, as well as additional plans submitted by parents. In the end, the staff unanimously opted for Plan C, the all-multiage configuration of kindergarten/first grade, second/third-grade, and fourth/fifth-grade classes. This was a fairly serious meeting; we realized that we were moving in a direction with which several parents strenuously disagreed; these parents not only had clearly voiced their objections at the community meeting but had presented their own plans to supersede those the staff had been developing.

Emerson may have died as an issue, but it lingered as a lesson. During and after that particular controversy and with the strike not far behind us, I think we pulled together, grasped the validity of our professional judgments, and felt strengthened by the easy, but hard-earned, collegiality and mutual support palpable in our building. We also had become more politically savvy and more sensitive to the potential effects of parent perceptions. Some of the staff had heard from parents who said they believed the teachers were seriously divided on the issue of multiage grouping. So even after the group had indicated its support for Plan C, Clare and Jo each pointedly asked everyone to be certain: "I want to be sure we all agree with this decision," Clare pressed. "I don't want us to go out of here saying we have consensus and then later hear parents say they've heard that some of the teachers don't agree."

Someone then asked if we could go around the room and have each individual indicate his or her position on the issue. We did this, and most of us simply said yes; others added comments to explain their preference. When it was Fran's turn, all eyes shifted in her direction. By now she had significantly distanced herself from the rest of the staff, and most of us were aware of her alliance with the parents in her classroom who were opposed to multiage grouping. I remember that Fran was sitting at a corner of the horseshoe. "I have taught regular classes and multiage classes," she said, "and I think both of them work." That was all she said; we assumed agreement with the larger group, and moved on to the next person.

Going around the room and individually expressing support was not enough. We drafted a brief letter to the community, expressing the staff's unanimous support for Plan C, and saying that consensus had been reached through a fair process of full and open discussion, that no one had been coerced or in any way pressured into this decision (this last assertion was specifically in response to those who contended that the principal had been manipulating the process). After the meeting the letter was circulated among the teachers, who were spread throughout the main building working in small groups and individually. You could easily have chosen not to sign the letter; no one was checking and there would have been no repercussions even if it was noticed. Fran signed the letter.

WE'RE STILL TEACHING

By this time we had become accustomed to teaching in the midst of controversy. Given all of the activity surrounding the multiage decision and the undercurrent of tension related to Fran's position, it is remarkable how life continued apace. At the end of April, Ellen and Kay were dismantling the student-constructed savannah from their large bulletin board and preparing to leave Africa and head to Japan. In addition, they had been working "forever," as Ellen moaned, on place value—"So, now if you have 12 ones, can you do any regrouping?" "How many tens are in 704?" "Please keep your beans in the cup!"

Kay and Ellen had helped most of their first and second graders discover that the Wolf and Red Riding Hood were following a sequence of events that would lead into something called "plot." I was working on a similar project with the older children, giving names to some of the plot pieces, such as climax and conclusion. But the focus was largely the same. More than once, Ellen, Kay, and I discussed story structure, how children gradually learn to ferret the structures out of what they read and apply them to their writing, and why some students have such difficulty understanding that stories tend to have plots. Each year I have boys who write sports stories that include pages and pages of intricate play-by-play narrative, but lack any hint of an actual story, even a clichéd story.

"So, why was this such an important game for the team?" the teacher asks, with hope in her heart.

"Um, they had to win."

"What was so important about winning this particular game?"

"They wanted to beat the other team."

" . . . Okay. What else is in your writing folder?"

My big effort in May was a unit on human biology, focusing on the circulatory and skeletal systems, including work with the microscope. At the end of the year I gave my class a survey; one of the questions was, "Which experience did you most enjoy this year?" There were several different answers, but the most frequently mentioned was "acting out the circulatory system." I try to remember this as I teach today, because it reminds me that even 9-year-olds look for and need learning experiences that can engage them both physically and mentally. "Acting out the circulatory system" meant my beating time on a drum as the "blood cells" carried oxygen and carbon dioxide through the body to and from the heart. What you actually saw out on the basketball court were children toting large red cards and dropping them off with Marcia, the "big toe," then picking up blue cards to carry back to the "heart," where our "valves," Murray and Alex, would push the "cells" through to the "lungs," and so on. I almost didn't have the children do this activity because I dreaded the organization and tedious explanation I thought it would entail. As things turned out, I was wrong. I had to explain everything only once, and we rehearsed just once. The children did the rest; I just concentrated on beating the drum in time.

I still make the mistake of trying too hard to push children into activities for which they lack the interest or inclination. It is too easy to step into that teacher trap of wanting children to do something because "I said so" or "the rest of the class is doing this" or "how will you learn anything?" I have to work at not getting stuck in ugly ruts, dismissing ideas because they don't seem "academic" enough. Teaching and learning inherently are too pleasurable to dilute into blandness. The "doing" is usually worth more than a predefined product, and such doings, while educational, also can be great fun.

CONTINUING THE PROCESS

Once the staff made its decision on class configurations, the School Council held an extra meeting to hear a report from Clare, in which she explained the process that the staff had followed and how we had thoroughly discussed all of the proposed plans, including that of the parents. Clare was an especially ardent crusader for multiage classes. In her first year at Jefferson, Clare was assigned to a straight fifth grade. All classes have behavior problems, but this particular class of fifth graders included a combination of students that never should have happened. There was a group of boys who could make strong teachers wince and weak teachers weep. They could effectively bully both students and unsuspecting substitute teachers, out-yell and challenge anyone in whom they sensed the slightest tentativeness. Clare had managed to win their respect and usually could keep them fairly civil. Others were not remotely as successful. Our art and music specialists, for example, found their weekly sessions with this class were more battle than instruction. After having a fourth/fifth-grade class that year, Clare was convinced that the fifth graders benefited by having younger children with them in the classroom. In a letter to parents, Clare argued that multiage grouping

> nearly eliminates the attitude of "older grade" superiority and intolerance. The brakes are put on "growing up too fast." Children in these classes become much more respectful and accepting of others. This spring in my classroom there has, again, been much more time for academics because we are not going through all the "wanna-be-teenagers" behaviors of the past years. "But will the fifth graders be ready for middle school?" you ask. Do you mean, "Have they learned what they should have learned in their fifth year of school so they are ready to go on to the next?" The answer to that is yes. If, however, you mean, "Are you treating them like middle school students so they can behave like middle school students when they get there?" I am going to tell you that I am not and should not. Why are we in such a hurry to have these kids behave like older people? Believe me, parents, you don't want that period of time to last any longer than it must! You know, many middle schools have a lot of multiage opportunities for their students and that is a goal for [our district's] middle schools.

Following Clare's report, the SC members continued with a discussion of the staff's recommendation, the parent concerns they had heard, the future implications of Plan C (eliminating the need to discuss configurations every year), appreciation of the decision-making process, and the need for communication between teachers and parents. They then decided that the parent representatives would compose and disseminate a letter to all of the parents, in which they would present the staff's position on Plan C and share the staff's responses to the parent concerns. This two-page letter was sent home on Friday, May 17. The final paragraph read:

> We . . . urge you to utilize the comments section below. The reasons for your views are very important to us. Your reasons for support are just as important as your expressions of concern. If you do support some aspects of the staff proposal, but have concerns about others, let us know. . . . It is our desire to reach ALL families. We realize that many of you have been unable to attend the meetings and have not had the opportunity to vocalize your opinions. It is our hope you will use this forum to do so. (*SC Parent Newsline,* May 17, 1991)

Clare's letter offered three additional reasons for multiage grouping besides the benefits to the fifth graders. She explained how multiage grouping more accurately reflects our everyday world ("adults do not work in age-specific groups"), how children have more latitude for maturing and progressing at their own rates, and how weeks of time are saved because students come in familiar with routines and teachers know half of their class. Our Emerson experience seemed to linger in Clare's mind as she added another paragraph:

> Dedicated, professional educators, who have spent years researching the issue, have found that multiage grouping is beneficial to the learning and growing process of children. Sometimes, perhaps, the public loses sight of the fact that those of us in education are doing for kids what we think will provide them with the very best learning environment possible. Based on 25 years of teaching experience, more than seven years of college (for an M.A. in instruction and curriculum), and my experience of the past year with a multiaged classroom, it is my professional opinion that the benefits of the configuration are compelling.

Clare's final sentence perhaps summoned up the Emerson ghost most directly: " . . . *I guess that I expect that some credence would be given to my opinion and that of the profession at large."* In other words, we had found our professional voices and expected to be both heard and respected.

Other voices, just as forceful and thorough, were joining Clare's. The three first/second-grade teachers collaborated on their own letter, specifically addressing parents' reservations about the proposed kindergarten/first-grade combination:

> There is no reason for concern that the first graders will not be sufficiently challenged, as the whole kindergarten/first-grade curriculum is designed to promote inquiry, exploration, and development of skills, thus enhancing the individual growth of each child. We feel that with our strong educational background in child development and many years of experience in working with children at kindergarten/first-grade level, we can provide a rich, nurturing environment in which each child can reach his/her fullest potential.

Judy sent home a three-page, single-spaced letter describing her extensive training and experience teaching in multiage situations. She was especially eloquent explaining how such grouping supported whole language teaching as well as children's personal and social growth:

> This classroom of six, seven and eight year-olds [referring to her previous teaching assignment] was truly a "community of learners." They cared for and responded to each other in a warm and respectful way. They were proud of themselves, their teachers, and their classroom environment, because the burdensome pressure of "keeping up" and meeting the grade-level expectations had been removed. They were freed to celebrate even the smallest growth and the giant leaps that often occur in this three-year age span. It worked both ways—if a student was a bit behind or was ready for greater challenges, he/she felt comfortable changing roles from the challenged to the challenger and back again. This is truly what the "successful" classroom environment means to me.

Betty and Mary wrote their own letter, describing the benefits of multiage grouping and, as with the others, emphasizing their own personal experiences as support. Every teacher's letter to parents seemed at some point to follow Clare's example in stressing professional judgment, genuine conviction, and how conscientiously we had followed the decision-making process to arrive at consensus on this issue. It was a fully deliberate effort to eliminate any possible grounds parents might have for charging lack of staff unity, coercion by the principal, or lack of a serious rationale. We were determined that this time around, we would be riding the train and not lying on the tracks.

Letters to Parents

A side thought. During the year we found ourselves writing a lot of letters to the parents in our classrooms. When Anne began her tenure at Jefferson, she strongly encouraged all of us to write letters to parents to describe what we were doing both in our classrooms and in the school as a whole. I remember how most of the teachers resisted this, usually claiming lack of time or an inability to write. I could understand the former reason, but the latter was more difficult. As a latecomer to teaching, I had spent considerable time in other pursuits, and I imagine I had always assumed that teachers, including elementary teachers, knew how to write. I have always felt that writing is one of the most important skills of an educated person, and that people not only should be able to write but should love to write. It was thus truly disconcerting to hear one of my friends, a fourth-grade teacher, actually say, "I hate to write. I make the children write, but I don't write."

Our staff began with this attitude toward writing. But as they became more immersed in writer's workshop for their students and began to integrate more writing into all of their curricula, I think they also began to see that writing was not just to be taught between 10:00 and 10:45 A.M. every day, that it is a functional, satisfying, sometimes soulful pursuit. The other factor making a difference in our staff's attitude toward writing was, ironically enough, technology. Put a computer at each teacher's desk, load it with a manageable word-processing program, and you go far in setting fire to the teacher's traditional role.

We began slowly. I will always remember sitting with Mary and Betty for their first word-processing lesson using one of our klunky but indestructible Apple IIs. Their first parent letter took a lot of perspiration and over an hour to produce. As they finished, Mary accidentally erased half of the letter so they ended up writing it by hand. It had been laborious, but they were hooked; they grasped the potential benefit of using the computer to make up classroom materials and communicate with others. When we each received our own Macintosh workstations loaded with a more efficient word-processing program, Mary and Betty were off and running. Most of the other teachers were right by their side.

Elementary school teachers, all teachers, have to be able to communicate. They have to be able to stand up in any gathering and precisely explain their program. They also have to be able to describe it all in writing, in concrete terms not smothered by cliches and jargon, because they have to have some way of "talking" to the majority of parents who never set foot onto a school campus. Granted, much that goes home never gets read; however, parents in our school repeatedly tell us how they immediately will toss every flier and school bulletin into the recycling bin, but actually will look for that letter from their child's teacher.

It is incumbent upon us as teachers to keep parents informed about what is going on in their children's classrooms. Too many parents work and cope with unyielding schedules to have time to visit the school. And visits do not always reveal everything about what is happening in a classroom. Walk into almost any one of Jefferson's classrooms and you will see so much activity going on that visitors comment on the difficulty of distilling out the organizing concepts, themes, and underlying goals and philosophy. Unfortunately, some observers assume that what they cannot see does not exist. Most of the teachers in our building send parent letters home at least once a month, some more frequently. It is the cumulative effect of these letters that makes the difference. All of those different writing activities, for example, begin to make sense when you can think of them as a whole, and especially when teachers squeeze in a few pithy explanations here and there. We need to create the picture and provide these explanations, a piece at a time. On an especially quiet morning, we can sometimes write a letter that will make a difference with one parent. That is enough.

The School Council Decides

Meeting more often probably than the National Security Council, the SC met again on Tuesday, May 21. The parent reps reported receiving 56 responses to their Friday, May 17, letter. Two classrooms did not receive the SC letter until Monday, so their responses were not included in the 56. A lengthy discussion ensued without the group approaching a decision. Some of the SC parents asked for more time to go over the surveys and to wait for additional responses. Another special meeting was scheduled for May 23 at 3:45 P.M. (regular meetings were held at 7:30 A.M.).

I was not a member of the SC that year; I don't know exactly what occurred at each meeting. Most of the staff in the building, however, was keenly aware of the tenor and direction of those meetings. Ellen usually emerged looking as if she needed to run around the block or hit something. It was not a normal year; we faced too many complex issues with sharply conflicting views. Given the extraordinary and ongoing stress, it is to the credit of all the parent and staff representatives that the process held, and that the group managed to maintain calm, respectful relations throughout its deliberations.

In some ways, the parent reps had the more difficult responsibility. While the staff position was generally clear and unified, the parents were often at a loss as to how to judge the weight of opinion among the general parent population that they were supposed to represent. As with almost any group of constituents, the naysayers are often the most vocal even if they number only a few. The genuinely supportive or indifferent individuals go about their business, feeling there is no need to become involved. The parents— John, Kathy, Sandy, and Wendy—seemed constantly engaged in their own searches for truth. Was that angry phone call just one voice or was it representative of many parents? Were the concerns they were hearing valid or misinformed? What were the silent parents thinking? Did it matter?

The parents were a mixed group themselves. John, a physician, had a third grader at the school. Kathy had two boys attending Jefferson; in addition, she often helped in the office when a regular staff person was out. Sandy helped with her husband's real estate business while tending to SC matters and keeping track of her first grader and another little one. Wendy, a counselor with a private practice, had a fourth-grade son and a middle-school daughter, who had attended Jefferson. John and Sandy seemed the most flexible, while Kathy was more cautious and needed additional convincing on each issue and extra reassurance that she was following the weight of parent opinion. Wendy appeared to maintain her own personal view of the world regardless of any alternative, no matter how compelling.

May 23. Everyone was in attendance. According to the minutes the SC parents had reviewed all of the surveys and had shared them with the staff. John noted that the surveys indicated strong parental support for the staff, but that a large percentage of the kindergarten/first-grade population was expressing concerns. The parent SC reps indicated support for multiage grouping for grades 2 through 5, but not for the kindergarten/first grade. At this point there is a single paragraph in the minutes describing several stipulations that were tacked onto Plan C, such as adding a half-time teacher to support the six full-time teachers who would be assigned to the K/first classes. The minutes close with: "After hours of discussion, it was determined that we had sufficient consensus for Plan C." The height of secretarial succinctness.

Those "hours of discussion" included so much that was *not* captured in the minutes but that was important when thinking about and understanding the process of consensus decision making. As recalled by some of those attending, the meeting was indeed long and emotionally taxing. Still, people listened and genuinely tried to work through the impediments to consensus. The staff respected the reservations of the SC parents, who themselves were trying to respond to the kindergarten/first-grade parents; and the SC parents worked at listening to the opinions of the teachers regarding the educational merits of the proposed plan.

After all of this discussion, each individual in the group indicated in turn whether she or he "could live with" Plan C as amended. Everyone could, except Wendy. She was adamant that acquiescing to the plan would be contrary to parent opinion in the school. The group was at an impasse. Anne then asked Wendy whether she objected to the proposal on moral or ethical grounds; she indicated she didn't. At that point Anne exercised her authority as principal, as stipulated in district and Association guidelines for reaching consensus, and declared that there was "sufficient consensus" to move forward with Plan C. (Shortly after this meeting, Wendy resigned from the SC. The following year she transferred her child to another school for his fifth-grade year.)

The SC parents sent home a letter the next day, announcing the group's decision to implement a fully multiage program the next year. They explained the process that had been followed and acknowledged the particular concerns expressed by the kindergarten/first-grade parents. In response to these concerns they described some specific steps that would be taken:

- Hiring a half-time teacher to support the six full-time kindergarten/first-grade teachers
- Providing released time for the kindergarten/first-grade teachers to visit other K/first classrooms and to outline a curriculum that would be presented to parents
- Holding a parent meeting before July to present the curriculum and other activities
- Setting aside Twenty-First Century funds to provide additional materials for the kindergarten/first-grade classes

The issue was settled; it was time to move on. Even Job would have felt sorely tested. We were already late in conducting placement of students for the next year. This particularly nettlesome process usually occurs during the first part of May, but we could not do anything until the multiage issue had been resolved.

THE WILL OF THE FEW

The end of May. The ground was soggy with spring rain. Parkas and boots were left at home. I kept asking my class whose white mitten and blue umbrella continued to sit under the coat rack. We were moving into the last days of the school year, with much left to do but eager to put the year behind us. The multiage decision had been made; we were feeling a tinge of satisfaction and pride that we had worked so well as a staff, had taken a clear position on the issue, and had done so early enough to make a difference. It would have seemed farfetched to suggest that, as long as we continued to support each other and were patient enough to let the full process take its course, we again would find ourselves in such an untenable position as that in which we had been in the fall. The chink in this sense of group well-being was that we had no idea what was going on in the principal's office.

Fran and the Parents

As indicated by their letter to the superintendent back in February, many parents in Fran's classroom supported her and wanted to see her contract renewed. The multiage decision came shortly after the decision not to renew Fran's contract, and for some of those parents this seemed to represent another setback. They believed in traditional, back-to-basics instruction, and multiage classes seemed to mark an irrevocable school commitment to a different kind of teaching and learning experience.

People will often say, "You didn't listen," when they mean, "You didn't decide the way we wanted you to." When decisions are made according to a simple majority, there is usually no formal obligation to accommodate or even listen to the minority. Consensus decision making, in contrast, by definition requires not only listening to every faction but also making "an honest attempt to design a direction acceptable to all parties responsible for its implementation without sacrificing the primary objective" (from our union's collective bargaining agreement). In other words, consensus decision making is a formal, extended process, with several checks and balances to ensure respect for all parties involved. Thus, when consensus is finally reached, the assumption is that, while the decision may not be exactly as everyone had envisioned, no one feels they were excluded from the process. The conclusion then should be, "You listened, and I understand how and why my own position wasn't precisely followed." In the best of all consensus worlds, that is how it works.

For the most part, our decision-making process worked; moreover, it helped most of us to grow individually and strengthened the internal community of the school. We learned both to understand and to respect the process, regardless of how exasperatingly long it took or how frustrating it could be. All of this could not have happened, however, without the exercise of bedrock common sense, personal responsibility, and an acknowledgment of the appropriate channels for registering dissent and shaping decisions.

Unfortunately, there were a few who decided their own cause was sufficiently right and just that they could take unilateral action on behalf of the entire school community. (One of the more perceptive parents in my room once observed that parents who seem to have the most difficulty with school decisions are those who focus on the interests of their own children rather than of all the children.) Once the multiage decision was made, the Olsons, parents in Fran's classroom, wrote a letter to the school board. Citing mishandling of Fran's review and the multiage issue, they demanded that Anne be dismissed as principal for reasons of discrimination and mismanagement (using "intimidation and coercion").

The board first shunted the letter over to Ted, the superintendent. He attended a meeting with the Olsons and other parents in Fran's classroom on June 6, the evening of our school art fair, at which time they again expressed support for Fran and questioned both Anne's recommendation and the board's decision. The Olsons also arranged to speak to the board at one of its regular Tuesday meetings. Although the Olsons apparently had tried to get as many parents as possible to attend that meeting, only five others were there. Later even a few of these parents would say they felt they had been misled, that they thought they were going to discuss only Fran's, not Anne's, tenure. The board heard enough that it charged the superintendent to investigate.

INVOLVED PARENTS

While we struggled with the Olsons, we were at the same time blessed with parents such as Kathy, Sandy, and John, our SC parent representatives, who worked vigorously to hold the center. They too were concerned about the welfare of their own children, but the Olsons seemed incapable of extending their perspectives beyond their personal biases and unwilling to pursue their grievances through existing in-school channels. The three SC parents, in contrast, appeared more sensitive to the views of the total parent community and worked to balance those views with the interests of the school, its staff, and students. As they struggled through each of the many, many discussions they had during the year, they also kept faith with the process. With their willingness to listen, to both parents and staff, and their patience in letting the process take its course, I think Kathy, Sandy, and John earned the trust of most of the members of both groups. When they continued on with the SC the following year, I think most of us felt reassured that the decision-making process would continue to evolve into a coherent, effective, and integral part of our school community life.

Jefferson benefits from having many Kathys, Sandys, and Johns. They may doubt, they may worry, but they have a basically positive outlook and generally are willing to "wait and see." This has been especially crucial in the first years of our Twenty-First Century program, as changes seemed to roll in relentlessly, one on top of another. We have been especially fortunate to have a small core of parents who are enthusiastically supportive, share our philosophy and goals, and fully understand what kind of program we are trying to create for their children. These are the parents who have tended to work on the Twenty-First Century proposal, participate on SIT, attend principal coffees, and actually read all the informational material sent home from school.

HANNAH

Hannah is in her mid-30s, tall, slim, and usually dressed just differently enough to stand out from the other moms at the school. Often in denim jumper, white socks, and sneakers, Hannah generally can be found, five minutes after the final bell, standing at the front of the school, balancing a child on one hip and holding onto another one at her side. She trades off daycare with other parents, but takes time to meet her own two boys after school.

Hannah's parents were in the U.S. Foreign Service, so she spent much of her childhood seeing parts of the world most of us only read about in social studies texts. She is bright, articulate, and openly passionate about almost everything. I sometimes think she was born about a half dozen years too late, just missing the clamor and fervor of the '60s.

Hannah is a stay-at-home mother, which was a deliberate, thoughtful choice, as were the choices of schools she and her husband made for their three sons. While the third grader has been at Jefferson since kindergarten, the first grader attends a private school, which his parents believe provides the more personal attention and latitude that he needs. They plan to start their youngest child at Jefferson in the fall, feeling that the regular public school environment will be just fine.

Hannah and her other parental kindred spirits seem not only to treasure their children, but to recognize each child's individuality and to appreciate having an environment that is flexible and yielding enough to nurture the differences. They seem to have in common a wide-open view of the world, which includes an interest not simply in one school but in all schools, and beyond that, in other issues impinging on our lives—the environment, government, social needs. It rubs off. Hannah's third grader probably knows more about politics and world affairs than most 18-year-olds.

Parents such as Hannah have contributed much in the way of ideas, insights, and support for the staff. It does seem true, however, that these parents who have been more thoughtful about issues and who have tended to examine matters carefully, have also tended to be quiet activists rather than publicly outspoken. This is why they have been so effective working on our Twenty-First Century proposal, and moving among other parents on an informal, one-to-one basis. These parents, as much as the staff, were unprepared for the public level of controversy generated by the Emerson issue. Their hearts were with us, but they were overwhelmed by the dissenting noise. They, too, would be gathering in lessons over the year.

Somewhere between the Olsons and the SIT parents is a large mixture of other parents. In addition to the single-parent homes or families where both parents work, we also have many students from more traditional families, with mom at home and dad at an outside job. As a result, many of these moms, and many who hold part-time jobs, are scattered through our building virtually all day long, helping in all kinds of ways. They help in the classrooms, especially crucial for the primary grades, and they lend many extra hands in the office and in the library. They drive and chaperone students on field trips, set up assemblies, and visit classrooms as "picture persons" who present a work of art once a month. We have, in addition, an extremely active PTSA, which garners the help of more parents for such services as producing the annual school play, coordinating the year's big fund-raiser, and planning and running an all-school field day in the spring. Fiscally sound, its passbook something to be proud of, the PTSA also provides Jefferson with supplemental funds for such things as materials and field trips. All of these activities involve invaluable contributions of time and effort. I am always amazed at how much time these parents, usually mothers but increasingly fathers also, are willing to give to the school without any tangible compensation.

As wonderful as all of these activities are, however, they are not especially different from the ways that previous generations of parents have helped out in the schools. What *is* different is that over the past three years Jefferson added another layer to parent participation. In more traditional schools, parents generally don't need to become highly involved in decision making, given that most decisions are fairly routine and tend to maintain the status quo. As the district has mandated building-based decision making, however, and as Jefferson has instituted more than just one or two substantive changes in its program, parents cannot be left observing from the sidelines.

ALICE

> Four years ago, Alice and her husband moved from a large city to our community expressly "for the schools." They did not want their sons to attend what they considered inadequate city schools. They expected orderly classes, conscientiously focusing on skills, teaching in straightforward traditional ways. When their children first began at Jefferson, that's exactly what we were doing. Alice could not know, however, that this picture was about to change drastically.
>
> As bright and as committed as Hannah, Alice is different in her complete willingness to wade into dissension, and she can be impressively blunt. She has not been happy with the way we have changed our instructional program (whole language, cooperative learning, etc.) and she was adamantly opposed to Jefferson moving to Emerson as well as to our shift to multiage classes. While Alice has pointedly questioned each specific initiative, the overarching issue simply may be that of change itself and a fervent reluctance to give up what is perceived as tried and true.
>
> In characterizing differing responses to change, someone once talked about "the pioneers," "the settlers," and "the stay-at-

homes." Hannah is a pioneer, unafraid of trudging into new territory, confident that we will gain something significant in the journey. Parents such as Kathy, Sandy, and John, are the settlers. They don't mind moving, but before they dismantle anything they want to be assured that moving will bring a better life. Once you can convince them to set off, they are the ones who keep the wagon train steady and unified. The stay-at-homes, such as Alice, pretty much want to stay put. They like their lives just as they are, thank you very much. Only by hog-tying them and throwing them into the wagons can you get them to budge. And usually, once they're on the road, they decide it might not be so bad after all.

Schools such as Jefferson could probably do without the kind of challenges presented by the Olsons, but they need their Alices as much as their Hannahs, and especially parents such as our SC representatives. Hannah and the other pioneers help us sustain the vision; they help us to focus on overall purpose and major themes guiding change, and provide ongoing support and good spirits. The settlers bring up the details that visionaries often overlook and then wonder why they failed. "Exactly how will you implement this?" "Where is the funding going to come from?" "Have you thought about how to persuade parents?" "How long will it take?"—all good questions, the kind that need to be answered to make a program work. The stay-at-homes keep us honest. They remind us that we are not alone, that we have a responsibility to allay fear and to mitigate uncertainty, that we cannot arbitrarily force people to go where they don't want to go. We don't want this to be reason for giving up, but we have to do as much as possible to work with Alice, give her a voice and opportunities to participate and to learn. We also learn from Alice. She, perhaps more than any of the others, will ask the questions that will force us to be most clear about our purposes and beliefs, most precise about our plans, and most certain of our commitment.

WHOSE CLASS?

In simpler times when there was more trust in the schools, many parents sent their children off in September with the admonishment, "Listen to your teacher," often with no idea of who "your teacher" would be. Times are no longer so simple and schools no longer so trusted. In many communities today, parents not only may be more interested in which teacher their child will have each year, but become activists in the placement process. Some parents "teacher shop" in the spring; they visit all of the prospective classrooms, making notes of what they like and dislike in order to choose the "best" teacher for their child (I always wonder how these parents can have no clue as to how demeaning this is for teachers). Some schools routinely meet all parent requests for specific teachers. Of course, our building doesn't do anything as simple as that. Instead, for the sake of equity (not all parents are so actively involved), parents at Jefferson may not request teachers by name; rather, they can stipulate in writing any special considerations that should be applied in making their child's placement (e.g., an ITC classroom to meet special computer abilities). Besides the equity issue, we have enough in-and-out movement of children during the summer that enrollments shift, and students often are moved from one classroom to another to balance the numbers as well as maintain evenly heterogeneous classes (girls and boys, special needs children, etc.). There is the additional factor of fairness to the staff. Placement should not end up as a popularity contest among teachers. The belief is that our teaching staff, while different in styles and areas of interest, is a competent, caring staff. With rare exceptions, most children do fine with whichever teacher they are placed with in September.

Despite all of our efforts to create fair policies, placement is a ticklish affair. Over the past few years we have developed a still imperfect, less-than-satisfactory system by which teachers take their current class lists and divide the students into "friendship groups," groups of three to five students who generally get along and work well together. Then, with our bundled student cards in hand, we gather in the library to set up classes for the next year. The second-grade teachers, for example, meet and set up the classes for the third-grade teachers. This particular year was slightly easier in that some of us would be keeping most of our students another year (I was moving from third/fourth-grade to fourth/fifth-grade, for example), except for those who requested another teacher or were transferring.

Each grade meets on a different day, so the process is spread through most of a week. We are told, not advised, more than once that the placements have to remain confidential. In the past, when parents prematurely managed in June to discover their child's placement for the next year, the result often was unreasonable anxiety mixed with tears and fears, and all usually based only on some slim hearsay of what the assigned teacher was like. New teachers seem to have to go through this more than others. Pam had an especially demoralizing start to her year when two parents pushed enough to have their children moved to other classrooms. The parents did not even know Pam, and yet they were willing to have their children go through the disruption of leaving one class and getting settled in another. If left alone, most children generally adjust wherever they are placed. In only a few instances are there some conflicts of personality or other factors that might prevent a child from having a successful year. When that is apparent, Anne quickly arranges for another classroom assignment. (At the end of Pam's second year, parents were trying to figure out how to request an "environment" that would exactly match Pam's classroom.)

When the third- and third/fourth-grade teachers met to conduct placement for what would become all fourth/fifth-grade classes the next year, Fran was there with her student cards. As the teachers were setting up the class groups, Fran was making notes about where her students were being placed. This was not for her own information; this was to be relayed back to the students' parents. It seemed a blatant, perhaps sad indication of Fran's lack of close relations with the staff and her reliance on parent goodwill. Pam, so kind and nurturing but also capable of old-fashioned indignation, took Fran aside and tried to explain to her the inappropriateness of what she was doing. A few minutes later, Anne reiterated the caution, probably in more forceful terms. (We had to meet a couple of weeks later to readjust some of the numbers for the fourth/fifth-grade classes. Fran again tried to make notes and was again given a firm reminder from Anne.)

VISIT FROM THE INTERVENTION TEAM

While the Olsons were instituting their own action against Anne, a few other parents wrote letters to Ted protesting the multiage decision. (This latter track of protest was separate from what the Olsons had initiated against Anne, but the two actions melded into a single disheartening, painful challenge for the staff, and probably more so for Anne.) Ted sent these letters to the board, which referred them back to Ted, who then gave them to Martin L., executive director of elementary education. Martin proceeded to form an "intervention team" to visit the school and investigate the issue. The collective bargaining agreement between the Association and the district sets out specific criteria defining "sufficient consensus." When a serious grievance is received, a team of Association and district representatives can visit the particular building to determine whether, in fact, all criteria have been met and followed. The intervention team basically asks if the participants followed a process characterized by:

- A reasonable effort to obtain, examine, and consider information (both internally and externally available) germane to the making of the decision
- Active listening and consideration given to alternative points of view expressed by any participant
- Open consideration of alternative proposals in an effort to identify a direction acceptable to all
- Reasonable attempts to persuade without coercing persons holding varying points of view in a conscious effort to reach true consensus
- An honest attempt to design a direction acceptable to all parties responsible for its implementation without sacrificing the primary objective or flying in the face of reason
- Acceptance (but not necessarily advocacy) of a decision by a sufficient number of persons to ensure successful implementation, and willingness to implement the decision

According to the collective bargaining agreement, failure to meet any single criterion above is adequate reason to indicate that sufficient consensus has not been obtained and/or the process has not been a valid one.

An intervention team consisting of the Association's local executive director and president, plus two district representatives (Martin and the director of employee relations) visited the school on June 12. They read through all of the SC minutes and interviewed the SC representatives as well as members of SIT and some PTSA parents. In an effort to review the entire history of multiage grouping in our school, they went through our original "Schools for the Twenty-First Century" proposal, which included multiage grouping as a goal, and they read through each year's written evaluation for the state department of education, in which we described the progress made on this particular goal. The team agreed, without reservation, that our building had followed the stipulated procedures and that we had reached sufficient consensus as defined by the guidelines.

CHECKING THE SYSTEM

Although Martin took the reasonable step of forming an intervention team to investigate the multiage decision, according to Anne he skipped a crucial step. He did not ask the parents whether they themselves had participated in the decision-making process, whether they had spoken with the parent SC reps or with Anne, whether they were fully cognizant of how consensus had been reached, whether they understood what consensus meant in our building. If they had done all this, it is difficult to believe they would have felt so excluded from the process or, as some seemed to believe, that the decision had been railroaded through by a small minority, or by one principal.

Personal responsibility, good sense, respect for the process—when these elements are absent, even a very few individuals can disrupt the well-being of many. It is worse when there are no safeguards yet built in, when the system is so new that the participants have had time to piece together only the most visible, daily operating parts of the structure. No one thinks about who will bear the responsibility if something breaks down. In our case, it was not that our decision-making machinery had broken down; rather, some parents simply did not use it but circumvented it, either willfully or out of ignorance. The question, however, was the same—who would be responsible for maintaining the integrity of the process?

Anne became the lightning rod for parent frustration and anger. The irony is that neither the Olsons nor the other parents ever contacted her or asked for a meeting. They made major assumptions with which they never bothered to confront her and instead went directly to the board and the district. It is true that some of our parents are not comfortable talking to Anne. She listens, but does not let you get away with shaping your argument to your own benefit. While many parents have been accustomed over the years to taking advantage of more compliant, eager-to-please administrators, Anne is not a woman easily fooled or intimidated. My personal feeling is that the Olsons knew this and realized that if they actually went to Anne they would not get very far. Whatever their reasons, they presumed that they could reach over Anne with impunity.

The board and district have their own in-house reflecting to do. How do they remain responsive to parent concerns without mitigating their support for the schools and school personnel? Do they respond to every parent and parent group that chooses to write an irate letter? Can they distinguish between legitimate grievances and groundless personal bias? The board and district have mandated building-based decision making, but have they considered whether and how their own attitudes and procedures complement and support what goes on at the building level? Is there at least an initial phase in which the board and/or district ensures that parents (or any other complainant) have both acknowledged and worked through their own local channels before knocking on the board's door?

Many schools across the country are grappling with change, not the usual band-aid change of a new textbook series or reading software program, but broad and deep change that promises to upend much of what we have accepted for decades as "basic education." Nostalgia, however, often traps us into clinging to old behaviors, where we can find reassurance in what is familiar and predictable. Facing all of the changes today is daunting enough for teachers and principals, but we have the advantage of learning on the job. We can move along, learning from what we do each day, learning from each other.

Outside of the school, the immediate world sometimes seems to be standing still. Parents and other members of the community receive only bits of information, usually late. Someone is tampering with one of their most personal institutions, and they don't understand; not surprisingly, they become angry and distrustful. They do not understand the changes per se, and they lack experience with the consensual/participatory processes engendering those changes. Each school is responsible for communicating with and involving its parents in the process of change, involving them in decisions, helping them to understand how to make those decisions. This is a staggeringly difficult task; and schools cannot educate parents effectively except with the practical and moral support of their districts, and probably every level of governance beyond that. Are school boards and district offices sufficiently sensitive to this facet of school change? I think not, at least not yet.

The district office seemed to move on the assumption that something had gone awry in our building. Thus came both the intervention team and Ted's charge from the board that he investigate the complaints against Anne lodged by the Olsons. The intervention team completed its work with dispatch. Ted's work took a little longer.

OUR TURN

Schools are like sieves; news and gossip filter through constantly. Anything going on that's worth knowing about is general information within days, even hours. It's just the nature of an elementary school: a small space holding a group of people who tend to be exceptionally gregarious and always want to know what's going on. It was through this informal in-house grapevine that we found out about the efforts to remove Anne. The Olsons apparently weren't communicating with anyone at the school (except Fran); the district and the board weren't directly or immediately communicating with the staff; and Anne herself could not openly discuss the situation. So, I was typical of most of the other staff members: I heard the news offhandedly, while talking to Kay, a primary teacher, who in turn had heard about it while chatting with a mom at a Campfire Girls function.

Up to this point we were vaguely aware that the district and the Association were engaged in sensitive discussions with Fran and her lawyer (a complaint had been filed simultaneously with the Association, which conducted its own parallel investigation). Karen H., district counsel, was handling the case for the district and served not only as an effective negotiator but also as a vital conduit of information for Anne. Because of the potential for formal litigation, Anne was precluded from mentioning any aspect of the case or her own views on the issue. Through May, June, and into July, Karen had several meetings with Fran and her attorney. Each time they met, there were additional allegations, mainly against Anne and a few against the staff. The latter included the claim that we had unduly pressured her into signing the multiage letter addressed to the community.

Thus, during the first half of June, Anne faced extraordinary pressure, exerted simultaneously by the proceedings between the attorneys on Fran's behalf, the efforts to have Anne herself dismissed, and the questions about the validity of our consensus decision on multiage grouping. The allegations of mismanagement and discrimination constituted severe personal and professional criticism of Anne, which must have been unduly difficult to bear, given the ethical standards she has set for herself. Since Anne could not discuss the issues with the staff, we could only guess, from how little we saw of her in the classrooms and hallways, and from the clipped response to a question, the agitated look on her face as she emerged from her office, at the stress she was experiencing. It was June, a time when the atmosphere in a school usually relaxes considerably, as everyone looks forward to the rejuvenation of summer. Yet there we were, walking another tightrope with no visible safety net.

We saw how isolated a principal can be within his or her own building. When a teacher has problems, she can walk next door and talk to another teacher, or to the principal. A principal, on the other hand, has no immediately available peers. Anne was especially isolated; she was new to what previously had been a fraternity of elementary principals (there were now six women, including Anne). At the district level Martin provided some support, but he was also investigating the multiage decision, and, I assume, had to retain a certain impartiality.

So, who becomes a principal's major source of support? In a school such as ours, we expect the staff to be there. However, how does a staff go about demonstrating support? There are no guidelines, and we felt totally at a loss as to how to help someone whom we were accustomed to viewing as totally independent, as the one to whom we took our own problems. A few of us met in my classroom one morning. Should we march on a meeting of the school board? Circulate a petition? Send scathing letters to the Olsons? Yell at Fran for allowing things to go this far? Finally, some clear-headed soul suggested that we talk to Joan, our school counselor. Joan would be the ideal person, given her objectivity and her position straddling both administration and the teaching staff.

Joan and Anne have been friends and associates for more than 20 years. Joan was familiar with what was going on, including the work of the Olsons. She offered to talk to Karen, district counsel, asking her what action the staff could take that would help, not harm, Anne's position. Joan did this and, relaying Karen's advice, said that we should write letters to Ted or Martin. Karen had emphasized that we had to do this on our own, not allowing any suggestion that we were somehow being mobilized by Anne into a group action against Fran. It was a relief to have some direction, something concrete we could do. Word spread. Write letters. Try to address issues of management, knowledge of instruction, fairness; confine yourself to your own experiences with Anne, your personal perceptions of her leadership and dealings with people.

So we wrote, not all of us at the same time. Some wrote immediately; others needed more time to think, get the words just right. Some wrote drafts and asked others to read them before sending them on; some letters were typed, while others were carefully written in longhand. All of us, however, most likely wrote from personal experience, each having at least one story that testified to Anne's skills and understanding as an administrator, instructional leader, and close advisor. Teachers were not the only ones writing. As parents found out what was happening, several of them also began to write. The letters became a quiet but powerful response to an action that should never have been taken.

LAST PHASE

Ted had been charged by the board to look into the various allegations of mismanagement and intimidation made against Anne by the Olsons and a handful of other parents. Although Anne had been with the district much longer than Ted's seven years, he didn't know her well, and had little direct, personal knowledge of her abilities as an administrator, supervisor, or instructor. There was a lot to find out. He talked with Anne; he talked with Anne and Martin together; he went through all of the material that had accumulated on Fran, including Anne's detailed notes and meticulously detailed record of events. Ted also talked to teachers and parents, surprising several of them with phone calls. Finally, before Ted went back to the board with his findings and recommendation, one additional step was taken. Anne had a videotape of one of Fran's earlier lessons, used during a standard observation. Fran requested that Ted review the tape. He did, and copies of the tape also were sent to three different elementary principals in the district for their separate evaluations. None of these principals had "any knowledge of or involvement with [Fran] or with [Jefferson]," as stated in Ted's later letter to parents. In each case, the evaluations were consistent with Anne's observations and conclusions.

Ted did not make his final report to the board until July 9. At that time he confirmed Anne's original recommendation that Fran's contract not be renewed, based on his assessment of both Fran's teaching performance and his review of how the evaluation process had been conducted. Ted also sent a letter to the parents in Fran's classroom informing them of his final recommendation and describing the process he had followed to reach his conclusions. He emphasized that he had considered not only material from Anne and the district but also material provided by the parents and Fran herself. While the letter did not mention it specifically, the implication was that, in upholding Anne's recommendation, Ted also confirmed the validity and soundness of her management decisions, the appropriate fulfillment of her obligations as principal. The board accepted Ted's recommendations. They, too, relied not only on Ted's recommendation but also on the "considerable written material" submitted by Fran.

Fran, with her attorney, had been threatening an appeal and legal action against Anne, but with the board's decision in July (and a comparable decision from the Association), the issue seemed finally and mercifully to dissolve into the haze of summer.

FINAL BUSINESS

With the school year extended five days because of snow days and the teachers' strike, we began to joke about planning units for the

Fourth of July. For its part, the SC was working hard to tie up loose ends. A marathon of meetings was held through June— June 4, 11, 18, 25, 28. The agendas included everything from the building's disaster plan to goals for the 1991-92 school year, revision of the by-laws, participation in the district's language arts/math assessment project, activity pay for the music teacher, selection of a new SC chairperson, and updates from the "5-1/2 day committee."

The 4-1/2 day committee had changed its name. The final plan was to begin school 10 minutes earlier each day, thus "saving up" minutes. The required number of contact hours would remain intact, and students could be dismissed each Wednesday at 1:00 P.M. To help parents requiring daycare and also to provide children an opportunity for enrichment experiences, we would provide various kinds of classes during the afternoon until our usual 3:30 P.M. dismissal time. Susan, chairing the committee, became program coordinator and eventually arranged for a grand array of classes, including folk dancing, a baseball clinic, cooking, rocketry, computers, Japanese culture, newspaper writing and production, and enough other classes to accommodate about 300 out of some 500 students. The committee felt that the half-day of enrichment classes, added to the equivalent of five school days, warranted a name change from 4-1/2 day to 5-1/2 day committee.

The SC even held a final meeting on July 9, a week after school was out. At that time, Susan reported on the 5-1/2 day plan, which was on its way to becoming a reality in the fall. The remaining kinks were with the transportation department. The logistics eventually would be worked out, and the first 5-1/2 day week would come to life in mid-October of the next school year. It had taken almost a full year to conceptualize, present, revise, and win acceptance, but there was hardly a discouraging murmur from the community.

In the Classrooms

We were squeezing in as much as we could. My own class managed two field trips—one to a brick factory and another to a city newspaper. The students were much more impressed with the thundering machinery and gritty surroundings of the brick factory than they were with the neat and clean operations of a modern newspaper. We pressed on with fractions, pattern blocks, Father's Day projects, poetry, and bones; and we did not forget buddy reading. The children continued to read their own books, write their stories, and piece together their projects almost to the last day. One group spent hours spread over several days on their own in the art room, planning and creating a magnificent tempera mural as a follow-up to their reading of Madeline L'Engle's *Wrinkle in Time*.

The year in the classroom had been a good year. It was spent getting to know my third graders, all of whom would continue on with me into my fourth/fifth-grade class the next year. In September we would not have to spend any time "getting acquainted." They would be familiar with my expectations and I would know right from the beginning who needed an extra encouraging word, more structure, more latitude, added explanation, no explanation, extended time, less time. Except for one student who joined our class this year, the other fourth graders were completing their second year with me. Erna had qualified for and would leave Jefferson the next year for a self-contained "gifted" program. Sharon muddled through well enough, but, with her parents and me in agreement, she would move on to another teacher. Gentle Tom, too, would move on. In two years I had never quite succeeded in helping him to be academically independent. I asked his grandmother to have a talk with him and they agreed that perhaps he needed a teacher with a more nurturing approach. Decisions were made and I ended up looking forward to seeing five of my fourth-grade boys back for a third year. All of the fifth-grade girls the next year would be new.

These are the natural rhythms of a classroom—children change, teachers change. Lives touch and diverge. Having students for more than one year, however, is a special opportunity to slow the rhythms a bit, have a chance to get to know children almost as well as you know members of your own family. I believe that I can have more of an impact on children's learning and personal development if I can work with them beyond a single school year. Danny had come far this second year. Less volatile, more open and willing to talk through problems, he also was becoming a "student." Despite periodic lapses, I generally could count on him to fulfill his classroom responsibilities without me hovering and nagging. He could work reasonably well in small groups, given an appropriate mix of temperaments, and he was beginning to feel more self-confident, periodically popping up with questions and comments during class discussions. Toward the end of the year I told him that he and his mom should talk about whether he might want a change of classrooms for his fifth-grade year. "I'm staying right here," he said. And so he did.

The final weeks of school are like a locomotive charging down the tracks, braking into a sudden stop. One day we were knee-deep in unfinished projects and children at our elbows; the next day we were staring at empty desks and bare walls. The children were gone. We boxed up our teaching materials and stashed the classroom flag in the closet. We loaded our car trunks with all of the potted plants, "Best Teacher" mugs, boxes of chocolate, and other good-bye treasures from our students. Some hugs and wishes for a good summer, and we were out the door.

We were tired, and we knew it had been an exceptional year, but I don't think we fully realized then just how much had happened and how remarkable it was that we had held together. What we did know, with certainty, was that the children had had a wonderful nine months. They had worked hard, helped each other, and taken 12 steps forward in their learning. They had spent their days at school immersed in joyful happenings and becoming thoughtful human beings. We could not have asked for more.

The year had been an incredible test of how one school makes decisions and maintains the integrity of its program, goals, and human relationships. The gift is that we became neither cynical nor despairing, that we learned and gathered in bits of hope to sustain us for all of the days and years yet to come.

4

Distillation

> One, two, whatever you do,
> Start it well and carry it through.
> Try, try, never say die,
> Things will come right,
> You know, by and by.
> —Traditional nursery rhyme

Selected by the state as a "School for the Twenty-First Century" in 1988, Jefferson Elementary committed itself to a course of major innovation and reform. After just two years, 1988–1990, we had implemented, to varying degrees, almost every element of our proposed program—site-based management, multiage classes, mainstreaming, cooperative learning, problem-solving math, whole language, and a new discipline plan. Visitors from other schools and districts began to appear at our front door, perhaps as eager for reassurance that change was possible as for any specific ideas on what to do. Within our own building, however, not everyone was cheering. For some staff and parents, certain habits of schooling were too ingrained to be given up or even modified.

With its confluence of singular events and sensitive issues, 1990–91 provided the opportune moment for active dissent. This was the year that we confronted parents on the Emerson proposal and the multiage plan; as a staff we struggled to cope with an estranged teacher and efforts to have our principal removed. The Gulf War added its own layer of tension and anxiety. Then with barely enough time to decide "for or against," a statewide teachers' strike emerged to provide a difficult distraction. Even nature made her own wry contribution by sending a blizzard to close the schools for three days. In spite of everything, Jefferson survived.

Schools attempting to institute change that is both wide and deep inevitably face a moment of crisis when everything seems to slide to the center, threatening to obviate every hard-earned accomplishment. How to survive that moment and continue forward without sacrificing substance and soul seems to depend on the inherent strength and adaptability of the new structures. If a new plane is precipitously sent airborne before all of its parts are carefully forged and welded together with enough tensile strength, it surely will come apart when subjected to exceptional pressure and external forces.

Jefferson did not come apart. We survived the pressures of the 1990–91 school year, because by then we had had enough time to create a school that worked. We knew who we were and where we were going; we had a formal process in place for making decisions; we actually had time to talk with each other; we had a hugely capable and thoroughly involved principal; and, especially important, a sufficient number of staff and parents was willing to hang on through the hard times, transforming the abstraction of "commitment" into tangible effort and hard work. No single factor in itself, however, could make the difference. Everything had to work together, all the gears grinding at the same time; stop one, and the rest would cease turning. For Jefferson Elementary, we were indeed fortunate that nothing stopped, that we could grapple with obstacles and keep stubbornly chugging forward. Jefferson Elementary thus may serve as an opportunity to examine how one school tries to become and remain a "good" school, with our experiences constituting a kind of crash course in institutional survival.

DEFINING OURSELVES

Where does the culture of a school begin? What provides the framework for consistency and commonality of purpose combined with tolerance for individual quirks in temperament and work style? How does a school create a context that nurtures a common set of beliefs, which values learning and growth for both children and adults, while at the same time supporting constructive dialogue and disagreement? Such questions have kept researchers and their tape recorders busy for years. For Jefferson, everything simply may have begun in a plan that was genuinely our own.

When parents and staff members first gathered to conceptualize and write our "Schools for the Twenty-First Century" proposal, we knew each other mainly as casual acquaintances. I don't believe any of us previously had shared with each other our specific beliefs about education and learning in a direct way. The opportunity to have a more personal exchange extended over several months, involved wide-ranging, often self-revealing discussions, substantial outside reading, and frequent consultation with the full staff (parents attempted to reach the larger parent community through newsletters and small meetings). I believe this process in itself, together with the formal proposal, provided the initial context in which we eventually were to create one voice out of many and learn how to make that a strong, clear voice.

Many schools and districts over the years have chosen site-based management as their path to reform. Great attention is given to the particular organization of decision-making bodies, procedures, and equitable representation of parents, teachers, staff, administrators, and sometimes students. Often missing from these efforts are the *what* and the *why*. While engrossed in the intricacies of structural change, schools don't always consider what all the newly formed or reorganized bodies are supposed to be making decisions about. Even if they identify areas of focus, participants may lack an agreed-upon framework in which to forge common goals and make decisions. It's the old tale about the blind men and the elephant. Not having a sense of the whole beast, each man interprets his piece as something familiar only to himself.

The state's Twenty-First Century project therefore may have benefited participating schools as much by requiring an explicitly described innovative plan as it did by providing supplemental funding. Several schools that did not have their proposals accepted still proceeded to implement at least some portion of their ideas. The implication is that schools often lack a clear sense of who they are. Accustomed to being defined by district and state guidelines, they are like overly dependent children waiting to be told what to think, what to do, how to be. The Twenty-First Century project, in a sense, liberated many schools with its mandate that they come up with plans not only original in concept but also reflecting their own specific interests, needs, and resources.

Our own concept of a *developmental community school* represented ideas that gradually crystallized into some basic beliefs about learning opportunities for every individual within a school, about children being best served if they are exposed to learning opportunities even before they begin school, and about the importance of understanding how each child's development proceeds at a different pace and in different ways. We also became convinced that the school had to be a community, where individuals assume responsibility for themselves as well as for the well-being of each other, rather than an institution.

Parents were not to sit on one side of the table with staff on the other; teachers had to leave their classrooms to find out what was going on next door; the custodians and other classified staff were to participate in building decisions; and the principal was to listen and facilitate, more than direct and control.

Our 1988 proposal thus embraced the total entity of the school—students, staff, parents—in developing a rationale for change, ultimate goals, philosophy about learning and human development, and clear plans for bringing everything to fruition. Consistent with long-held district policy, we intended to take hold of the entire complex of factors determining what a child experiences in a single day at school. We were not interested in a piecemeal approach to change, such as trying out a technology program, experimenting with whole language, or starting with site-based management.

An especially important consideration as we developed our program was that we tried to keep our sights on children's learning. You may reorganize your building to a fare-thee-well, but unless something changes for the better in your classrooms as a result of all the revisions in the organizational chart, then it is an empty exercise, and, yes, another passing fancy for education. Schools need to be clear about the kinds of educational experiences they want to provide their students. Because schools reflect specific communities, this may look quite different from one school to another, daringly adventuresome in some, less so in others. At some point, however, I believe each school has to decide where it is on that continuum; it has to develop some initial consensus among parents and staff about what children should be learning and how that learning is to be fostered and assessed. Complete understanding is not going to come about through a single 75-page proposal, but you must at least begin the discussion and establish certain broad goals within which you agree to work through the details as they are implemented. Having such goals does *not* mean setting minute objectives and working backward to predetermine instructional procedures.

The fact that our program was not pinned down by lists of outcomes or objectives gave us the necessary latitude to be creative in how we developed instruction and solved problems as we went along. Yet ours was not a random, wandering effort; we kept our aims in sight and our actions deliberate. Noisy calls for specific objectives in order to measure performance often reflect not simply an interest in student learning but a need to keep teachers accountable. Like production quotas—turn out a specified number of buttons to demonstrate good use of time. Being content with broad goals and a thoughtful plan for a school requires a certain degree of trust; however, it also reflects the realization that learning and teaching are joyfully malleable endeavors that thrive best on imagination and flexible intelligence.

Jefferson began with its goals and a coherent plan, on paper. Over the next many months, that plan truly became our own as we dealt with each component within our classrooms, in our meetings, with parents, and among ourselves. In the process, we developed a better understanding of what our program actually meant in practice; and as we became accustomed to working with individual issues it was with the reassuring sense of where and how things fit together. Having this kind of larger reference serves as a continuing and reliable rationale for all of the separate struggles. When we made our case for multiage grouping, for example, it was with reference to how it would support the instructional approaches we had already implemented, how it was consistent with our philosophy of shaping learning experiences to meet individual differences, and how it was an extension of cooperative learning to help children work in heterogeneous groups for common purposes. The danger lay in doing anything to avoid conflict, simply giving up, or charging out in full battle gear ready to attack at the first sign of demurral. We were not always entirely successful in taking the high road, but I believe that, for the most part, we managed to keep our egos behind us and our program goals ahead of us.

Schools are like living organisms, moving forward, backward, sometimes getting stuck, then pushing forward again. Change therefore requires time, time for schools and their constituents to absorb changes, learn lessons, and find ways of adapting. Eventually, if they are even partially successful, schools should emerge with programs that are very much their own, implemented in ways that are consistent with the expectations and norms of their individual cultures. We not only had the gift of time, we had a carefully considered plan, implemented essentially on our own initiative; and that may have given us something especially valuable in working through the year's challenges. It may have helped us to believe that everything we did and experienced together, no matter how difficult, eventually would be worthwhile. Some people like to call this *vision*.

CHANGING ROLES, SHIFTING POWER

When a student joins my class in the middle of the year, he or she needs time to adjust to the new situation, but sometimes the adjustment requires a bit more than expected. Some typical questions: "What should I do now?" "How should I write this?" "What color paper should I use?" My response is generally the same: "What do *you* think you should do?" and that leaves most students slightly awash until they realize that it really is okay for them to make such decisions independently. Students who have been with me for a while know this routine; they have learned to make their own decisions, but consult with each other or me when they need help. I believe it is a relationship between students and teacher that many of us rarely experienced in our own schooling. Shifting power in this way has been a gradual process, not always consistent, sometimes frustrating, but in the long term it has benefited both students and me. In addition to obvious results such as freeing me from minute-to-minute monitoring of each student's activity, this altered relationship engenders mutual trust, collaboration among students, greater responsibility for oneself, and, with that, increased pride in one's accomplishments.

My class fits in well at Jefferson Elementary. We reflect a norm that has emerged over the years not just in the classrooms but throughout the school. This norm of diffusing power arises naturally out of our conception of a school as a community, a place not constrained by a rigid, intrusive hierarchical order. In current parlance, the issue is *empowerment*. From among the many and varied definitions of empowerment bandied about in the literature, Lightfoot's (1986) interpretation may be most sensibly apt in this instance. "Empowerment," she says, "refers to the opportunities a person has for autonomy, responsibility, choice, and authority" (p. 9). Especially important are her added assumptions that empowerment is a "dynamic process," involving an "ethos of self-criticism" and dialogue and, as such, should be in evidence at every level of a school. We may not have succeeded in fully realizing these assumptions, but they accurately define our efforts. And these efforts have resulted in the kind of learning and growth that embolden individuals and shake up institutions.

A Principal

Power within a school traditionally has been concentrated in the principal's office. Even if weak or ineffective, the principal still is formally vested with central responsibility for major decisions affecting the affairs of a school. Assuming that the kind of school reform generally envisioned today requires a significant transformation of this role, how is such a change instituted, and how is it specifically manifested in everyday decision making? Again, so much depends on each school, its own expectations and norms, and the individual participants. Implicit, too, is the question of whether such a revised role for the principal must precede, even precipitate reform in a building, or whether most of the change can be effected at the same time that a school is changing. Judging only from my experience at Jefferson, I find it almost impossible to imagine reform occurring without the principal's direct involvement from the earliest possible moment. We were fortunate, I think, in that Anne arrived at Jefferson not simply open to the idea of sharing power but prepared to be a catalyst to such a shift.

Already an experienced teacher and principal in several different settings, including an alternative middle school and teaching overseas, Anne exuded quiet self-confidence and made it clear that a school's first priority was to provide an environment most conducive to children's learning and well-being. Her earliest efforts focused on staff development and a positive, nonthreatening discipline plan for students. She was not preoccupied with staking out the boundaries of her principal's territory. In fact, she invited us to share the view from her side of the mountain. Still, Anne wasn't shoving; she is too savvy about and respectful of the existing culture of a school and how individuals participate within the boundaries of their own temperaments and work habits.

Any leader replacing another, whether as coach or CEO, faces the problem of placing his or her own stamp on the organization, while demonstrating reasonable respect for the previous order. Anne was eager to move in new directions, but she was a very different personality from her predecessor. Her initial years at Jefferson thus required subtlety and a good sense of timing. Anne had to know when to suggest, when to nudge, when to wait. She had to be assertive enough to push us a few steps forward, but indirect and patient enough to let us find our own way. The price Anne paid was to be accused of manipulation, which seems to be one of the more venal sins for a principal. The alternative for Anne would have been to do nothing but let us mosey along as before. That would have been the easier, much less painful way, but Anne does not duck a challenge, and she decided that pushing at the status quo would be worth a try. The results probably yielded more than even she expected.

Anne's persuasive powers and active encouragement were perhaps primarily responsible for our plunge into school reform and the emergence of a document outlining a vision for Jefferson's future. This guiding role could not end quickly. While everyone in a school bears some responsibility for creating and hanging onto such a vision, the principal perhaps more than anyone else must continue to hold the lantern aloft. Tucked into each issue of change is the potential for complete unraveling. Jefferson easily could have sunk before it sailed when we began to revise our schoolwide discipline plan to be more consistent with the other changes envisioned for our program. Differing personal philosophies and values came crashing into each other, and many of us reacted as if this were the only issue of consequence. In this and other critical moments, it was usually Anne who helped us to identify our commonalities and negotiate our differences. In every school, so much happens every day, at every level, that change only complicates and intensifies all of it. Someone has to be there to help ensure consistent direction.

Although elementary schools generally are considerably smaller and organizationally less complex than most high schools, they are not simple places. Even in the relatively unfettered days before the current wave of school reform initiatives, principals were responsible for an intricate mix of administrative functions, teacher evaluation and other personnel decisions, student discipline, and an array of public relations activities, such as appearing at school plays and pancake breakfasts. Rather than eliminating or reducing the number of such duties, school reform only complicates the principal's role. Building-based decision making changes the structure of governance, makes it more inclusive and expands the number of participants. At the same time, instruction experiences its own upheaval, with accompanying shifts in the role of the teacher. Stir in technology and assessment, and the challenge is complete. Changes initiated during the first years of our program were difficult to manage in themselves, even without vocal or overt opposition. With 1990–91, Anne perhaps confronted her own personal crucible year, while we continued to rely on her to mediate among the various groups, keeping them on track and working in tandem. We trusted that she would help us to retain some overall perspective and keep us moving forward. It was a well-placed trust.

Anne survived the year because of her extended experience and skill as a principal in dealing with sensitive, controversial issues, while not neglecting the daily minutiae of principalship. In dealing with Fran, in particular, Anne knew how to handle the detailed corroborating paperwork, how to be sure that every procedural requirement was adequately met. Most important, she was able to maintain her balance and continue to conduct the affairs of the school without being overcome by the stress of dealing with the personal charges being levied against her. What would have happened with a principal less experienced in evaluation, less knowledgeable about instruction, less cognizant of policy regarding contract review? What would have happened with a principal less committed to the overall goals of the program and to the people who had invested so much time and work in implementing that program? Unfortunately, we have too many schools that can serve as illustrations of what happens when an "Anne" is not there to hold the pieces together.

Principals are not always successful at negotiating the intricate steps of removing an ineffectual teacher. Such a teacher then may remain at the school, which can lead to a constant undercurrent of tension and make it impossible for genuine staff cohesion and collegiality to develop. The principal's position also can be weakened, suggesting diminished authority and competence, and that easily leads to a loss of confidence on the part of staff and parents. The total result is a school demoralized, and, if it was in the midst of attempting major reform, it could end up where it began, with changes gradually re-exchanged for the old status quo. Fortunately, this was not Jefferson's fate.

Time and Support. Effective principals appear to have some specific skills and areas of knowledge that are absolutely essential in helping any school to function efficiently and to provide quality instruction for students. At the same time, however, as much as a school can and should be responsible for defining and implementing its own course of change, it can be readily constrained by externally set policies and decisions. A common practice in this country has been to routinely rotate effective principals from school to school with the expectation that they will "fix" problems at one stop and then move onto the next. If we believe, however, that schools are healthiest when they develop a strong internal culture that supports learning among both children and adults, then we must believe that one of the individuals most pivotal in this process should be given time in which to turn this into a daily reality. "Time" in this case has to be more than a year or two. Even 3 years, in certain schools, may be long enough only to lay down a slim foundation. Districts need to understand how long it takes to institute substantive school change and how continuity in school leadership is a critical factor in both initiating and sustaining such change.

Principals need additional support in such areas as personnel (hiring staff supportive of building changes, facilitating justified transfers) and funding (Jefferson received some supplemental monies during its initial restructuring efforts). District support also should be available for more adventuresome innovation. This may be logistical, such as providing transportation services for a shortened school day to make inservice time available. Or it may involve a larger policy commitment supporting, for example, a school's decision to mainstream its special needs students over objections of the district coordinator for special education.

Sometimes timing is everything. Anne arrived at Jefferson as the district was committing itself to supporting site-based management and innovative instruction in all of its schools. This commitment included stability for principals and some initial efforts to accommodate individual school needs in personnel decisions and noninstructional services. Most established bureaucracies, however, cannot transform themselves overnight, and Anne still had to work her personal sleight-of-hand to go over, under, and through the customary impediments.

Anne's Vision. Anne's managerial skills were both deft and determined; but what served us best was the extra piece not usually included in job descriptions. Anne was on a personal mission. She wasn't delivering speeches or sending out memoranda listing dozens of objectives. Instead, she was starting at the edges—in informal conversations, the agenda topics for staff meetings, how teacher evaluations were to be conducted, her daily wandering through classrooms, Principal's Awards for positive student behavior, articles on instruction attached to our weekly bulletins, and complimentary notes and comments to teachers and staff. Anne was sending us a message. In essence, it said: "What is important to me is learning, teaching, and how well we treat each other"—a seemingly obvious message but one usually obscured by managerial priorities and administrative directives. Sergiovanni (1992) observes:

> The head of leadership has to do with the mindscapes, or theories of practice, that leaders develop over time, and with their ability, in light of these theories, to reflect on the situations they face. Reflection, combined with personal vision and an internal system of values, becomes the basis of leadership strategies and actions. If the heart and the head are separated from the hand, then the leader's actions, decisions, and behaviors cannot be understood. (p. 7)

With her efficient, sometimes clipped style, Anne often seemed a principal working exclusively by head and hand. The "heart" of her efforts would become apparent only gradually, and not to everyone. I believe that Anne arrived at Jefferson with an already clearly formed image of the kind of education she believed children deserved to have and of the kind of school that would make that possible. Central to this vision was exceptional instruction provided by reflective and competent professionals, with parents, teachers, staff, and administrators planting their feet in the same direction.

The peculiarly difficult task for Anne was to establish her personal vision as a flexible framework within which the school community could shape a vision of its own—we ultimately give our best when the goals are of our own making and not someone else's. Believing so strongly in her own vision, Anne had to walk a thin line between encouraging and coercing, manipulating and guiding. Such is the special responsibility of being a leader. I think what helped Anne to maintain this balance was her own particular set of values and beliefs, which Sergiovanni (1992) sees as underpinning "moral leadership." Anne could encourage and guide because of her trust in each individual's potential for growth and for learning. She could wait for us to create our own vision for Jefferson because of her belief in the benefits of community and cooperation. She could listen because of her respect for the views of others, their personal anxieties and concerns. She could persevere because of her deep and abiding concern that children be allowed to learn in a stimulating, utterly safe and caring environment. For all this, however, she was certainly not "St. Anne." She could be stubborn, brusque, unapproachable, and inadvertently manipulative; but she recognized such shortcomings, accepted them in herself and in others, and always moved on.

A principal's work moves in neither a straight line nor at a constant pace. When shepherding a school such as Jefferson through significant reform efforts, a principal should expect that each phase will require changes in his or her own behaviors and expectations. When helping a hesitant student, a teacher may begin slowly, nudging and encouraging until both share a modicum of trust. The teacher then may begin to set some higher expectations, suggesting options and new tasks. Principals should be engaged in a similar process with their schools. As staff and parents come to know each other better, a principal can begin to introduce the really tough issues of change, feeling relatively reassured that relationships and processes will be strong enough to handle the most difficult disparities of opinion and belief.

Whether consciously or subconsciously, Anne knew when to coax and when to wait. Her sense of timing seemed to grow sharper over the years as she came to know staff and parents as individuals and developed her own core of trusting relationships. In the process of helping us to deal with the more unsettling aspects of change, Anne extended her own understandings and skills as a principal. And I believe that she became a better principal as she went along. Part of this was the result of practice and experience, but a large measure of it seemed to emanate from a basic desire to do something good for people she cared about.

Schools engaged in change rely on the commitment, intelligence, and measured judgment of talented principals. It should not be far-fetched to suggest that radical reform cannot occur without them. At the same time, however, they cannot do everything by themselves. The district provides certain crucial help, and Anne was about as determined a principal as a school could have. But that was not enough. Although she may have succeeded in finally getting us into the boat, we had to learn how to row together.

The Teachers

A multiage, mainstreamed classroom welcomes a wide range of abilities, skills, and personalities. A traditional approach to instruction is one way of coping with the complex diversity. Everything is teacher-directed; students are grouped by ability and quickly accept narrowly circumscribed definitions of what they can and should do. Inevitably a few leaders emerge, usually those accepted as "the smart ones." The rest of the class tends to drop back into inconspicuous roles, rarely invited to demonstrate individual talents. Worse, they are denied opportunities for discovering their talents or for engaging in extended learning experiences. Teachers historically have been just as constrained as these students. Strongly pressured to follow detailed curriculum guidelines, many teachers resign themselves to passive roles without seeking to enrich their own learning or become centrally involved in professional activities.

As we worked to create more democratic classroom environments, using such approaches as cooperative learning and whole language, students at every level found many opportunities to demonstrate special talents and accomplishments. We also tried to create a sense of family, in which children could root for each other and celebrate individual academic and personal success. As these changes began to slip into our classrooms, similar changes occurred among ourselves as teachers. We created our own version of cooperative learning and pulling together as a staff. At the same time, individuals began to assume some risks and expand their lives beyond the classroom. Even a few of our more timid staff members stepped onto the stage, finding supporting roles to play in the ongoing drama (with welcome comedic moments) of Jefferson Elementary.

As Leaders. Anne practiced this art with fair skill and conviction, right from the beginning, as she handed us our individual budgets and invited us to say what we thought. For a while most of us didn't know what we thought. Sometimes we knew, but wouldn't or couldn't say. Eventually, however, with time, practice, and opportunity, we clarified the ideas and found our tongues. Teaching has tended to be a mute profession; but our experience suggests that, given sufficient purpose, trust, and latitude, teachers will try on some new hats and become more directly involved in school decision making.

Consistent with the multiple definitions that researchers and theorists have ascribed to the concept of "teacher leadership" (e.g., Wasley, 1991), staff in our building demonstrated their commitment in many ways other than publicly taking the floor to make a point. In some cases leadership was attached to formal decision-making positions on the SIT or SC. But it also was evident when individuals volunteered to help on school committees, became enthusiastic participants in team planning, piloted alternative assessments, joined district groups to develop new language arts SLOS (student learning objectives), wrote parent newsletters to explain certain issues, or even gingerly interjected their own perspectives into informal daily discussions.

As Curriculum Planners. Perhaps the most critical exercise of leadership within our building came in staff's commitment to and active implementation of innovative curriculum. In rejecting "teacher-proof" manuals, teachers subverted traditional behaviors and laid claim to their classrooms. The abstraction of *teacher empowerment* turned into the practical reality of responsibility. Spend any length of time visiting classrooms in our building, and there is a clear sense of teachers exercising options, making reasoned judgments about what to teach and how to teach, and not being intimidated by the central office.

In elementary schools, the norm has been to follow the norm, as teachers quietly set about meeting traditional expectations—"April showers bring May flowers" to grace the bulletin board; 27 matching yellow ducks on the wall; three ability-based reading groups; "If it's 10:00 it must be math." So tied to a factory-model approach to instruction, teachers merge with the institution of the school, and, while they may gain a nod of respect, they give up professional prerogative. Stay with the scope-and-sequence charts, check off the SLOS, fill the planbooks a week in advance, and follow district directives. I think it has been true that while teachers may have been eminently successful assimilating and acculturating students, often they also have sacrificed inventiveness, intellectual integrity, and gumption within both their students and themselves.

Blessed with a district that supported site-based decision making, an innovative state program, and a visionary principal, we had a huge opportunity to reverse this pattern. In informal discussions, in grade-level teams, on the School Council and School Improvement Team, in special committees (building and district level), and as a whole staff—teachers talk to each other about important matters, about children's learning, about integrating instruction, about how to communicate with parents. We know more about instruction and child development than we ever did before. We are learning how to plan creatively and collaboratively in order to develop authentic and challenging curricula. We teach as we do, not out of lockstep mentality but because we personally believe in the validity and worth of our program.

As Decision Makers. We also assume we are an integral part of the decision-making process in the school, and we fuss when we perceive we are not. We are becoming less afraid of confrontation or of difference in opinion. At this stage of school reform it seems almost axiomatic that any building attempting significant change will not achieve totally uniform understanding of its goals or actions to support those goals. Typically, one end of a staff seems to be dominated by a few highly adamant, sometimes even subversive resisters, often trying to pull in a larger group of the apathetic or undecided. At the opposite end are the "stalwarts," the ones with endless energy and optimism, drawing in the "leaners," those who basically like the new directions and just need a little nudge to flop over into the water. How all of these groups interact and the effect they have on the dynamics of change will necessarily vary from one building to another and from one phase of change to the next. Our own experience seems to indicate that there can be a critical phase in which a program's continued viability and growth will depend on the existence of a strong foundation of staff (and parent) support.

Our own staff did not enjoy complete or consistent unanimity in direction and purpose; but while there were doubters, we did not face significant overt opposition. Those most uncomfortable with the new directions tended to take the quieter routes of transferring or retiring. (This was not an insignificant number—by 1990 at least half of our regular classroom faculty of 20 was new to the building.) Among those choosing to remain for the long haul were outspoken and knowledgeable teachers and staff committed to what we were doing. Because our program evolved from the inside rather than as a district-imposed mandate, I think most of us gradually developed a sense of personal investment. We became accustomed to being centrally involved in decisions that initiated, then shaped, our program, and it seemed only natural that such involvement later would extend to the most tense moments as well. As resident SC stalwarts, Mary, Clare, Ellen, and Jo, our librarian, could almost always be counted on to offer an argument, an explanation, or a telling reason for any important proposal. In full staff meetings additional voices often were heard from Betty, Judy, and Neil. But what seemed more important than the activism of a few teachers at critical times during the year was the willingness of the larger staff to be patient, to have faith, and to listen and learn. It seemed the professional thing to do.

As Professionals? Physicians are professionals. So are attorneys, architects, and dentists. But teachers? Teachers sometimes believe their professional status is viewed as only slightly above that of a daycare worker. After all, teachers as a group don't monitor their own performance, set their own standards for competence and licensure, or even appear to possess a specialized body of knowledge (many politicians, businesspeople, and parents regularly claim to know as much or more about education as teachers do). Reports from the Holmes Group (1986) and the Carnegie Forum on Education and the Economy (1986) provided official national recognition of this issue. They also led to what has been an almost decade-long proliferation of theoretical papers and research on specific issues of teacher preparation, the quality of teachers, and their status, roles, and working conditions.

Perhaps Jefferson Elementary can contribute a small piece to the continuing discussion. There were no marching bands, no media announcements, and no one ever came to our school with a certificate declaring us to be "professionals." And yet I believe that by the end of the 1990–91 school year, we knew that we were. There were tangible signs: direct participation in school governance, development of our own classroom curricula, collaborative teaching, using our own expertise in staff development, providing parents with frequent and informative descriptions of our instruction, increasing efforts at peer coaching, and participation in hiring of new teachers. While each of these efforts earned us another notch of professionalism, I don't believe that we were aware of them as anything more than logically necessary to our program. No one was asking, "What else can we do to be professionals?"

There is a substantial literature (e.g., Darling-Hammond, 1985; Lieberman, 1988) on teacher professionalism, exploring both definitions and influencing factors. Within the scope of our own experiences, our sense of professionalism perhaps can be more simply described as a matter of fellowship and mutual respect. During the extended period in which we worked to implement a new program and, especially, in coping with the issues of the 1990-91 school year, we gradually came to know each other beyond daily pleasantries. We helped each other through all of the changes, learned to live with each other's more irritating habits, and recognized how each person had something to contribute to the larger effort. I think, too, that as we worked together, unsuccessfully at first, on the Emerson proposal, but later successfully on the multiage issue, we developed increasing confidence in our own skills and knowledge. David Wallace (1993) talks about what he calls "facultyness," suggesting that teachers who come together in this way gradually build collective purposes and healthy interdependence. Our professionalism seemed to derive less from individual self-satisfaction than from identification with a group for whom we had developed great respect and even affection.

Parents, Too

One of the major adjustments I had to make when I began teaching was getting comfortable with my students' parents. My teacher-preparation program didn't mention how parents could be so anxious about the daily happenings in their children's classrooms. Initially, I didn't want parent helpers in my classroom, and I didn't even know what to do with them. It took me several years to see them as regular people who happened to have a particular concern: their children. Once I learned not to be reflexively defensive, my class was able to benefit from parents' enthusiastic participation in classroom activities. As an unexpected bonus, several of these parents became good friends. This was especially true of parents whose children I taught for two or three years; they had enough time to understand my approach to teaching, trust my decisions, and eventually become wonderful supporters. This was an experience to keep close to the heart as we began to involve more parents at the school level.

Jefferson Elementary's daily life is premised on values of community, openness, and healthy relationships among all constituencies. While it was crucial that teachers developed their own identity and norms for working together, they also had to find genuine ways of collaborating with parents. Teachers, principals, and staff have not been the only ones dissatisfied with the old order and struggling to make room for creative, effective change. Many parents want to be included in this work. We are long past the days when parents stayed home and left their children's schooling entirely to "the educators."

A staff may create a wonderfully enlightened vision for its school, but changes required to fulfill that vision cannot become fully rooted without substantial parent involvement and willing, dedicated support. None of this is a given; nor can it be demanded. Parents not only have to be welcomed into the business of school change—they have to be treated as genuine partners, trusted and respected. This is different from earlier tendencies to exclude parents for "not knowing anything about education" or, in some instances, teachers abrogating all professional responsibility in timid deference to parent preferences.

Over the years parents became increasingly more conspicuous in the flow of Jefferson's decision making. Once usually limited to PTSA meetings or appointments with the principal, parents now have substantial representation on both SIT and the SC, the two major internal decision-making bodies of the school. In 1991 parents and staff were allotted an equal number of representatives in each body. It is assumed that, with certain exceptions (e.g., a staff committee to plan curriculum), parents will be represented on every decision-making and planning group. This has included a mix of topics, including technology oversight, budget approval, school assessment, playground improvement, and emergency planning.

As their involvement in school decisions expanded, many parents learned what the staff has learned: Decision making is often a slow and prickly affair. Parents have had their own struggles reconciling differences and managing to stand still for confrontations. In addition, just as the staff had to learn to manage its internal dynamics and motley makeup, parents discovered that they have their own diverse factions and interests. For parents, the process of finding common ground is a formidable task, given the fact that the parents most involved in school life constitute a relatively small group. The SC parents, for example, discovered most acutely during the year how difficult it is to judge the trend of opinion in their constituency.

One of the most powerful obstacles to school change is the collective memory of many parents and the general public. That collective memory is a rosy mental picture of noiseless classrooms, where children did their equations, filled in blanks, circled answers, and wrote each spelling word five times with perfect penmanship. Everything was very clear. When your reading group was the Speedboats, Sailboats, or Rowboats, you knew exactly where you stood in the class (and everyone else knew as well). School reform has blurred the picture and replaced old scenarios with new ones. The result is often disorientation, insecurity, and the feeling that if the images are different they cannot be good. Anne understood this, and she made sure that parents were included in each phase of change, not just as observers but as contributors to the process.

Parents helped to write the original Twenty-First Century proposal, and over the years they became involved in most other facets of school life. Simple participation was not enough, however. One of Anne's constant priorities was to help parents learn about all elements of our program, from philosophy and rationale to actual program pieces such as hands-on math and cooperative learning. She made it a point to invite parents to staff inservice meetings that focused on areas such as assessment and cooperative learning to help them acquire a better understanding of our curriculum and instruction. The result of this extended involvement was, in a sense, to demystify our program. In addition, we gradually acquired a core of parents both knowledgeable and generally supportive of what we are doing. In turn, of course, we hope they will convey information to other parents and demonstrate that active participation in the life of their school is not only welcome but necessary. And when there is disagreement, it will be on the basis of informed opinion rather than rumor or personal bias.

During the 1990-91 school year, we overcame some of the most formidable challenges to confront any school, and we did so with the considerable help of parents who were tolerant, patient, willing to learn, and even willing to lend their own eager efforts and voices in support of our program. No school can survive otherwise. Change is difficult enough for a staff to manage among its own members. If, in addition, they confront continuing parent opposition without any balancing parent support, their efforts may suffer the fate of many earlier well-intentioned reform efforts: failed and forgotten.

"Followership"

Although a school's reform efforts may rely heavily on the leadership of an adroit principal and a small cadre of committed teachers and parents, the eventual outcome of these efforts still rests in the hands of the wider school community. In Anne, Betty, Clare, Sandy, and John, for example, Jefferson Elementary had no dearth of leaders. Just as important, however, was that it also had thoughtful, courageous followers. For several years, discussions of school change have emphasized leadership, especially on the part of teachers and principals. Recognizing that parent leadership has yet to be fully appreciated and examined, the other neglected element in the discussion is "followership." Who are all of these leaders supposed to be leading? And can they really be leading so perfectly that virtually anyone and everyone unquestioningly falls into marching order? Effective leaders provide inspiration, clarify issues, mediate among differences, deftly suggest directions, and help to create environments in which every individual can take risks and gradually accept change. Yet no matter how supportive such environments may be, it seems inevitable that groups will end up with a few recalcitrant members who are nailed to one spot. Leaders can do a great deal, but they still must rely on individual good sense, flexibility, and some deep, personal motivation. They must trust that these qualities eventually will be demonstrated throughout the process of change, whether by the teacher almost paralyzed with indecision at every turn or the cautious parent earnestly asking his question for the fourth or fifth time.

Not everyone can or wants to be a leader. This does not mean they become irrelevant or that the nature of their participation is diminished. Just as leaders in a school, or any institution, have certain moral obligations and responsibilities, so must those standing to the side of them. Sitting passively, in either assent or dissent, is not acceptable.

Pam could have opted to take silent refuge in her first-year status at Jefferson; instead, she listened hard during staff discussions, asked questions, joined in informal after-school conversations, and struggled to reach conclusions with which she felt comfortable. A 20-year teacher, Libby agonized over each change. Whether approaching the proposed move to Emerson, multiage classes, mainstreaming, or any other new bend in the road, Libby openly expressed her anxiety. Despite her continuing trepidation, Libby did not shut down. She listened enough that her own understanding gradually grew and she was able to entertain the prospect of new possibilities for her teaching. Tears flowed often during the year, but she never gave in to apathy or hostility. Libby instead reached inside herself to combine a personal transformation with a school transformation. At the end of the year, she seemed to have become a more self-confident and happy teacher, even revitalized in her outlook for the final phase of her teaching career. In contrast, Ella was mainly a warm body in decision-making meetings. Her detachment was palpable. Generally she nodded in agreement with the consensus that was forming, smiled, and was pleasant. But she then trundled back to her classroom to continue on as if nothing had changed. Ella was waiting for retirement; in a sense, however, she had already retired.

Many of our parents were quiet parents. They attended every meeting, read every article, memo, and school letter, but they rarely uttered an assertive statement. Like the staff, the parents were learning about both the content and process of school change. Their willingness to listen, to be present at the most difficult times, to sift through information among themselves, and to ask critical questions, provided Jefferson with enough breathing space in which to manage each change. These parents resisted reflexive reactions even as a few parents did not. As critical as the parents' roles were on SIT and especially the SC, I don't think I can overestimate how much we relied on the steady, measured participation of the many other parents involved in the several layers of our school life.

Followership includes different kinds of followers: the passive, nonthinking followers; the grumbling "Chicken Littles" who follow along despite themselves; and the followers who join in only after they are fully convinced that they should. The latter group, the cautious skeptics, were deliberate participants. They were neither mindless nor coerced and their dedication was based on values and beliefs, not on habit. An eager crusader may have announced, "We'll go this way!" but others stood calmly and patiently at the gate asking, "Why? What's over there?"

Jefferson Elementary was supported by exceptional followership as well as leadership. Most of the adults in the school community seemed to grow into their individual roles; they wiggled around to find their niches, gaining confidence as they went. For a developmental community school, this seemed the way our story should go. Not only did the children have opportunities to develop and learn at their own pace and as appropriate to their own needs and styles, so too did the adults. We could feel comfortable about choosing to be listener instead of talker, helper instead of initiator, pragmatist instead of idealist. We could take center stage or hug the wings, pilot the plane or grease the engines. In each case, however, the responsibility was the same—to be a fully engaged and thoughtful participant.

In discussions of school change, the question eventually seems to arise: Why are some individuals open to and able to cope with significant change, to become "engaged participants," while others hold death grips on the status quo? I have come to see the latter group as much less interesting than the former. Familiar explanations for their recalcitrance now seem too facile, but fear of change, unshakable beliefs in the traditional, resentment toward the eager "pioneers," all seem to ring true and have a certain broad generalizability. I don't mean to dismiss the personal crises that these individuals may encounter when thrust into the storm of school change, but my sense is that discussions often tend to focus too much on the Ellas and not enough on the Libbys. On the other hand, Libby's willingness and ability to grapple with the panoply of changes marching across her path, cannot be explained in any general terms. The reason for Libby's growth simply may have been Libby herself. We could attribute her resilience and eventual acceptance of change to the learning that emerged out of an unexpected divorce, or to her earlier career change. But these were events, and one wonders what it was within Libby that allowed her to survive the events. As much as we rely on the communal support of others, we inevitably make our own decisions, and these seem to be based more on individual traits, gathered experiences, and values than simply on the persuasive weight of external factors themselves.

Schools are communities, but they are also collections of individuals, some more complex than others. When forced out of their classrooms to face the sharp light of conflict and the deep unease wrought by change, teachers are not likely to respond in predictable ways. Similarly, parents, startled by changes occurring in the schools, will respond with varying degrees of relief and delight, or horror and outrage. When a school is poised at the edge of the Rubicon, each individual may face his or her moment of decision. We can only hope that when a school chooses to make the crossing, there will be a sufficient number of self-aware and strong individuals to join in the journey.

MAINTAINING ORDER

Visitors to our classrooms typically see students moving around a lot, having spontaneous conversations, and engaged in a variety of tasks.

The impression often is of a hodgepodge of activities, of children doing what they like without any unifying purpose. In actuality, for most of us, there is more structure embedded in that flow of activity than in any traditional classroom we have ever taught. To work independently as they do, students have to be absolutely clear about expectations, about how they are to conduct themselves and behave with others, about what is constructive activity and what is not. Little of this would be necessary if I were directing each step of instruction. Similarly, within the larger school, the expectation is that you assume responsibility for your own actions, are respectful of others, and follow established guidelines for decision making. All of that means, of course, that however lofty our visions, we still need a sound organizational structure and enough time in which to make good decisions.

Structure

School reform has assumed many shapes and guises over the years. Among the most recent and most familiar are district mandates for site-based decision making—an interesting bureaucratic irony. When such initiatives are not accompanied by thoughtful efforts to create substantive goals for learning and instruction, a coherent internal governance structure may provide schools with at least a framework in which to conduct daily business and maintain order. In our own building, whatever the degree of agreement or disagreement, issues almost never slithered through without being discussed inside and out. The precedent was set early when Anne established staff meetings as a time for discussing instructional and curricular issues rather than where to put the copy machines. Representatives of the classified staff (e.g., secretaries, custodians, aides) soon joined these meetings, as Anne felt that in order to do their own jobs better, they needed to know what the teaching staff was doing. With parent members joining the table, the SC began to handle the more pragmatic school matters. Keeping a core of parents who helped write our 1988 proposal, the School Improvement Team began its own monthly meetings, charged with overseeing the goals and implementation of our "Schools for the Twenty-First Century" program.

Specific bodies were established for specific roles and arenas of decision making. It is telling, I think, that in subsequent years some of the most peckish moments between staff and parents arose from issues involving the PTSA. Over the years we have benefited substantially from the work of a highly active PTSA. As a successful fundraising body, a sort of booster club for the school, the PTSA has been responsible for providing us with new equipment and supplementary materials, in addition to handling functions such as planning the fifth-grade graduation events. It has never directly participated in school governance issues, nor has it sought to replace its own parliamentary rules with consensus decision making. The PTSA is thus a very different body in form and function from the rest of the school governance structure.

As the SC and, hence, parents became a more integral part of building decision making, the PTSA began to express a desire to be included in this process. This was first addressed by having the PTSA president attend SC meetings and give a report on PTSA activities, soliciting questions and other input. Not being a formal member of the SC, the PTSA president was, like other nonmembers, not allowed to vote or to speak on other issues. This arrangement appeared satisfactory for a couple of years, but eventually the PTSA requested full voting representation on the SC. SC parents resisted, because they felt they represented the parent community and the PTSA's presence would be redundant. Staff was resistant to the prospect of being outnumbered by parents; and if an additional staff member were added to balance the numbers, then the body would seem too unwieldy. After almost an entire school year of deliberations, the SC parents finally decided that one of them would attend PTSA meetings so as to carry information from one body to the other. This final compromise may seem almost petty, but for those involved it meant preserving the basic structure of the SC.

Beyond this relatively painless moment to clarify one aspect of our governance structure were the far more complicated procedures set into motion regarding Fran's teaching evaluation, Anne's recommendation for nonrenewal of her contract, and subsequent parent efforts to have Anne removed as principal. For the staff there were no organizational mechanisms to guide our participation, and so we created our own. We met in one of our classrooms and played out ideas ranging from the innocuous to the drastic. Eventually, the appropriate people were consulted, and our successful letter-writing campaign began.

The staff moved to support Anne in her evaluation of Fran's teaching performance, not so much confirming Anne's assessment but wanting to avoid her dismissal. Our support was, in truth, based more on previous experience with and trust in Anne's instructional skills than on firsthand observations of Fran's teaching abilities. This was not deliberate bias but the result of an odd system in which teachers, unlike members of other professions, generally lack formal, built-in roles for participating in and shaping their own evaluations. I believe most of us on the staff agreed that much of the frustration during the year came from our having virtually no information about Fran's situation. Excluded from the evaluation process as a matter of policy, we were not able to provide Fran with collegial support or help to alleviate the problem in any way. Given the current emphasis on teacher empowerment, this stands as one particularly conspicuous gap in school reform efforts.

As schools across the country take up the challenge of site-based decision making, explore different organizational systems, and develop their own internal structures, perhaps they also should examine more frequently whether there is a place for staff self-governance related to professional rather than simply program issues, and how it might work. The unions have clearly delineated procedures for processing grievances of teachers, usually against administration. The new wrinkle is the notion of teachers more directly and immediately managing their own on-site issues. Factory workers have assumed greater responsibility for "quality control" in production, and they also use on-site grievance committees to mediate differences among themselves. Teachers, in contrast, are subject to performance evaluation by administrators (many of whom lack a sound understanding of or experience in instruction); and disputes tend to involve mediation by district and association representatives rather than professional colleagues. The question is whether site-based decision making eventually can lead to teachers assuming primary responsibility for their own evaluation and in-house problems.

Building-based decision making still means that more decisions leave the principal's office to be sifted through several additional hands. Without clarity of roles and appropriate sharing of responsibility, the danger is confusion and a constant struggle for territory. Goals are forgotten; the program collapses. While we may have had a small problem with the PTSA, and a larger problem involving the status of one teacher and our principal, our building's overall governance structure was sufficiently well-defined that it remained intact.

Processing

More important than the flowchart organization of the various groups were the procedures and expectations guiding their actual functioning. With district and association support, we replaced the formal restrictions of Robert's *Rules of Order* with the more messy, often highly personal process of consensus decision making. In this kind of decision making, you cannot disappear into a minority vote, then later enjoy the luxury of claiming no responsibility for the majority decision or, worse, become subversive with impunity. Consensus building requires that every individual come front and center. If you disagree with the majority view, why? Articulate your objection. What compromise can be devised to minimize your objection? How can the issue be shaped such that you can at least "live with it"? The intent in its best form is not to intimidate or coerce anyone into artificial consensus, but, instead, to provide everyone with extended opportunities for fully understanding an issue and the differing viewpoints, and then to forge consensus based on the group's perception of common needs and goals.

None of this, of course, came in one sitting. We needed several years and considerable teeth gnashing to learn how to work through difficult issues fairly and honestly, to be accepting as well as respectful of opposing views. It is not a one-time learning event; whenever the issue changes or new people join the discussions, you face the possibility of beginning again. What was critical during the year, however, was that staff, SIT, and, especially, the SC kept faith in the process and continued to work to make it better. Wendy's attempts to make end runs around the SC in the fall engendered a series of special workshops for the group to set some guidelines for itself and become more comfortable interacting with each other. (In subsequent years such workshops became standard events for the SC as well as for SIT and the whole staff.)

The staff had its own learning to do. When the Emerson issue emerged in the fall, we were unprepared to deal with major parent/community opposition. Up to that point our attention was concentrated on issues of curriculum and instruction; these seemed usually to require only staff discussions and generated no strong parent objections. Thus, while we had become adept at building internal consensus, we were not experienced in taking on more public controversy. The Emerson proposal was indeed public, and I think we lapsed into some old shuffling of feet, not wanting to take a firm, fully articulated position. Somehow, we hoped, it would all work out. Well, it didn't; and we consigned ourselves to an indefinite tenure in an unpleasant, inconvenient facility.

The multiage issue could have been another futile effort, except that it emerged much later in the year. We remembered our lessons from the Emerson experience, and probably we also were experiencing the afterglow of a successful statewide teachers' strike and months of close instructional collaboration. Professional pride was alive and well. In addition to feeling confident in our knowledge of how multiage grouping contributes to learning, we were also eager to set the pace of the discussion. Anticipating possible parent opposition to the addition of more multiage classes to our school, we met early in the spring, more than once, to have a thorough discussion of the issue, examine different plans, and come to strong consensus on recommendations for the following year.

Instead of indulging in polemics or self-pity about not being understood by the public, I think we had learned that the process could be our ally, if we were willing to begin early, work steadily, find consensus, and then explain and support our position through ongoing conversations with parents as well as written statements. Our efforts were not isolated. We benefited from the simultaneous hard work of SC parents and staff reps to obtain input from the larger community, to weigh alternatives, and to stay with their own agreed-upon procedures. Although not overwhelmingly unanimous, parent support was judged sufficient for final SC approval.

Despite this happy ending to the multiage saga, it did not come without a difficult walk through the woods. Among parents objecting to the all-multiage configuration, a few were unwilling to accept the final decision, claiming that the process had been biased and somehow manipulated. (This is a reason for schools to work hard to communicate with and involve as many parents as possible in major decisions.) Their complaints to the district led to an on-site investigation by an "intervention team," comprising both district and Association personnel. After interviewing parents and staff members who had been centrally involved in the multiage decision, the team confirmed that proper procedures had been followed for reaching consensus. Again, the process continued to be the means for negotiating and resolving differences, keeping personality differences and special interests in check. In this case we were fortunate that our own on-site decision-making process was complemented by participatory procedures laid down by the district and Association.

Some wider implications may be drawn from all of this. Accepting the critical importance of genuine consensus building means that schools adopting site-based management need to provide participants with some training in group processing. Dealing with confrontation, listening, working through to compromise—none of this comes naturally to most teachers and many parents. Our building was fortunate in that Anne already had such skills. She spent considerable time during her first years at Jefferson helping various groups learn to work together, whether that meant simply ensuring that every individual had a specific opportunity to express an opinion, or having us work through informal inventories to become aware of our quite different personal styles of interacting with others. Districts need to help schools with such efforts, and teacher education programs need to be redesigned to provide teacher candidates with decision-making experiences in their own courses as well as through abundant well-considered field experiences.

Once committed to school change, you can expect the worst of times without always the best of times, and because there are no exact precedents, you need something reliable to help you maneuver through the unique challenges. With administration no longer making all of the tough decisions, with a covey of parents and staff now sharing responsibility for every major issue popping up along the way, no school seriously engaged in reform can afford to rely on ad hoc measures. Pitfalls abound: Individual personalities can overwhelm the issues; reason can be sacrificed to impulsiveness, with the majority served up to a voluble minority, or a reticent but wise minority ignored. In the most difficult instances, tenaciously clinging to the process can make the difference between an overly emotional reaction and deliberate, inclusive decision making. Holding to each step can be excruciating, but the general integrity of your program should remain intact and relationships still constructive; progress should not be undone by a single issue.

Taking Time

Staff collaboration and a sense of collegiality were essential in meeting our instructional goals as well as in providing mutual reassurance when faced with critical issues during the year. All of this, however, took time. At the most crucial junctures of the year, when we had to decide what to do about multiage grouping or moving to another building, we could use our inservice meetings (Twenty-First Century funds provided substitutes for 2 release days each month) for extended discussions and consensus building. We could thoughtfully evaluate different classroom configurations, work through the pros and cons of moving, revisit our program goals, and talk about different avenues of action. Without these regular meetings, I don't know if we would have maintained our unity as a staff, continued to feel confident about our choices, and taken the reasoned actions that we did.

Of all the elements mentioned as critical to implementing school change, time is probably cited most often and may be the most difficult to provide. Buildings can manage their decision-making processes, create innovative, intelligent programs, and even become directly involved in the selection of personnel, including their principals. What most schools cannot do is unilaterally expand the time they have available to them. Schools have been endlessly creative in managing the time that they do have—for example, adding minutes to each day for an early student release once a week. There are also many schools that make dramatic changes to their programs without any manipulation of time. They simply give up evenings, early morning hours, even weekends, usually without compensation.

Obviously, this latter route is unsatisfactory. Even when a school successfully initiates substantial program change, maintaining the momentum may take additional effort and a continued expenditure of time. Total staff exhaustion seems inevitable without some external support. Given Anne's dedication, leadership, and sheer physical stamina, we probably would have set about making the changes that we did, even without the Twenty-First Century funding. I doubt, however, that we would have been able to move as far and as quickly as we did without that support. And without the generous time we had for decision making, would we have been as successful as we were in anticipating the multiage issue or maintaining our unity as a staff through each of the other stormy events of the year?

The caveat about time is that time in itself does little to make a difference. When you gather for that extra team meeting, something substantive should be on the agenda. I have seen teachers use their additional time to exchange worksheets and run off handwriting practice sheets for the year. Additional time for staff meetings and inservice can be professional treasure or simply padding to the school calendar. If gifted with more time, schools must have very good ideas about how to use that time. This will occur most readily for schools that have coherent programs and clear goals. For these schools, the additional time can support continuity of efforts, lead to greater understanding of change, and provide enough long pauses for self-reflection and ongoing assessment.

I would like to think that somewhere at the state capitol, someone actually is paying attention to our experience at Jefferson and even making a few notes. Our school and, I am sure, the many others contemplating broad change are confirming over and over again that the larger system has to kick in. One school can do a great deal, but usually only with Herculean effort, substantial luck, and a few individuals idealistic and crazy enough to work for the love of it all. But they, too, eventually will walk away unless there is additional support. For example, we need a longer school year, more staff development time, adequate compensation, and training in both leadership and group-processing skills.

Districts, associations, and state legislatures must free themselves from the yoke of the 6-hour day, the 5-day week, the 180-day school year, and begin to entertain some extravagantly creative ideas for how to restructure a school's schedule. Tampering with the traditional 9-month school year often draws active opposition from parents, in part because it complicates scheduling family vacations, but mainly because of understandable problems with childcare. As difficult as these issues are, the fundamental issue is still the education and welfare of children. This country cannot continue to bemoan the "failure" of public schools without realizing that courageous, difficult steps need to be taken to help rather than criticize the system. We cannot keep taking "nips and tucks" here and there, hoping that something may take hold. We need more time in the schools, but time is running out on the policy makers who can make the decisions that could potentially alter our educational system radically, irrevocably, and for the better.

STAYING CENTERED

During times of crisis, people may wash the dishes or vacuum the rugs—anything that will keep them anchored in the security of familiar, mundane activity. I don't think we were ever close to a crisis level, but we experienced our share of anxiety and helplessness. Given all of the controversy and discord that marked the school year, it seems a wonder that we kept moving forward, most of the time even in good spirits. Program, process, principal, parents—these all helped, but the most effective deterrent to anger and despair was simply teaching and hobnobbing with children every day.

At 8:00 A.M. you sit in a meeting wondering if you should have gone into real estate, and at 9:30 A.M. you are helping 28 minds to grasp fractions through pattern blocks. One evening you're in the middle of a testy community meeting in the school gym, and the next morning you are coordinating seven groups of children in devising creative demonstrations of the water cycle. During recess you hear that some parents have gone to the school board to protest a building decision. You are allowed 5 minutes of indignation and irritation, then you must present a mini-lesson on quotation marks and squeeze in writing conferences with five students before the end of the day.

In other words, we had no time to brood. As a mind-boggling mix of the profound and the trivial, the daily doings of our classrooms offered a lifeline to normalcy and a constant reminder of why we had plunged into the maelstrom of school reform in the first place.

By June, we were tired but not discouraged. And by early August most of us were already planning for the next year, eager to get back into our classrooms to put up the new bulletin boards, rearrange furniture, and fill up the bookshelves. Some of the distaste of the previous year would linger, but it would not interfere with instruction. Teaching was and is our priority. Anne understood that, and I believe she did a good job of keeping us focused on our classrooms. She accomplished this in large part simply by keeping the building functioning as normally as possible. She continued to emphasize instruction and inservice in our regular staff meetings, and when it was necessary to bring up contentious issues, it was done calmly, reasonably, and with reference to our larger program goals. After we decided to give up on the Emerson proposal, I think that we were able to move on quickly because Anne had set a tone of acceptance without resentment. She also helped us to accept our own responsibility in the fiasco and glean lessons for the future. Anne was never about to let us get bogged down in petty carping or be distracted by personal antipathies. Even at the peak of her own problems with Fran, the parents, and the school board, she managed to keep all of that removed from the scope of staff business.

The staff was not helpless either. It served itself and the students well. Even in the middle of the most difficult issues of multiage grouping and the Emerson move, the pace of planning for instruction never seemed to falter. Team meetings continued; individual teachers collaborated. We attended our workshops and district meetings on assessment and curriculum. We grappled with the technology creeping into our classrooms; we took field trips, planned science experiments, orchestrated group and independent projects, and kept up the pace of writer's workshop.

When the school year began in September 1990, most of our textbooks and manuals were already stacked in the district warehouse. "Planning" had come to mean more than what pages to cover the next day; we were actually responsible for developing instruction, selecting materials, and integrating skills and content areas. We were completely engrossed in instruction and learning, and each side issue became almost an intrusion into this preoccupation. After Emerson, however, we learned that we had to take note. How we did our jobs could indeed be influenced by issues outside the immediate curricular areas, and we had to assume our share of responsibility. Despite that acknowledgment, I believe that our daily school lives held the center, that what we did with our students from minute to minute usually took precedence over almost anything else.

CONTINUING ON

The most effective teachers are never completely satisfied with their teaching. They understand that teaching is a lifelong process of learning. And it is not simply learning more about plants, energy, the Civil War, or geometry. It goes beyond accumulating large repertoires of teaching strategies and file cabinets full of activities. Instead, the most important learning comes from within. It has to do with self-knowledge, capacity for growth, and taking delight in the company of others. As teachers, parents, and administrators begin to let these ideas shape their actions and relationships, schools should become better places for children. Children will thrive in a school that values individual progress over grades, cooperation over mindless competition, and that sets high expectations for humane behavior as well as for academic performance. All of this, however, is in a perpetual state of becoming; and in the trying is the learning. We resolved specific issues, each time learning and trying to be better prepared for the next challenge. We were far from self-congratulatory at the end, feeling relieved to have survived but also grateful for the caring companionship that graced the year.

We should not underestimate this extra factor of human beings caring for and about each other. I think a school cannot thrive as a learning environment unless individuals, both children and adults, demonstrate genuine concern for each other's well-being. Such caring engenders trust, and with enough of that trust you can accept change, survive setbacks and conflict, and grow into a community stronger for your diversity, tolerance, and compassion.

5

An Activist School

> The only freedom that is of enduring importance is freedom of intelligence, that is to say, freedom of observation and of judgment exercised in behalf of purposes that are intrinsically worthwhile.
> —John Dewey, *Experience and Education*

During the 1990-91 school year, Jefferson Elementary survived the changes and tensions associated with major school reform. But mere survival cannot be enough. The process of coping with the singular challenges of broad change eventually should lead to an enduring transformation of the school. Clearly, this does not always happen. Schools confronted by determined and effective opposition too early in the reform process easily can give up and fall back a dozen paces. Jefferson was fortunate in having had the time to build a program that could hold fast during the travails of the year. And by the end of the nine months, we discovered that our school had not simply held fast; we were, I believe, a more secure, self-defined community. We were also leagues beyond the historical and traditional image of an elementary school.

As an institutional constant through the generations, the organization and culture of the American elementary school functioned to maintain familiar habits of schooling rather than to promote participatory self-governance. Schools historically have not been encouraged or expected to engage in an active self-defining process. Despite the constant press of change throughout the wider society, schools generally have managed to sneak through the decades with their structures and habits virtually intact. They have done so, fully abetted by shortsighted policy as well as by public nostalgia for the Dick-and-Jane classrooms of our collective memories.

School reform arrives as the bear at the party. It threatens the ingrained amenities of schools and rattles community tranquillity. Ideally, reform begins as a school decision, the result of internal initiative and a compelling desire to engage in deliberate change. It is a declaration of independence—a school intentionally sets itself outside of broad policy swaths in an effort to determine its own goals and means of fulfilling them. Such a commitment means not only that a school begins to redefine and re-create its role, but also that the larger community must join in the re-examination of historical assumptions about what schools should do and be.

Although the district and Association provided a supportive context, Jefferson Elementary's decisions and efforts to engage in significant change emerged from well inside our school walls, with a new principal and a committed group of parents and staff. In assuming primary responsibility for determining what and when to change, implementing change, and working constructively with the doubters and dissenters, Jefferson also needed to develop substantially different systems and behaviors than are inherent in traditional school organizations. This became even more essential given the removal of the principal from the center of decision making. While Anne provided a firm guiding hand, we still had to look to ourselves as a school community for managing issues and conflict. In fulfilling this extended role, we could not be simply spectators in school reform. We were now players at center field, and Jefferson would never be quite the same again.

INDIVIDUAL SCHOOLS, PRACTICAL SOLUTIONS

Transformation of the established order—in the way teaching and learning are conducted, in expectations for individual participation and conduct—such changes have the potential for engendering new school traditions. These traditions should reflect healthy changes in the culture of the school, and, in the best of all educational worlds, that culture will assume an ongoing activist approach to problems and challenges.

Activism seems to imply certain traits: commitment to a cause, a belief that individual actions can make a difference, and a willingness to confront formidable obstacles. Each of these traits eventually became part of Jefferson Elementary. Our motivating commitment was straightforward: We hoped to improve the quality of learning and school life for all of our students. This seems almost an educational cliche; however, unlike administrators creating formal policy for a group of schools, we were focused on one school—our own. I believe that this personal identification sharply intensified our belief in the value of change and allowed us to grasp the immediate daily implications of a revised instructional program.

With the advantage of time for extended and continuing discourse, we gradually acquired and improved our skills in reflective decision making and problem solving. These skills, in turn, contributed to our ability to function as a fully engaged school community, allowing us to sort through problems, shape solutions, maintain our collective balance, and continue to move forward. We did so, to a large extent, on our own terms, with decisions and changes reflecting the particular circumstances and relationships within our school.

American elementary schools have tended to look the same, whether two blocks from a beach in Honolulu or on a flat, treeless plain in Kansas. Desks, chalkboards, crayons, basal readers, workbooks, and worksheets—the familiar trappings of elementary school life. This comfortable familiarity, however, belies the variety of experiences and human differences sheltered within each building. Fully recognizing this facet of schools is crucial to understanding the failure or success of school reform (Barth, 1990; Sarason, 1982/1971, 1990; Schwab, 1978; Sergiovanni, 1992).

Sirotnik (1989) notes that attempts at school reform historically have tended to be "top-down exercises," which, he argues, represent an American penchant for applying positivist approaches to solve complicated problems. As institutional microcosms of some of society's most intransigent problems, schools have become inherently unpredictable and almost impossibly complex environments in which to solve problems by simply applying textbook management techniques. The basic contradiction of attempting to apply predetermined, standardized procedures to what Sirotnik calls "messy social systems in the process of evolution" (p. 93) should not only be apparent—it should be virtually blinking in neon.

As Jefferson's example should clearly demonstrate, effecting a program of major school change will almost inevitably run headfirst into conflicting views and interests. So much of such dissension is based on strongly held beliefs of what is right and wrong for schools and for children to be doing. Many school board meetings across the country have become livelier and, occasionally, angrier gatherings when constituents decide to protest changes that appear to contradict their personal beliefs about the role of schools. Schools therefore need to be realistic about the kinds of change they can institute and how far they can proceed at any given time. A school may find it easier to begin gradually, giving individuals time and latitude to become accustomed to new behaviors and procedures. In the process, preconceptions and expectations also may shift sufficiently that the school can continue with its next steps. As Fullan (1992) has observed about school reform, changes in behaviors tend to precede changes in beliefs.

None of this is to suggest, however, that schools should become less than bold in implementing reform. Nor does a suggestion of judiciousness imply timid, piecemeal change. Even when moving at a measured pace, schools still must maintain an overall sense of direction and a defining set of values. Within such a framework, each school can approach reform with a deliberate but comprehensive approach that touches the key elements of its program all at once.

Jefferson Elementary did not wait until all individual belief systems were fully aligned before we instituted broad changes. If we had, we most likely would have ended up as a case study in failed school reform. Instead, change and all of its related problems were folded into our daily school lives. Each of these problems may have sounded familiar in general reference, but in application and within the specific context of our school, each was unique and unto itself. As such, we could not expect to find prepackaged procedures or administrative cookbooks for resolving issues such as the Emerson proposal. Lacking ready-made solutions, Jefferson gradually developed a tradition of problem solving consistent with what Reid (1994) calls a "method of the practical." Such an approach relies on deliberative decision making and inquiry to determine the best actions to take in practical situations, which, as Reid points out, eventually may have significant moral, social, and political implications.

A particularly knotty issue for Jefferson was its discipline plan, which Anne chose as the first real testing ground for our ability to discuss and institute change. Of all school issues, discipline is among the most value-laden and most weighted down by traditional norms. During our tense and emotional first meetings on this subject, Anne helped us simply to express our views, which were substantially rooted in personal experience and expectations. The basic division within the staff was between a program of progressively more punitive measures and a program encouraging individual responsibility. The latter was not as definite or distinct in its consequences, which could vary with the student and the offense.

We easily could have ended at an impasse, without a consistent schoolwide policy and with each teacher doing whatever he or she pleased. Instead, we focused on the kinds of behavior we wanted to encourage from our students, which was fairly easy to agree upon.

Out of this discussion came the school refrain, "Be kind, be safe, be responsible." Each of these three "be" statements included several facets—"be safe," for example, referred to conduct on the walkways, where to run and walk on the playfield, and appropriate behavior when playing soccer. What this initial agreement did for us was to provide a starting point of specific action grounded in a concern for what was most right for our students. The slogan went up in each classroom, was posted in other common areas of the school, and was included in parent newsletters. It took two years, but we eventually developed a comprehensive schoolwide discipline plan that accommodated different values while doing the job of teaching and reinforcing appropriate student behavior.

Another difficult situation occurring early in the implementation of our Twenty-First Century program concerned our efforts to mainstream our special needs students—Chapter 1, special education, ESL (English as a Second Language). Not everyone agreed that every identified special needs student had to be mainstreamed into the regular classroom. To some extent the attendant discussions involved explanation and clarification of educational positions; however, most of our time and effort were spent on crafting innovative but feasible ways of accommodating the varying needs of teachers and students. We then spent the rest of the school year individually and collaboratively fine tuning and revising. By the spring, teachers, students, and parents had become sufficiently accustomed to the revised special needs program that it was difficult to imagine that it ever had been an issue. Again, this situation was typical of the course taken with most of the changes we initiated. Our concerns were of the moment, how to maintain order while continuing to move forward in ways that appeared to be in the best interests of our students and the larger community.

Given the almost constant tension and uncertainty about how to manage conflict and resolve issues during the 1990–91 school year, I think that we came to view the challenges as immediately practical situations, specific to our own school. Our foremost issues may have had philosophical disagreements at their heart, but when those issues manifested as tangible problems, resolutions depended less on changes in beliefs than on the gradual evolution of customized solutions. We learned how to let differences co-exist while we proceeded with some form of action that could alleviate tension and lay the foundation for continuing change. We unknowingly were following a course of "continuous improvement," as advocated by W. Edwards

Deming. Although historically applied in business contexts, Deming's ideas more recently have been successfully generalized to education (Holt, 1993).

For Jefferson Elementary, the factors that seemed most important in sustaining us before, during, and after our difficult year were factors that, functioning in concert, directly enabled us to make thoughtful decisions and take specific actions to solve the large and small problems accompanying school change. As we progressed through the 1990-91 year, we became more adept at this deliberative process and deepened our understanding of what needed to be changed for the benefit of our entire school community. When this kind of learning and growth become endemic rather than occasional, a school becomes more than just another school. It draws out the best from each individual, respects their differences, and takes pride in minding the affairs of its own house.

FLOURISHING

As schools commit to substantive reform and assume more control over their own issues, they should not be surprised or intimidated by conflict and dissent. They also should understand that conflict, if confronted and managed well, has the potential to benefit more than harm.

Conflict is inherent in change, whether it be the known versus the unknown, habit versus innovation, or present versus past. When we opt for change, we in effect look past something in favor of something else. In that choice, and with its ensuing actions, we juxtapose differing philosophies, needs, and expectations. When we speak of "the process of change," we are often talking less about how to adapt to the new order itself and more about how to manage the conflict that arises in the course of committing to actual change. Confronting and successfully resolving contentious issues during the 1990-91 year required us to regularly re-examine our directions; and through this process, we acquired the confidence to let go of expected ways of doing things, alter attitudes, and become more tolerant of differences.

For all of its progress, Jefferson still grapples with tensions wrought by change; but the difference is that we are no longer afraid of joining the fray. Jefferson has evolved into a strong entity in itself, with parents, administrators, staff, and students constantly and exuberantly tugging at worn-out structures and habits.

Until this particular school year, I think many of us felt that although we supported the changes that had occurred in our building, we still were, at least indirectly, following someone else's lead, whether signals from Anne, guidelines attached to the Twenty-First Century proposal, district policies, or even national trends. By June 1991, however, I think we finally understood the fact that all of us were responsible for each significant change as well as its consequences; we not only accepted that responsibility, we tried to make it an inherent part of our daily school life.

As each school embarks on its own path to change, each school creates itself. Given enough time, critical support, and latitude to make its own way, a school can develop a shared history with an internal ethic and culture to provide consistent direction and stability while each change is being absorbed. In the process, individuals within the school community begin to develop a bone-deep commitment to the program that they themselves are helping to shape. And to the extent that this commitment becomes practical reality, they discover that they perhaps can make the impossible possible.

Afterword

I finished my second reading of this book during a weekend spent with the principal of one of the new schools struggling to survive New York City's multilayered bureaucracy. Despite all the differences, Laraine Hong's final paragraph resonated throughout our weekend of talk, talk, talk. It seemed irrelevant as I read this account that one school served adolescents with a history of school failure in the midst of a large northeastern city, while the other served a more heterogeneous population of young children in a small western community. Despite many painful moments, and even some despair, this New York City high school had over time, like Jefferson Elementary School, finally begun to build "an internal ethic and culture," resting on the "bone-deep commitment" of its own community.

In contrast, I often listen to other colleagues and friends who also have stories that share, at moments, the same qualities the author describes in this account, yet they got stuck at one of the many obstacles she describes and never moved beyond it. What made this book so important to me is that it is an honest and almost brutally frank revelation of the humiliations and confusions that strew the path of school change. It allows us to ask the specifics of why some overcome while others are overcome by similar obstacles.

It was hard to put the book down because Hong was telling the story as I know it, yet as I have not yet heard it told publicly, in all its detail, including the personal toll it takes on its players. Teaching is a very personal task when done well. There is almost no room for distancing ourselves from our work—or its subjects. Teaching requires precisely this sensitivity to others that is the flip side of such vulnerability. As a result, criticism of one's practice too often feels like criticism of one's person. One's habits of work are not superficial teacherly traits. Long-standing habits often go back to our own early schooling. Teachers are dismissively called upon to give them up long before they have adequate replacement habits. If they have doubts, they are considered "resistors," as though teachers are capable of only one of two stances—to resist or "go along." The assumption is that neither is rooted in rationality or legitimate experience. Teachers are not legitimate designers of their work, nor are they expected to show publicly the doubts they are feeling privately.

We pay an enormous price for this cover-up. By silencing the voices from the field we both undermine the growth of professional judgment and starve our public debate of the real stuff. We leave public discussion to public policy makers on one hand and the often irritated anecdotes of dissatisfied customers on the other hand. Myths and rumors replace reason. Every experiment works and is defended with glowing accounts until it is ridiculed out of existence as an utter failure when a new fad, or new superintendent, arrives. We build no history, we just recycle with new jargon. But it need not be so if we looked at our work in a different way, the way Laraine Hong has in this stunning book.

I'm sorry that this story had to be told with altered names and places. But it rings so true that maybe it doesn't matter. I know each of these moments and, like a good piece of fiction, maybe it's more true to the reality than the story with the proper names would have been.

In its particularity she helps us answer the important question: In what circumstances does change take root? What enabled this school to go down the well-worn path, exposed and uncertain at each step, without turning back? What enabled this author, along with most of her fellow teachers, to deal day in and day out with the anger and sometimes thinly disguised contempt of some powerful parents and not give up?

We're sometimes told that the answer lies in "charismatic leadership," or "outside pressure," or perhaps just a school so near the bottom that it runs no risks trying to do things differently! Yet this is a school that fits none of these descriptions.

What Jefferson had was good leadership—meaning smart, thoughtful, serious, patient, and above all else courageous. But, we get no sense of "charisma"—or even of unusual political or public skills. What Jefferson had were a staff and families who were prepared to make compromises with each other, to hear each other say things that were not always comfortable, and then absorb what they learned and keep going. They had a history of this kind of mutual respect. In fact, the author's pain was related to her surprise that this mutual respect hadn't translated into greater willingness to trust the teachers' best judgment. No one steamrollered these changes, no one made ultimatums, yet no one backed off either. They learned to do what is at the heart of a democratic community—argue respectfully, if not always comfortably. At least most of the time. The basic good fellowship that apparently was part of the history of this school—a staff used to being supportive of each other—paid off over time. But it took time. Understandably, the policy makers and reformers sometime scoff at this kind of mutual support network among teachers. Yes, it can turn into a mutual-defense society that avoids all self-criticism, shuts out outsiders and dissidents. But a staff that "gets along" is the necessary, however insufficient, starting place, and once it's lost no amount of coercion can substitute for it. No good school can be built, however clever its design, however clever its faculty, and however charismatic its leadership, on the basis of mistrust and disrespect for each other.

The shift from "they" to "us" that the author painstakingly details is far more difficult than we want to acknowledge. Going from being a staff that likes and supports each other as friends to becoming a staff that takes joint responsibility for its shared work—the school— is to leap over a lifetime of experience. It's counterintuitive. Conventional wisdom tells us that the expertise and the authority emanate from somewhere else. The "who me?" innocence of many good teachers when asked to account for "their" school's failure is a habit not easily dislodged.

The particulars of this story reconfirm for me that good schooling rests on principles that do not differ much whether children are 5-year-olds or 15-year-olds, African American, Asian, or white, live in big cities or small towns. It helped that Jefferson was what we are accustomed to think of as small. People seemed to know each other well. That it was not merely one school in a huge impersonal bureaucracy, where critical decisions rested far from those most affected, helped it get through the tough times. The "community" to which it was responsible was stable and visible—and its primary actors were people with a personal stake in the school. These were also important ingredients. That its staff had years of working well together, and of good relationships with the community, was critical. And its choice of school leader, a woman seen by the staff both as "principal teacher" (not principal administrator) and as carrier of ideas (not just techniques and policies), may have been the key factor that turned all these advantages into powerful tools for change.

So, what can we do to change American education? We might *start* in places where many of the above ingredients are present, and then work on creating, inventing, or locating the missing ones. In some cases it's size or autonomy that is the roadblock. In other cases it's the climate of mutual distrust among the faculty or between faculty and the community. In other cases it's the absence of appropriate leadership within the school. It's rarely "all of the above," and besides, we can't change everything everywhere anyway. My late mentor at City College, Lillian Weber, used to tell us, over and over, Start where you are, with the strengths you have as a foundation for tackling the ones you don't have. That's as good a way of "educating" schools to reform themselves, as it is for educating our students to reform themselves. It's a pretty good principle for being a lifelong learner—one of those things we claim to want for all children, but need as well for all schools. Laraine Hong described a school that was a learning community—that's the glue that unites the separate ingredients.

—Deborah Meier

References

Atwell, N. (Ed.). (1990). *Coming to know: Writing to learn in the intermediate grades.* Portsmouth, NH: Heinemann.

Barth, R. S. (1990). *Improving schools from within.* San Francisco: Jossey-Bass.

Carnegie Forum on Education and the Economy. (1986). *A nation prepared: Teachers for the twenty-first century.* Report of the Carnegie Forum on Education and the Economy's Task Force on Teaching as a Profession. Washington, DC: The Forum.

Darling-Hammond, L. (1985). Valuing teachers: The making of a profession. *Teachers College Record, 87*(2), 209–218.

Fullan M. G. (1992). *Successful school improvement: The implementation perspective and beyond.* Philadelphia: Open University Press.

Holmes Group. (1986). *Tomorrow's teachers.* East Lansing, MI: Holmes Group.

Holt, M. (1993). Dr. Deming and the improvement of schooling: No instant pudding. *Journal of Curriculum and Supervision, 9*(1), 6–23.

Lieberman, A. (Ed.). (1988). *Building a professional culture in schools.* New York: Teachers College Press.

Lieberman, A., & Miller, L. (1990). Restructuring schools: What matters and what works. *Phi Delta Kappan, 71*(10), 759–764.

Lightfoot, S. (1986). On goodness in schools: Themes of empowerment. *Peabody Journal of Education, 63*(3), 9–28.

Nelsen, J. (1987). *Positive discipline.* New York: Ballantine Books.

Reid, W. A. (1994). *Curriculum planning as deliberation* (Report No. 11). Oslo, Norway: Institute for Educational Research.

Sarason, S. (1982). *The culture of the school and the problem of change.* Boston: Allyn & Bacon. (Original work published 1971)

Sarason, S. (1990). *The predictable failure of educational reform.* San Francisco: Jossey-Bass.

Schwab, J. J. (1978). The practical: A language for curriculum. In I. Westbury & N. J. Wilkof (Eds.), *Science, curriculum, and liberal education: Selected essays* (pp. 287–321). Chicago: University of Chicago Press.

Sergiovanni, T. J. (1992). *Moral leadership.* San Francisco: Jossey-Bass.

Sirotnik, K. (1989). The school as the center of change. In T. J. Sergiovanni & J. H. Moore (Eds.), *Schooling for tomorrow* (pp. 89–113). Boston: Allyn & Bacon.

Wallace, D. (1993). From a focus group discussion on "Teacher Leadership" co-sponsored by the Danforth Foundation and National Education Association, St. Louis.

Wasley, P. A. (1991). *Teachers who lead*. New York: Teachers College Press.

Watts, G. D., & McClure, R. M. (1990). Expanding the contract to revolutionalize school renewal. *Phi Delta Kappan, 71*(10), 765–774.

Index

Alice, 136
  as a person, 135
Anne
  as change initiator, 5-7, 20
  and interpersonal relationships, 65-66, 70-71, 116-117, 158-159
  as a person, 114-119
  supervision and evaluation of Fran, 77-78, 87, 93, 112-113, 138, 155-156
  and teacher evaluation, 74-76, 77
Arnold
  and teacher evaluation, 75
  as traditional principal, 5
Association
  executive director of (Jack), 105
  as professional organization, 14-15

Betty
  and Emerson move, 50-51, 52-53
  as a person, 53
Boys and Girls Club, 31, 43, 46
Budgets, teacher, 117-118

Change, 37-38, 185, 189
  as part of district and school culture, 14, 185
  and responses to, 18, 51-52, 135-136, 141, 166-167
  See also Instructional change
Clare, as a person, 61-62
Class meetings, 82-83
Collaboration, 161
  of Betty and Mary, 6-7, 126, 127
  of Ellen and Kay, 28, 79, 85, 97, 122
  examples of, 36, 60, 67-68
Collegiality, 19, 91-93

Community meetings
  on Emerson move, 50-52, 62
  on multiage grouping, 120
Conflict, 101, 152, 184
Consensus decision making, 44-45, 131-132, 171-172
  and multiage grouping, 122, 129-130, 173
  and School Improvement Team, 73
  and "sufficient consensus," 138-139

Dailiness of teaching, 176-178
Danny, 25, 64, 146
  as a person, 81-82
Deming, W. Edwards, 183-184
Developmental community school, 9, 59, 96-97, 150-151
  and multiage grouping, 108
Discipline, schoolwide plan, 65, 155, 182-183
District reform initiatives, 10-11

Ellen, as a person, 28-29
Emerson move
  and Anne's role, 49, 50, 51
  parent letter against, 47-48
  reasons for, 30-32
  and staff decision making, 44, 52, 63, 172
  teachers' letter in support of, 52-55
Empowerment, 153
  of students, 96-97
  of teachers, 160

Followership, 166-168
4-1/2 Day Committee, 30, 71, 86-87, 107, 112, 145

Fran
  and claim of discrimination, 113–114, 132, 142
  and district contract, 93, 114
  hiring of, 118
  and issues of instruction, 33–34, 87–88
  as a person, 34
  position on multiage grouping, 121–122, 142
  relations with parents, 88–89, 91, 93, 112–113, 131, 138
  relations with staff, 88, 91

Hannah, 135
  as a person, 133–134

Inservice days (Wednesdays), 119–120
  disadvantages of, 30, 86
  purposes of, 20, 35, 36, 73–74, 174
  See also Staff meetings
Instructional change, 12, 39–40, 151–152
  and integrated curriculum, 60–61
  and math, 78–79
Intervention team, 138–139, 141, 173

Jane
  and instruction, 60, 85
  as a person, 68–69
Jefferson Elementary
  new teachers, 16–17, 41
  student population of, 4
  teacher teams, 21
Jo
  as a person, 27
  and teachers' strike, 103
Joan, 118, 143
  as a person, 83–84
John, 129
  and Emerson move, 49, 50, 61
Judy, as a person, 100

Kay, as a person, 97

Mary
  as a person, 21–22
  and teachers' strike, 99, 103

Math
  and district student learning objectives, 33
  and teacher leaders, 13
Mentoring, and Fran, 40–41, 78, 79, 87
Multiage grouping, 24, 107–109
  and Anne's letter to parents, 98
  and staff decision making, 107, 120, 121–122, 152, 172–173
  and teachers' letters of support, 124–126

Neil, as a person, 35–36

Office staff, 116

Pam, 137–138, 166
Parent conferences, 57–58
Parent protests
  against school decisions, 132–133, 138, 140, 141–142, 143
  follow-up investigations and recommendations by superintendent (Ted), 112, 113, 132, 138, 143–144
Parents, support from, 80–81, 132–135, 163–165, 167. *See also* Hannah; Alice
Principal
  as administrator and instructional leader, 74–75
  isolation of, 142–143
  See also Anne; Arnold
Principal's Award, 65–66
Professional development, district supported, 12–13
Professionalism, 162–163
PTSA, 59–60, 134–135, 169–170

REACH Program, 24, 29–30

School Council (SC), 14, 20
  and Emerson move, 32–33, 43–44, 46–47, 55, 61, 63
  and group cohesiveness, 55, 63–64, 85–86, 172
  meetings of, 26–33, 71–72, 86–87, 107, 111, 128, 129–130, 145
  and multiage grouping, 123–125, 128–130

representation on, 26–27, 129, 164. *See also* John; Wendy
School culture, 149, 180
School Improvement Team (SIT), 17, 46, 72, 169
  and decision making, 72–73, 164
  and Emerson move, 31, 42
School reform, xii, 179–180, 181–182
  and principal's role, 118–119, 153–155
  and role of the Association, 15
  and site-based decision making, 150, 169
  and teacher decision making, 13–14, 161–162
Schools for the Twenty-First Century
  development of proposal, 7–8, 108, 149–150
  provisions of grant, 9, 20
Shirley, 109
  as a person, 110–111
Site-based decision making (SBDM), 45–46
  and budgets, 71–72
  lack of precedents for, 48–49
Staff meetings, 44
  as inservice, 5, 169
  to revise discipline plan, 65
  See also Inservice days
Strike, teachers', 99
  Anne's response, 102
  and the Association, 69–70, 99, 103, 105
  community's response, 103
  and Jefferson teachers, 102–103
  membership vote, 100–102, 104–106
  and PTSA, 103
  and state budget, 69, 99, 100, 104, 105
Student progress reports, design of, 56–57

Students
  assessment of, 17–19, 58
  class placement of, 136–138
  descriptions of, 24–26, 94–96, 146
  special needs, 81, 82, 84, 183
  See also Danny

Teacher Appreciation Week, 106
Teacher evaluation, 37, 71
  district-association program, 76–77
  variability among districts, 78
Teachers
  communicating with parents, 38, 89–91, 126–128
  as curriculum planners, 160–161
  as leaders, 13, 160
  See also Betty; Clare; Ellen; Fran; Jane; Judy; Kay; Mary; Neil; Pam; Shirley
Teaching
  pressures of, 41
  reflections on, 38–39, 64, 123
Technology
  school technology plan, 86, 111
  and teacher expertise, 13, 17
Time, 156, 174–176

Union. *See* Association

Vision, 152
  as held by Anne, 157–158

Wendy
  and Emerson move, 48, 49, 50
  and multiage grouping, 130
  as a person, 42–43

About the Author

Laraine Hong is a language arts curriculum specialist in the Bellevue (Washington) public schools. She took her doctorate in early-middle childhood education from Ohio State University. Reversing the usual order of professional events, she began as an assistant professor in education at a small liberal arts college. After three years, she realized she needed regular classroom experience in order to be fully effective as a teacher educator. What was to be a short stint in the classroom became eight years of teaching every grade from second through fifth, and being an active participant in her school's efforts at reform. She recently tried academia again, but returned to her district after a year as a language arts curriculum specialist. She still thinks about going back to the classroom.